THE F PLACE

THE F PLACE

CHRISTINE STROBUSH
&
SONAL TRIVEDI

como

The F Place

Copyright © 2021 by Christine Strobush and Sonal Trivedi

The COMO Group, LLC.

Library of Congress Control Number: 2020952734

ISBN (hardcover): 9781662907470
ISBN (paperback): 9781662907487
eISBN: 9781662907494

Dedication

We dedicate this book to the millions of people around the world who lost their jobs and those who have struggled with all the challenges that resulted from the global pandemic of 2020.

The pandemic continues to impact everyone in one way or another, and some more drastically than others. For a number of people, it could mean making big changes in everyday routines due to loss of friends and family, financial hardships, or simply having to cope with the uncertainty of the future.

In most cases, your job has been your livelihood, but it should not define you.
Losing your job is incredibly scary, but your value is not dependent on a company or others.

Your value is defined by WHO you are!
You were created for a purpose!
You are a beautiful, one-of-a-kind person with unique talents, skills, and gifts that the world needs to appreciate.

Please don't let fear dictate your next right move because fear is a liar!

"When one door closes, another opens; but we often look so long and so regretfully upon the closed door that we do not see the one which has opened for us."
—*Alexander Graham Bell*

Contents

Foreword

MANY INDIVIDUALS AND companies glamorize and attempt Transformative change, but few succeed. Most of the time this can be directly attributed to the individuals or leaders who are driving the change. At best, a few new ideas or work methods become part of the individual's practice or company's structure. At worst, they do not achieve the basic requirements to survive and grow because there was no real embrace and required skills of the change. As a result, individuals, leaders, and employees of the organization become irreparably disillusioned with the revolving door of change and the mixed messages. The problem is that those changes address neither the individuals nor the corporate culture. They often look only to the superficial behaviors rather than amending the root cause or mindset.

Having worked extensively with both Sonal and Christine, the lessons that they share in this unforgettable story are drawn from over forty years of leading and driving successful Transformation. These authors show us how individual adjustments from the CEO and executive leadership team can make or break not only the individuals but the company. If you want to look for the role model who reflects passion for their work, I recommend you meet Sonal and Christine.

This book is not about telling a particular individual's or company's story, but about learning real-life Transformative lessons through creative storytelling. It is truly an engaging story of why leaders consciously make a controversial leap, as well as what they had to do to take risks to achieve their values and goals. It clearly illustrates that when done for the wrong reasons it truly unravels the individual and organization, whereas when done correctly it has the ability to Transform individuals and organizations alike in a powerful way that yields exceptional enduring results and culture.

This paradigm-shifting iterative approach to undergoing the journey of personal and professional Transformation shows us that when an individual and a company achieves true Transformation the results are extraordinary both in the business world and on the personal front.

Remarkably, Christine and Sonal have produced a book that will inspire courage to those that are currently in a leadership role, those that are aspiring leaders or those that are looking for a impactful personal or professional Transformation. This is a unique book—a captivating novel—full of invaluable insights and practical lessons that you will relate to. I cannot wait to give this book to all my clients that want to undergo a True Transformation as a "must read."

Ashok Shah
Author of Emergence of the "Me" Enterprise
and Achieving Lifetime Employability

After serving in various C-suite roles and retiring from Alcatel-Lucent as President of their Global Professional Services organization, Ashok Shah spends his time serving as an advisor and as a member of the Board of Directors for a collection of public and private businesses and universities. He is the founder and President of CEPS Consulting, LLC.

Who Should Read This Book?

WHILE THE COMPANY, characters, and events in this book are fictitious, the personal and professional transformative lessons in this story are real. If you are seeking a personal or professional Transformation, you will find *The F Place* captivating. It is not simply our capabilities and talent that bring us success, but the wholistic mindset with which we approach Transformation. This book is for you . . .

- If life has ever thrown you curve balls and you need support on how to survive and grow through the pain. . . .

- If you have ever found yourself in or are currently in a season of fear, uncertainty, and/or anxiety but are trying to refuse to give in to the negativity around you. . . .

- If you are struggling now or have ever struggled against the toxic culture of your workplace, while determined to stay true to yourself. . . .

- If you have ever been consumed by chaos or are facing chaos now, but you are determined to find clarity and move forward. . . .

- If you have ever struggled or are struggling now with company politics and power struggles, but you prefer to focus on delivering value to your customers. . . .

- If you have ever struggled or are struggling with imposter syndrome, believing that one day you will be "found out"....

- If you have ever struggled or are currently struggling with "work/life balance," feeling like you are giving the best of yourself to your job and the leftovers to your family....

- If you have ever wanted to or are struggling to live by your values, even when circumstances around you have made it incredibly difficult....

- If you have ever wondered if you have what it takes to be successful while being your authentic self....

- If you've ever wondered why some incredible companies go under quickly even though they seem to have all the ingredients that it takes to be successful....

- If you are a leader who wants to further your Transformation journey....

- If you are a leader who has experienced the exponential speed of change firsthand and you want to stay on top of the curve and want a broad overview of what's possible....

- If you are an MBA student who wants to understand real Transformation lessons in a multi-perspective way....

- If you are looking for an inspirational tract on personal and professional Transformation and want a unique way to acquire new information, think creatively, and diversify your perspective....

INTRODUCTION
What Is The F Place?

THE F PLACE is a fictitious pharmaceutical company that was founded in 2001. The actual name of the company is irrelevant. What is relevant and meaningful are the transformative lessons that you will experience through the stories of these fictional characters whose lives are intertwined within the walls of The F Place.

Journey with them as they engage in political warfare, fight for their personal relationships, and apply the COMO Factor, choosing Freedom Over Fear during the unprecedented year of 2020 with the global COVID-19 pandemic, economic meltdown, unparalleled political division, peaceful protesting, and violent rioting.

Beneath the surface, there is a toxic culture at The F Place where the company is plagued by back-stabbing leaders, drama, lies, scandal, and unhappy employees to the point that both the performance and the well-being of the people in the company are affected.

The F Place Overview

The F Place was founded in November 2001 and, under the leadership of Alexander Wood, experienced rapid exponential growth, reaching $10 billion in sales in 2011 due to the incredible success of the HappyVITA product line. HappyVITA (florastine) is a selective serotonin reuptake inhibitor (SSRI) drug to combat depression.

The F Place continued to capture market share, and revenue peaked in 2015 at $20 billion. Due to fierce competition, revenue slowly declined between 2016 and 2019. In 2017, Alexander retired, and Michael Vitali was appointed as president and CEO. Michael's first major leadership actions included creating a new Executive Team and outsourcing a large majority of the manufacturing to China to mitigate profit erosion.

In 2019, despite the company's best efforts, The F Place dropped from the #3 to the #9 spot in the top 10 U.S. pharmaceutical and biotech companies. Rumor has it that they are doubling down on their next big product line, BalanceVITA (flaxopine), to address bipolar disorders.

The F Place Mission Statement

To become the global leader in pharmaceuticals by providing wholistic solutions that improve the mental health and lives of patients everywhere.

The F Place Core Values

The Five Fs are the foundation of our culture and influence every decision we make at The F Place.

FIRST: We strive to be number one in everything that we do.

FAST: We make decisions and execute them more quickly than the competition.

FOCUSED: We are focused on our shareholders, customers, and employees.

FLEXIBLE: We are willing and able to adapt to changing market conditions to deliver solutions quickly.

FUTURE: We make decisions today that will create a better future tomorrow.

The F Place Executive Leadership Team— Organization Structure 2020

An organization chart is a visual representation of the hierarchical structure of a team or organization. It shows the relationships of the leadership positions or roles within the company. It is also a tool to help company employees and stakeholders understand roles and responsibilities.

The organizational chart for The F Place as of the year 2020 is shown below. As indicated in the legend, there are two new leaders who have been appointed since the last organization chart was published.

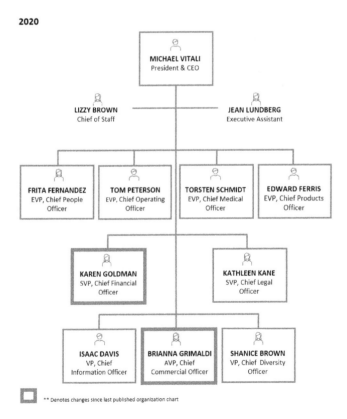

2020

MICHAEL VITALI
President & CEO

LIZZY BROWN
Chief of Staff

JEAN LUNDBERG
Executive Assistant

FRITA FERNANDEZ
EVP, Chief People Officer

TOM PETERSON
EVP, Chief Operating Officer

TORSTEN SCHMIDT
EVP, Chief Medical Officer

EDWARD FERRIS
EVP, Chief Products Officer

KAREN GOLDMAN
SVP, Chief Financial Officer

KATHLEEN KANE
SVP, Chief Legal Officer

ISAAC DAVIS
VP, Chief Information Officer

BRIANNA GRIMALDI
AVP, Chief Commercial Officer

SHANICE BROWN
VP, Chief Diversity Officer

** Denotes changes since last published organization chart

CHAPTER 1

What The F?

October 22, 2020

"Enron—although an extreme case—is hardly the only company with a hollow set of values."

—*Patrick Lencioni*

BRIANNA WOKE UP at 4:30 a.m., determined to get in a long run before heading into the office. She thought to herself, "This is going to be a day that will be remembered forever." She started feeling a little anxious and, as she always did, took a few deep breaths to calm herself.

As she stepped out on to the street and made her way to Central Park, the crisp, cold morning air hit her and further activated her mind. She wondered how the day would unfold and wanted to fast-forward a bit, and then she was reminded of a quote she had read from Vera Nazarian: "Would you like to know your future? If your answer is yes, think again. Not knowing is the greatest life motivator. So, enjoy, endure, survive each moment as it comes to you in its proper sequence—a surprise." Wise words, she thought, and she knew better than anyone else that life is fleeting and impermanent. As she ran, her mind drifted to the events that had taken place this year. The year 2020 was so chaotic, and it looked nothing like she had envisioned at the start.

While there were some bright spots in her life, as she thought about The F Place, it was all disquieted and repulsive—the global pandemic, the unnecessary layoff of thousands of employees, the corporate political warfare, the betrayals, the fraud, and the never-ending toxicity. "Is this really my life?" she asked herself. What Brianna wanted most was the freedom to author her one-of-a-kind life story without having to choose between a meaningful career that makes a positive difference in the world and being a loving and generous mother to her precious children.

Brianna thought about Michael. He was so intelligent and driven, handsome and charismatic, yet lacking in integrity and emotional intelligence. He had so much promise early in life, but somewhere along the way, he lost himself and had become a broken man who left a trail of broken people in his wake.

Her thoughts quickly shifted to Frita. Brianna's skin crawled at the thought of her. Frita was conniving, self-centered, boastful, vain, condescending, and plain evil. The way that woman stirred up conflict everywhere she went made Brianna incredulous. She seemed to grow in power every time she belittled someone else. She had sarcastic comments about everyone except for Michael and the Board. While at times they seemed small, these barbs were designed to hurt people.

As Brianna's pace evened out, her attention turned to Edward next. She thought of how Edward was a pawn in all this and did not even know it yet. Then there was Isaac. He was so young, and when he joined The F Place, there was such a promising future ahead for him. That kid has so much potential . . . all of which he wasted on The F Place. Brianna inhaled the fresh air deeply and cringed at the fact that each and every single one of them had crossed the line, one inch at a time. Well, today, they would all regret the day that they walked through the doors of The F Place.

Brianna made her way back to her place to get ready. Today's run had helped her to clear her head and give her an extra boost of much-needed mental energy. Given the significance of the day, Brianna decided to dress up and look her absolute best. She knew exactly what she would wear to make her entrance. Brianna thought about how, in her Indian heritage, white was the standard color for those grieving the deceased. She decided to dress herself in an off-white wool suit with a cream-colored silk blouse underneath it. She recalled that she had the suit custom made in Singapore during her last visit there with Michael. They had gone to see several potential customers, as Singapore's pharmaceutical market was anticipated to grow by almost double digits over the next fifteen years. Michael had insisted that Brianna meet with his tailor on that trip. Brianna still remembered that trip fondly. She could not believe how the tailor had turned around four custom-made suits for Brianna within twenty-four hours, and the price had been so reasonable. Brianna recalled how, during that visit, Michael would always look at her so appreciatively. Brianna had made it clear to him a long time ago that their relationship was going to be purely professional.

Brianna worked hard on her body. At 5 feet, 5 inches, and 127 pounds, Brianna looked like she was barely 30. She loved to dress up for work, and she often shopped abroad so that her wardrobe would not be replicated by anyone else in her circle. Looking at herself in the mirror, she knew that she looked professionally stunning. Her long brown hair glistened from the bright light from her closet chandelier. She quickly glanced at the time and slipped on her jewelry before she made her way to The F Place.

As usual, Brianna arrived in the boardroom early to do her final preparations before the executive leadership meeting. Michael walked in a few minutes before eight and went to his usual spot at the head of the table. He looked at Brianna admiringly and smiled. "Good morning, Brianna. Wow, don't you look stunning today."

Brianna smiled back at him, fully knowing that the suit she had on would remind him of their trip to Singapore. When they had gone to pick up the suits, Michael had told her that this was his favorite out of the lot. She joked to Michael, "I wish I would've known then to ask your tailor to make me a matching mask for each of my suits."

Michael laughed but could not take his eyes off Brianna. He thought to himself, "She truly is a stunningly beautiful woman." He admired the way that she was always so sure of herself. She was everything he wanted in a life partner, smart, gorgeous, funny, and one of a kind. Then, like an awkward schoolboy, he nervously whispered across the room, "Brianna, I have to confess. I cannot wait for tomorrow night!"

Brianna winked and flashed back a playful smile at him. "Thank you, Mikey. I am flattered. Indeed, tomorrow night will be very memorable and unlike anything you have ever experienced before!" Shortly after, the rest of the Executive Team walked in and took their places six feet apart in the boardroom. They were supposed to be wearing masks, but as usual no one bothered to do so. At 8 a.m. sharp, Michael kicked off the meeting and then handed it over to Frita.

"Thank you, Michael. As you all know, employee engagement has declined by 17 percent this year. This is not just an HR problem; this is a leadership problem," said Frita.

Brianna decided that she would jump right in and get

to it. "Frita, I wholeheartedly agree with you. This really is a leadership problem that needs to be fixed. How do you propose we fix it?" she asked.

Frita looked at Michael, expecting him to jump to her rescue, but he was nodding his head in agreement with Brianna. Irritated now, Frita looked away and turned to snap at Brianna "Well, sweet pea, we will get to that shortly. My team has worked tirelessly now for weeks to prepare this employee engagement packet. I need each of you to review it and put together your improvement plan," commanded Frita.

"So, Frita, if I understand correctly—and I certainly do as you've made it abundantly clear for everyone here—are you really telling us that you do not have a plan? You came into this meeting today simply to tell us that we need to create a plan?" The others looked on in disbelief. Someone was finally going head to head with Frita, and for the first time ever Frita looked a bit nervous. Brianna knew all eyes were on her now, and she had commanded everyone's attention around the table. For added effect, Brianna leaned back in her chair and crossed her arms. "Frita, please help us to understand exactly what value you and your HR team are adding to this process?" Brianna questioned confidently.

Frita started to twitch in discomfort. She regretted wearing her Spanx today. Between the wide Gucci belt that she had on her trousers, the Spanx, and the three-inch stilettos, she was feeling a bit suffocated. She had overslept this morning and was mad at herself for not taking the time to look as good as Brianna. She was having trouble concentrating on the conversation at hand and was taken aback by Brianna. She started to think to herself, "How dare she interrogate me like this? Who does she think she is?" After all this was said and done, she would make sure Brianna never returned to The F Place again. She wanted to lunge at Brianna and drag her out of the boardroom.

"I am sure that it was her looks that got her this far," thought Frita. Well, little did she know that Michael was on Frita's side. "Oh, yes, Michael," she thought to herself. Frita knew that Michael would back her up. All she had to do was give him the cue that she normally did. She cleared her throat and flashed him a pleading look as if she were a poor little puppy dog that needed a pat on the head. It worked every time, and she expected that he was going to jump in and shut Brianna up once and for all.

Much to Frita's dismay, he did not. Frita paused again and wondered what had gotten into Michael today. He seemed so distant yet content. She did a mental run-through of all the events that had led up to this moment. She had told Michael exactly what she planned on doing, and he had given her the green light. Yet here he was, just letting her fall down this slippery slope without even offering her a hand.

Frita decided she would play the video that she had asked the communications team to develop for her. Soon after this meeting she would ask her assistant to send it out company wide. It was Frita sharing the takeaways from the employee engagement survey. Frita was pretty proud of herself, and she was going to teach this group a thing or two about engagement. Before she asked Denise to play the video, she told the group that her HR team had the highest employee engagement out of all the departments at The F Place. The video was only a few minutes long, and that would give Frita the time she needed to collect her thoughts and recompose herself.

Why was Michael not looking at her, she wondered? Then Frita glanced in Brianna's direction and felt intimidated for the first time. "Look at her just sitting there so comfortably. She's busy looking at her phone instead of paying attention to my video," thought Frita.

Just then it was the army of footsteps coming down the hall

that caught everyone's attention at the same time. Michael turned to Lizzy and asked her to see what the commotion was about. As Lizzy started to get up, the doors to the boardroom were flung open, and suddenly a dozen FBI agents barged in. There was no mistaking that these were FBI agents. They were all dressed alike in dark-blue nylon jackets with the prominent yellow letters "FBI" on them.

Frita screamed out loud first. Tom blurted out next, "What the hell is going on here? Is that the FBI? Why are you here? What is happening?"

Kathleen jumped in: "Quiet, everyone." Brianna was so relieved to see the blue jackets coming in. She looked in Michael's direction first. He was looking around the room in total dismay and shock. She could see how scared and upset he looked. Next was Frita. There was an instant breakout of sweat on her face, and she looked like she was about to have a heart attack.

CHAPTER 2

The Frightening Past

2017 and Earlier

"Fear is the path to the Dark Side. Fear leads to anger, anger to hate, hate leads to suffering."

—*Yoda*

1988: The Grimaldi Family

NORTH OF CHICAGO in Kenilworth, Tina Grimaldi took her handsome 12-year-old son Antonio out to lunch at the country club for their weekly mother-son outing. Tina dressed in her almost uniform attire of Chanel, traditional collared shirt, and wool jacket with her leather skirt. She was dripping in her signature look with her Bulgari necklaces and 22-karat gold bracelets and 11-carat heart-shaped ring. "Antonio, do you see that woman and her daughter over there?" asked Tina.

"Yes, Mother. That girl goes to my school," said Antonio.

"Oh, do you think she is pretty?" asked Tina. All the while, in her mind she thought about how frumpy and plain this girl really looked. Tina thought to herself, "Why would a girl like that come into an exclusive place like this in a plain old white dress? Shouldn't she carry a signature couture handbag and drip herself in some bling? How could that mother or her daughter look the same way?" Despite how they looked, Tina couldn't deny how the duo captured her attention. It seemed like mother and daughter had an electric energy about them that no one could deny. Both had striking looks. They were dark-haired with oval faces, with eyes that could mesmerize anyone that encountered them and a smile that captured hearts. Just then, Tina's thoughts got interrupted by Antonio.

"Yes, of course. Anyone can see that she is beautiful, Mother," said Antonio.

Tina snapped defensively and started to whisper in fear of being overheard. "Looks can be deceiving, my love. You need to pay much more attention to detail. I mean, look at their shoes. They are faded, worn, and dirty. Look at her mother's purse. I just know that is a fake. Who would dare to wear a fake Cartier clutch in this day and age? Those two are trying to impress everyone with their beauty, but they are imposters! And we . . . the Grimaldis . . . we are better than them; we are better than everyone in this room, son! Look at us—look at how we are dressed; this is who we are. We know Mario Prada! We come from a circle of influence. You can tell in the way that we dress ourselves—the quality of the fabrics that we clothe ourselves in. You see those cheap women flaunting themselves in probably polyester?"

"Mother, you are absolutely right! We are better than them all! You are better than them all! You always look so beautiful and classy! My father adorns you in the best and puts you on a pedestal just as you deserve, my sweet mother!" shouted Antonio a little too loudly.

Tina glowed instantly. She smiled proudly and felt deep contentment at the fact that her son was embracing her wise lessons at such a young age. She remarked at what an amazing mother she had turned out to be. She thought to herself, "My boy is wrapped around my little finger, just like his daddy, and I've finally done something right. They're both going to be mine for life!"

Tina snapped herself back into reality. She realized that this was a never-ending process. She asked, "Antonio, what have I always told you about girls?"

Antonio was embarrassed and replied ever so politely, "Mom, do we have to do this right now? You ask me this *all* the time!" He hated when his mother tore into him this way!

All of a sudden, there was tension in the air. Tina did not need to say another word. Her look told Antonio everything he needed to know.

"Mother! OK. Fine. When I am 15 years old, I can start dating, but I promise to never let myself love anyone more than you. You will always be the number one woman in my life," said Antonio as he rolled his eyes.

Tina felt a warm feeling encompass her throughout. She relished how her son gave in to her every whim. Sweetly, she looked at him and commanded, "That's right, son. Now, continue with the rest."

"OK, Mother. Whatever you say. I know what's expected of me. After I graduate from university, I will marry the perfect woman that you have chosen for me in San Francisco. I know that it's important for our family and for you to make sure my future bride is from a Brahmin family line. I know that our lineage has to continue and that my children and their children will be from the same caste. I am grateful, Mother, for our lineage. I know that you have sacrificed so much to try to keep the family pure," said Antonio very quietly and with embarrassment. Antonio couldn't help to think about the fact that despite Tina wanting to be traditional, she and Antonio's father had something that was far from traditional for either of them.

Despite knowing all this, Antonio did not want to bother with any of it. He realized that someone else had captured his attention, and so he just nodded as his mother continued on. "That's right, my son. You can enjoy the playing field while you are young because your mother has already selected your perfect wife."

1991: The Failure After Annapolis

Annapolis, Maryland

Michael Vitali's parents beamed with pride as they watched their son give his valedictorian speech at the United States Naval Academy. Michael had majored in physics and planned to become a Navy SEAL after graduating from the Academy. While they had hoped he would follow in his father's steps as a businessman, they were pleased that he had succeeded in being first in his class and would become part of an elite special operations force.

Coronado, California

Michael gave everything he had, but he was unable to complete the twenty-four-week basic underwater Demolition/SEAL training. He departed in week twenty with his head hung low, ashamed to face his parents. This was the first significant failure of his life and he knew it! He wasn't sure how he was going to break the news to his parents. He remembered how his mother had thrown him a lavish party to announce to all their friends that Michael was accepted into this very elite program.

On his flight home, Michael needed liquid courage and

ordered a scotch on the rocks almost as quickly as he could settle into his first-class seat. There, in the seat next to him, he met Alexander Wood, a 30-something executive at a U.S. pharmaceuticals company. They quickly clicked as Alexander had had a tough day himself and also ordered the same scotch. Since they were strangers and Michael never expected to see him again, over a few drinks, Michael shared his life story with Alexander, including his SEALs failure. It felt good for Michael to say it out loud that he had failed. He knew deep down inside that he would not get a warm reaction from his parents when he broke the news to them. Michael was surprised at Alexander's reaction. He kept telling Michael how brave and talented he was to have gotten into the program in the first place. During that conversation, Alexander saw a young man with incredible potential and encouraged him. Alexander opened up to Michael and shared his passion for helping people and explained how the perfect balance of business and science could change the world. They had a dynamic conversation, and as the flight was about to land, they exchanged contact information, although Michael never actually expected to see Alexander again.

1994: Michael's Fate

Cambridge, Massachusetts

Twenty-five-year-old Michael graduated summa cum laude from Harvard with an MBA. As he walked to the stage to get his diploma, Michael realized he had finally redeemed himself from the failure of his SEALs program. He glanced over at his mother and gave her a beaming smile. Tears streamed down his mother's face as her only son walked across the stage to receive his diploma. The pride she felt for her son was also filled with sadness because his father hadn't lived to see this achievement. Michael Sr. had died of a massive heart attack six months earlier, just before his fiftieth birthday. Both Michael and his mother were devastated by their loss. To honor his father's legacy, Michael had vowed to his mother that he would be every bit as successful as his father.

After graduation, Michael secured a job with "The A Place" as a product manager, working in Alexander Wood's organization. He couldn't have imagined when he had shared a few drinks and some conversation with Alexander on that flight several years ago what would happen. That chance meeting on the tarmac had changed the trajectory of Michael's life.

2000: The First Meeting

Chicago, Illinois

Brianna worked two jobs during the summer after high school graduation. She wanted to save up her money so that she could focus solely on academics once she started university at Northwestern in the autumn. She was determined to work hard at university and create a secure future for herself. She had watched both her parents work hard all their lives to achieve what was considered "middle-class status." She had vowed to herself that she would make them proud of her and pay back tenfold all they had given her and her brother Grayson over the years.

She left her day job a few minutes late because she got stuck on a customer service call with an upset customer. Brianna never took any shortcuts in life, and work was no exception. Even though she earned an entry-level pay as a customer service representative at a call center, she made sure she always brought her best attitude and problem-solving skills to work with her. Brianna went above and beyond to support her customers, and because of it she was late arriving for her shift at India House, which was owned by her father. Her father was so proud of her for working so hard and always told her so. He also knew how seriously she took her job, so she knew that her father would understand

Brianna quickly changed into her uniform, which was a black dress with a brass name tag. While the rest of the wait staff wore black pants with a white shirt, Brianna preferred to wear dresses. They just seemed so much easier and certainly more feminine. She walked quickly to her first table, which was a four-top of young businessmen. She thought to herself, "This is a nice way to kick off my evening shift." In fact, a few of them were so strikingly handsome that she had to take a deep breath before taking their order. There's nothing wrong with having a little eye candy to make work a little more fun, she reflected.

"Good evening, gentlemen. My name is Brianna, and I will be your server tonight," said Brianna cheerfully. She smiled at them one by one and chirped, "I plan to make your dinner an unforgettable experience! What would you like to drink?"

The men ordered a bottle of 1992 Bordeaux. After serving the wine, Brianna shared the specials and asked for their order.

"Gorgeous! This menu looks so good that I need some recommendations. I'll bet you have great taste. What is your favorite thing on the menu?" asked Antonio, obviously flirting with Brianna.

"Why, thank you, sir. We pride ourselves on providing authentic cuisine and five-star service so that our customers come again and again. My favorite is the paneer tikka masala, extra hot and spicy! We can serve that with either rice or naan bread," said Brianna.

"Well, Miss Brianna, you just sold me on that. Paneer tikka masala sounds delightful. I cannot wait to try your favorite dish. I also can't decide between the rice and the naan, so let me have both, please," beamed Antonio.

"The lady has made it clear that it's the best dish on the menu, so let's make that two orders of the same!" said Marcus as he locked eyes with Brianna.

The four men enjoyed their dinner while also consuming several bottles of wine and stayed for nearly three hours. Antonio was clearly feeling pretty good and kept stealing glances at Brianna while laughing with his friends. Every time she would come to their table to ask if everything was OK, he would smile at her playfully and say, "The only thing that could make it better would be if you were having a glass of wine with us." To this, Brianna would politely respond, "I wish I could, but I'm on duty." When it came time to pay the bill, Marcus and Antonio tugged over the bill. In the end Antonio was able to grab it. He took the bill from his friends and insisted that he would pay it.

As they were leaving, Marcus was last to walk out and quickly slipped his business card into Brianna's hand and smiled. He winked at her and told her to give him a call.

Brianna blushed and gave him a stunning smile. "Wow, he sure is hot!" she thought to herself. When she glanced down at the business card, she discovered that Marcus was an attorney, and his personal number was written on the back of the card.

Upon returning to her table to pick up the check, she learned that Antonio had not only left her a $150 tip, but he had also given her his phone number and a note that said, "Call me tonight, beautiful!"

Brianna often wondered how her life would have turned out if she had called Marcus instead of Antonio.

The Dave Family

Brianna and Antonio had been dating for several months. With the holidays around the corner, they decided it was time to introduce each other to their families. At Antonio's suggestion, they started with Brianna's family first.

On a chilly Saturday afternoon in early November, Brianna arranged for an informal late lunch at her dad's house. She was excited for her father to finally meet Antonio. Brianna both admired her father and loved him dearly. His opinion meant so much to her. Brianna's thoughts turned to her stepmother, and she wondered what she would think of Antonio. "She will probably approve of him as soon as she knows how wealthy Antonio's family is," Brianna mused. She was fairly sure that her stepmother Valerie would have lunch catered because she couldn't find her way around a kitchen, let alone lift a finger to cook anything. Brianna often got frustrated with how different Sonia, her own mother, was from her stepmother. Sonia was a saint and worked so hard at everything. While Brianna was growing up, and even now, she cooked everything from scratch and was the perfect mother. She reminded her of an Indian version of Martha Stewart. Everything her mother created was just lovely in presentation, taste, and so on. Valerie, on the other hand, relied on her father for everything. She was too good to cook and clean. She would have him bring dinner from her father's restaurant almost every single day that they ate at home.

Brianna sighed deeply as she realized they had already arrived. As they walked through the front door, Brianna embraced her father with a big bear hug. "Daddy, this is Antonio," she said proudly.

Milan shook hands with Antonio and smiled at him warmly. Antonio replied politely, "Hello, sir. It's a pleasure to meet you. Brianna has told me so much about you!"

"The pleasure is all mine, Antonio. Anyone who loves and adores my only daughter is someone I am honored to welcome into my home," said Milan genuinely.

Then Brianna turned to Valerie and gave a quick hug. "Antonio, this is my dad's wife, Valerie," said Brianna.

"Hello, ma'am. It is so nice to meet you, too. Thank you for inviting me into your beautiful home," said Antonio, although he had already somewhat disdainfully sized up the house and its décor, deciding that it was a far cry from his family's luxurious home.

"You are most welcome, Antonio. It is so nice to meet you . . . finally!" said Valerie. Valerie had already noticed that Antonio had on a Hugo Boss sports coat and was sporting a gold, diamond-encrusted Rolex. She started to fuss over him immediately and made sure that she waited on him hand and foot.

Brianna and Antonio visited with Milan and Valerie for a few hours. The conversation was lighthearted and a little superficial, but typical of what one would expect with a first parental meeting.

After leaving Milan and Valerie's home, they walked down the street to meet Brianna's mother Sonia, who had just returned from her retail job at the mall. Brianna wondered why she had scheduled the introduction of Antonio with both parents on the same day. She knew the answer to that. She didn't want to hurt either parents' feelings by having one meet Antonio sooner than the other. It was starting to get windy outside, and they quickly walked into her mother's home.

Brianna hugged her mom hard, but she immediately felt that her mom was cold and distant. It was so unlike her mother to react like that to her. "Mom, I am so excited for you to finally meet Antonio!" said Brianna, trying to bring some energy to the air.

Sonia had been dreading this day for the last few months. She had an uncanny sixth sense for reading people. She could pick up on their energy and intentions within seconds of meeting them. Based on everything Brianna had shared about Antonio, Sonia knew that he was not right for her daughter. She knew that Brianna sensed that she wasn't herself. She didn't want to upset Brianna, so she quickly responded, "Hello, Antonio. Nice to meet you. Let's have a coffee together in the kitchen." She ushered him into the kitchen and realized she probably sounded a little terse.

"Good evening, ma'am. I am honored to meet you! Brianna has told me so much about you!" said Antonio eagerly.

Sonia was fuming inside. She couldn't help herself and immediately regretted saying, "Oh, really, Antonio! Well, what has she told you about me that would make you think I would approve of this relationship?"

Brianna couldn't believe her mother had just said that. "My sweet and soft-spoken mother just snapped at my Antonio, who she is just now meeting for the first time," Brianna thought to herself. Just as Brianna was about to say something, Antonio started without skipping a beat, "Wow! You are a feisty woman, just like Brianna shared with me. I know how much you love your daughter and want the best for her. I want to assure you that I love your daughter with all of my heart."

Sarcastically, Sonia responded, "That's reassuring, Antonio. Now, please tell me what exactly are your intentions for my daughter? You've been hanging out with her for quite some time." Sonia was proud of herself for standing her ground. She had been asking Brianna for months how serious it was between her and Antonio, and somehow Brianna couldn't give her a clear answer. She had also sensed that her daughter was starting to change, and she didn't like it one bit. It was almost as if overnight, Brianna was starting to second-guess herself.

What had made Sonia furious was when Brianna had shared with her that she had gone to Antonio's sister's wedding, and Antonio's parents hadn't even acknowledged Brianna's presence at the wedding. Brianna was seated in a table at the back of the room with a bunch of miscellaneous friends of theirs.

Antonio had not verbalized his true feelings to this extent, but he felt backed up against a wall. So, he said what was on his heart. "Brianna is my soul mate, and I am going to marry her one day," said Antonio as he looked into Brianna's eyes. Brianna blushed and closed her eyes, taking in this moment.

Sonia stood squarely in front of Antonio and then declared, "Over my dead body." She turned on her heel and stormed out of the kitchen. Brianna and Antonio stood there speechless looking at one another. Just then they heard Sonia slam the door to her bedroom shut.

Brianna was in tears. She was mortified at how her mother had just behaved towards Antonio. In all her life, she had never seen this side of her mother before. There were several times where her mother should have been angry, but she always retained control and was very careful not to react visibly. Brianna was stunned by her mother's behavior. Slowly, though, her shock turned into anger. As a result of this incident, she and her mother would not see each other or speak to one another for nearly twelve months.

The Grimaldi Family

Antonio had made dinner reservations for four at the Northshore Country Club for the following day. He had explained to Brianna that the country club tended toward formality, so she had decided to wear her nicest black dress.

Brianna had never been to a country club and didn't know what to expect. She did know that she very desperately wanted Antonio's parents to like her, especially after what Antonio had declared the day before about wanting to marry her one day.

After they arrived, the waiter seated them at a quiet table in the back overlooking the very manicured golf course. Antonio ordered Kir Royales while they waited for his parents to join them. It was nearly one hour later that his parents, Tina and George, walked through the doors with his sister Rhonda in tow. If you didn't know better, you would think that they owned the place. They marched in with such authority, all while nodding to some of the other guests. The maître d' was trying to guide them towards their table.

Brianna was so nervous that she felt uneasy and queasy. Nonetheless, she and Antonio stood up as they approached the table. Just as Antonio was about to introduce Brianna, Tina blurted out, "You must be Brittany."

"Mother, this is Brianna. Brianna, this is my mother, Tina," said Antonio, trying to smooth things over.

"It's a pleasure to meet you, Mrs. Grimaldi. Antonio has told me so much about you!" said Brianna with a nervous smile.

Tina did not return the pleasantries. Instead, she simply looked Brianna in the eyes and smiled a wicked grin.

Antonio continued with introductions of his father and sister. Inside, he was fuming because he did not want Rhonda to join them. He had specifically instructed his mother about this. After the way that she had treated Brianna at her wedding, Antonio had no tolerance for his sister. She insisted on seating Brianna away from him. Antonio had fought with his sister about the way she had spoken to Brianna at the wedding. She was so rude and short with her when Antonio had tried to introduce them. He wondered why his sister always stuck her nose into his business. Why couldn't she focus on her relationship instead of concerning herself with his?

The next two hours felt like two days. There was so much tension in the air that Brianna excused herself to freshen up in the ladies' room. Tina decided to join her. Once they were in the bathroom alone, Tina intercepted Brianna before she could move into one of the private ladies' restrooms. Tina moved closely and stood right in front of Brianna, just inches away. Brianna backed up and was literally standing against the wall.

"I don't know who you are or where you came from, but this is your first and last warning. You need to stay out of my son's life. Did you know that he already has a fiancée? Oh, by that look on your face, apparently you did not know that little fact, did you?" said Tina in the most hateful tone Brianna had ever heard.

"Antonio never told me about a fiancée! I'm sorry; I never meant to do anything wrong, Mrs. Grimaldi!" stuttered Brianna as she turned and ran towards the doors of the restroom crying. Her heart was pounding, and she was so confused. She thought Antonio had loved her and that they were going to spend the rest of their lives together. Luckily, the restrooms were located towards the front of the club, and she quickly found her way to the hostess to call her a cab. The hostess informed her that it would take a few minutes. Brianna could feel that her eyeliner was running down her face and so she decided that she would wait outside. The valet quickly came to her and brought her an umbrella. Brianna couldn't keep her composure. She stood outside in the rain crying her heart out.

Finally, even though it was only a couple of minutes, she was grateful that the cab had arrived. Just as she was getting into the cab, Antonio came running outside. "Brianna, what happened? Why are you leaving?" asked Antonio.

"Ask your mother. Better yet, ask your fiancée!" muttered Brianna between sobs. She gave the cab driver her address and asked him to hurry.

2001: The F Place is Born

New York City, New York

Eugene Wood and four other investors founded "The A Place," a privately owned U.S. pharmaceutical company, in 1962. Eugene's son, Alexander Wood, joined The A Place after completing his business degree at Stanford in 1980. Alexander worked his way up through the ranks and, at the age of 40, was appointed CEO in 1998. Unbeknownst to Alexander, his father had expanded his ownership throughout the years when the other investors decided to sell portions of their stake in the company. When Alexander became CEO, Eugene gave him the surprise of his life. He transferred all his shares to Alexander, leaving him with the majority ownership in the company.

Alexander was a visionary leader who liked to dream big. His passion for improving the lives of people everywhere was contagious. While The A Place was making an impact within the United States, Alexander's global vision would require additional financial investment of a significant amount as well as a shift towards wholistic, patient-centric medicine. To make his dream a reality, Alexander and his father successfully raised $10 billion in funding. This funding and the assets of The A Place were invested into a new publicly owned company called The F Place.

Alexander created a new leadership team, composed of top talent from The A Place as well as industry giants, such as Albert Weinstein, David Church, and Philip Speight. Michael Vitali had quickly advanced his career at The A Place, and

Alexander trusted him implicitly, so he gave him a prime seat at the table. Pat Pierson and Alexander had worked together for years. Alexander admired and respected Pat a great deal. Pat was perfectly positioned as the head of Human Resources. His love for people was truly remarkable, and Alexander knew that Pat would help him to create a one-of-a-kind culture where both their employees and customers alike would enjoy doing business.

"Pat, we need to create a brand-new company culture for The F Place. It should be the perfect blend of a successful, mature, domestic organization and a lean, global start-up company filled with passionate entrepreneurs. I want the legacy associates from The A Place and the new hires of The F Place to work as one integrated global team. How do you believe we can best accomplish this?" asked Alexander.

"Alexander, the fact that you are even thinking about our new company culture already puts you far ahead in the game. My recommendation is that we bring in a partner who has proven experience with business Transformation. They have industry-specific playbooks that can accelerate our progress. I already have a few consulting firms in mind. I would be happy to get the ball rolling. Just say the word," said Pat.

"Excellent idea, Pat. That's just the kind of thing that we need to get this launched. I love it, man. Please go ahead and proceed. Let me know your recommendation by the end of the month. That gives you several weeks, as we need to move on this quickly. I want to set the right tone from day one," said Alexander.

Pat Pierson then connected with each of his peers to discuss their ideas and requirements for a Transformation consulting partner. He curated all their input into a selection matrix and reached out to the top seven management consulting firms in the country. Pat interviewed each of the firms and created a short list of three.

A few days later, Pat quickly organized a two-day offsite meeting in Saint Thomas for Alexander and the Executive Team. During this session, each of the top three management consulting firms presented their plan for The F Place Transformation. Using the selection matrix, each of the executive leaders provided their input on which consulting partner would be the best fit for The F Place.

Pat facilitated a review of all feedback so that each leader had a voice in the process. In the end, The F Place leadership decided to hire The COMO Group for a twelve-month engagement to ensure that a strong, healthy foundation was laid during the first year of the new company. Their Transformation methodology, involving Clarity, Ownership, Meaningful Mindset, and One-Of-A-Kind Principles, or COMO, resonated well with most of the leadership team. In fact, all the leaders except for Michael Vitali were on board with the decision to bring on The COMO Group. Michael was politically astute and went along with the decision because Alexander supported it, and he was not about to ruffle Alexander's feathers.

Within the first ninety days of the engagement, The COMO Group partnered with The F Place Executive Team to solidify their mission, values, guiding principles, and five-year strategic plan.

Together, they created The F Place mission statement: "To become the global leader in pharmaceuticals by providing wholistic solutions that improve the mental health and lives of patients everywhere."

They also laid the foundation of the company culture by creating the Five F Values. Alexander, Pat, and the leadership team committed to living their values and leading by example.

The F Place Executive Leadership Team—Organization Structure 2001

Below are the key executive leadership team members and roles.

2001

```
                    ALEXANDER WOOD
                    President & CEO

                              DOROTHY CHAMBERS
                              Executive Assistant
```

BARBARA KUNKEL	DAVID CHURCH	MICHAEL VITALI	ALBERT WEINSTEIN
SVP, Chief Financial Officer	SVP, Sales & Marketing	AVP, Chief Products Officer	VP, Strategy

PHILIP SPEIGHT	NICOLETTE DEAN	JOHN BROWNING	PAT PIERSON
VP, Operations	VP, Legal	VP, Chief Information Officer	VP, Human Resources

2002: The Forced Prenuptial

Chicago, Illinois

Brianna could hardly believe that she and Antonio were celebrating New Year's Eve together this year, given everything that had happened just over one year ago. She remarked on how the year had flown by. She thought about how she had absolutely refused to speak with Antonio after learning that he had a fiancée. He tried for weeks to explain the situation, but she wanted no part in that. Brianna had felt so betrayed by Antonio. Between the cruelty of his mother and the shock of his engagement, there was nothing that he could say to change her mind. So, she focused her attention on her studies and work. With this winter semester's finals behind her, she was now working as many hours as she could to earn money over the holiday break.

She was sad, alone, and depressed, so she had decided to work at her father's restaurant for New Year's Eve. They always needed help on New Year's due to the big dinner dance that the restaurant would host. Midnight had come and gone. She thought to herself, "Just like that, another year has gone by." As she was walking to her car to go home, Antonio surprised her by walking straight up to her. Before she knew what was happening, he embraced her and kissed her. "Brianna, I have been trying and trying to talk to you. I need to explain the situation." At first, she thought she was dreaming, and then she realized he was still holding her in his arms. She had missed him so much and realized it felt so good to be in his arms.

"Well, you're here now. So, you have five minutes and then I am going home," said Brianna, holding back tears.

"Brianna, I have never loved anyone the way that I love you. And I have never asked anyone to marry me. I swear on my life. I am not engaged! My mother has had this dream for me to marry her friend's daughter since I was a little boy. They come from a super-wealthy, high-class family, and she wants me to marry her. In her mind, it was a modern-day arranged marriage. But I choose you. You are the only woman for me!" said Antonio.

Brianna's shoulders relaxed as the confusion and hurt started to melt away. It finally started to make sense to her. "Well, what does your mother say about us? If she will not accept me, we can never work! What's the point, Antonio?" said Brianna.

"Don't worry, my love. After that horrible day in November, I spoke with my father and explained my love for you. Father supports me in my decision. After all, he and my mother had a love marriage of their own. Father convinced my mother to accept you into our lives, even though we come from different backgrounds. My mother's parents had an arranged marriage for her, and she broke that arrangement to marry my father, who is Italian . . . not Indian. She should be the last one to object to our union," said Antonio firmly.

Brianna was taken aback by what Antonio had just shared with her. "Are you serious? How could she talk to me like that after what she went through to marry your father?" said Brianna, skeptical.

"Don't worry, my love. My mother has seen the error of her ways. She will not treat you like that ever again. In fact, I even think she is sorry for the way she behaved towards you. I know my mother, Brianna. All she wants is for me, her only son, to be happy, nothing else," said Antonio. He seemed so sure of what he was saying, thought Brianna, and was certainly convincing. She could see by looking into his eyes how much he loved her.

Brianna could not believe it was almost the year 2002. "It is so amazing what can change with one full rotation around the sun," Brianna thought to herself. She and Antonio were dressed to the nines and had taken a limousine to the most exclusive New Year's Eve ball in New York City to bring in the year 2002.

"Honey, it's almost midnight; do you want to dance?" asked Antonio. Suddenly, Brianna's mind shifted from last year to the present.

As they danced on the dance floor, Brianna felt like the most beautiful woman in the world with her knight in shining armor. As the song ended, everyone cleared the dance floor, but Antonio encouraged Brianna to stay next to him. And then, the orchestra began playing their favorite song, "Time to Say Goodbye" by Andrea Bocelli and Sarah Brightman. Antonio whisked her to the center of the dance floor while everyone looked on. They danced slowly, and he whispered in her ear how much he loved her and that he wanted to spend the rest of his life loving her. He wanted her to be his forever.

As the song neared the end, Antonio stepped back and got on one knee. "Brianna, will you make me the happiest man on the planet and be mine forever?" he smiled.

"Yes! Yes, I would be honored to be your wife, Antonio!" Brianna said tearfully.

As they embraced, the New Year's Eve ball dropped and the year 2002 began.

Over the next several months, Brianna, her mother Sonia, her future mother-in-law Tina, and her future sister-in-law Rhonda worked together to plan the traditional wedding in Mumbai, India, as well as the reception in Chicago, which was essentially their Western wedding. Brianna had offered to include her stepmother Valerie in the planning, but Sonia had shut that down quickly!

Tina seemed to be supportive of their relationship, and she had been cordial with Brianna ever since she and Antonio had gotten back together. But Brianna always felt like she had to walk on eggshells around her because she had seen firsthand how mean and nasty Tina could be.

Brianna and Sonia had worked through their relationship troubles once Sonia learned that Antonio had proposed to Brianna. At that point, Sonia knew that she could lose her daughter forever if she did not accept the man that she loved.

Late February, Brianna and Antonio met with Tina and Sonia to finalize the wedding invitations as well as Mumbai and Chicago logistics. Once they included all the Grimaldi family, friends, and business associates, they had a total of 1,200 people to invite to the wedding ceremony in India and another 750 people for the Chicago reception for those who couldn't travel. Adding people to the endless list seemed to please Tina very much!

It was the responsibility of the bride's parents to pay for the wedding, and Brianna knew that this was going to be a huge expense for both of her parents. Her father Milan had committed to paying for the Indian wedding, including travel for the wedding party, and her mother Sonia had committed to paying for the Chicago reception. Milan took out a $100k second mortgage on his home to cover his costs. Sonia took out a $80k second mortgage on her home to cover hers. Brianna felt so guilty for laying this burden at the feet of her parents, but she had no other way to pay for the wedding of her dreams.

Brianna truly struggled that semester with keeping up with her classes while working part time and planning a wedding. Tina had insisted on speeding up the wedding, so they had to plan and execute the whole thing within two months of their engagement. It was absurd. Brianna was burning the candle at both ends and was just ready for the semester to be over and her wedding to happen already. The stress was too much, and Tina insisted that Brianna put university on hold and focus on making sure the wedding went off without a hitch. Brianna knew that if she continued with university that she wouldn't survive the semester, not to mention, there was no way she was going to be able to able to take a whole month off to go to

India to prepare for the wedding. She decided to give in and promised herself that she would take only this semester off, and then she would take classes over summer so that she could finally graduate.

About a month before the wedding, Antonio came over to her place for dinner. She had cooked his favorite, paneer tikka masala, and was expecting a quiet, romantic evening. Instead, he explained to her that he needed her to sign some legal documents so that they could proceed with their dream wedding.

"Honey, this is a standard prenuptial document. Everybody does one these days. It was prepared by our family lawyer, Charles Radcliff. There is nothing in here to worry about because you and I are going to be married forever," said Antonio.

"Antonio, I trust you, I really do. But how can I sign something that I don't even understand?" said Brianna.

"Sweetheart, this is just twenty pages of legal mumbo jumbo to say that what's yours is yours and what's mine is mine . . . if we ever get a divorce. That's it. It's as simple as that. But we will never get a divorce, so you don't need to worry about it. I promise you!" said Antonio.

Brianna looked really uncomfortable but did not say a word.

"You can review it with your family lawyer, if that makes you more comfortable. But my parents need this to be signed by next week at the latest," said Antonio.

"Antonio, I don't have a family attorney, nor do I have the money to pay an attorney to review this for me. So, what am I supposed to do?" asked Brianna.

"Baby, do you know how much I love you?" asked Antonio, as he leaned in to embrace and kiss her.

"Yes, of course I do," said Brianna.

"Then, just trust me and sign the document," said Antonio.

And Brianna followed her heart instead of her head. She

signed the prenuptial agreement, and just over one month later they were married in May of 2002. Her wedding day in Mumbai was the absolute best day of her marriage!

Antonio's parents paid for a three-week honeymoon to Europe. When the lovebirds returned in June, they moved into the Grimaldi estate and lived in the guest house.

In November, their first child, Ari Deepali Grimaldi was born.

2006: The Friendly Grandma . . . Not

Chicago, Illinois

Brianna successfully graduated from Northwestern University with honors in December 2005. Despite having a 4-year-old daughter and a newborn son to care for and having so many long hours and countless sleepless nights, it was all worth it. It was so much later that her original graduation date, but she reminded herself that it just wouldn't have been possible to finish earlier with the wedding, kids, and her endless obligations to her in-laws. Antonio had also insisted that there was no reason for her to go to school when he was now going to provide for her for the rest of her life.

Sonia had insisted that Brianna get her degree and secure a job. She would always remind Brianna, "Darling, money will come and go. Once you have a degree, though, no one can take it away from you. You'll always be able to find a good job and take care of yourself." Sonia knew that Tina and Antonio always made Brianna feel bad about her humble beginnings. They would say things like, "If it weren't for us, you would never be able to live in a luxurious house like this or drive a Mercedes." Brianna knew deep down that her mother was right about being able to stand on her own two feet. Brianna hated that she was forced to rely on Antonio's family for all their financial needs. Despite Antonio begging her not to finish school and take a job, Brianna was thankful that she had decided to do an internship because it opened several doors for her. Upon graduating, she received a competitive job offer as a project manager in the Quality organization at The F Place.

"You are the mother of my children, and we have everything we need living with my parents. Why do you need a full-time job anyway, Brianna?" asked Antonio like a spoiled brat. Brianna was so disgusted with Antonio. Shortly after they were married, she realized that Antonio did nothing. He would sleep in every single day of the week till 10:30 or 11 a.m. He would expect food on his timing, and he barely helped with the kids. Aside from making a few stock trades here and there, he literally did nothing productive. He often went out with his friends and would come home in the wee hours of the night.

"Antonio, how many times do I have to explain this to you? I want to have a career; it fulfills me. We cannot live off your parents forever. We need to have our own home. And I want to help my mom out, too. She is too old to work as hard as she does!" said Brianna.

"Brianna, that is never going to happen! I am the only son of my parents, and we will live with them until they die. Then, I will inherit everything, including their import and export jewelry empire. Your parents have never truly accepted me, so they will never get a dime of my money. They are going to need to figure it out for themselves. Do you understand? You are such an ungrateful wife! Any other woman would kill to have what you have and live in a house like this," yelled Antonio.

"You think I'm ungrateful? What about you? You are lazy and have never worked a day in your life. Your parents give you everything. What do you do for them?" said Brianna, getting angrier.

"I have given them their only grandchildren, and I am there for them at a moment's notice whenever they need me. If you don't change your tone with me, I will take your car keys again and you will have to find your own transportation to work. Do you hear me, woman?" shouted Antonio.

Brianna realized that the argument was going nowhere, and she wanted to avoid upsetting Antonio further. He had already hit her in the face twice since they were married, and she did not want to experience that ever again. Were it not for her two children, she would have left him shortly after they were married. She had never imagined that her life would turn into this awful nightmare.

She quickly reminded herself that it was time to put the children to bed. "I am sorry for upsetting you, Antonio. Can you ever forgive me?" asked Brianna in submission.

"Oh, my love, of course I forgive you. You are the love of my life!" said Antonio.

While Brianna worked at The F Place, Antonio often golfed during the day. Grandma Tina happily provided childcare for their grandchildren, Ari and Eshan. Although she despised her daughter-in-law, she adored her grandchildren. And she never missed an opportunity to plant seeds of doubt into those little minds.

"Children, it's time for lunch," said Tina.

"What are we having today, Grandma?" asked Ari.

"Eshan is having his favorite bottle of milk. You and I are having your favorite, too, sweetie—tomato soup and grilled cheese sandwiches," said Tina.

"Yummy! Grandma, I miss Mommy. When is she going to be home?" asked Ari.

"Sweetheart, your mommy should be home by 5:30 in time to cook dinner for all of us. I am so sorry that she loves her career more than you two. I just cannot understand how a mother can choose her job over her children. But don't you worry about that. Grandma, Grandpa, and Daddy will always be here for you!" said Tina.

2010: Accelerated FDA Approval

Michael Vitali as well as Torsten Schmidt, Edward Ferris, and their team had practically moved mountains to obtain FDA approval for HappyVITA in September 2010. Torsten Schmidt, who joined the company in 2005, had exerted his "influence" with the regulators. Edward Ferris was the VP of Product Development and Michael's longtime protégé. Edward spearheaded the development of HappyVITA and was one of Michael's most trusted leaders.

The HappyVITA launch was a tremendous accomplishment for Michael at 41 years of age, but it still wasn't good enough. His father had become CEO at age 35, and Michael was determined to be just as successful as his father.

"Congratulations on a job well done, Michael! Our vision of helping people with their anxiety and depression is finally becoming a reality with the launch of HappyVITA! We couldn't have done it without you. What would you like to do next, Michael? Just say the word and I will make it happen," said Alexander.

"Alexander, I sincerely appreciate all of your support and the Board's support as well. What's next for me? Well, you already know that I want your job one day . . . when you retire, of course," said Michael.

"Michael, I have been very transparent with you and David

Church alike. You are both on my succession plan. However, I don't plan to retire any time soon. I love working at The F Place!" said Alexander.

"Yes, I appreciate your transparency. In the meantime, I would like to make a proposal to you, which will increase my value proposition to The F Place," said Michael knowing full well that he had piqued Alexander's curiosity by making this bold statement.

"Good. I'm listening, Michael," said Alexander.

"We all know that Philip is in over his head with Operations. I would gladly take his role and put him out of his misery to step in and serve as your true chief operating officer. There is so much opportunity to optimize our operations, and unlike Philip, I am prepared to make the tough decisions. If we don't get things under control quickly, we are going to lose some major customers. Afterall, you did say that I could ask for anything. So, what do you think?" asked Michael.

The next week, just like that, Philip Speight (VP, Operations) quietly departed from The F Place, allowing Michael to take one step closer to his goal of becoming CEO. In the meanwhile, Michael's protégé, Edward Ferris, was promoted to the C-suite.

The F Place Executive Leadership Team— Organization Structure 2010

Below are the key executive leadership team members and roles.

2010

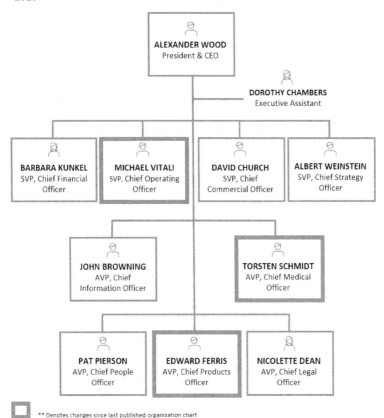

** Denotes changes since last published organization chart

2014: The Fractured Marriage

Chicago, Illinois

After enjoying a full day of golf on a beautiful Friday in April, Antonio walked through the doors of his house. He was famished and looking forward to one of Brianna's delicious home-cooked meals. It was nearly 6 o'clock, and he was frustrated that she was not home yet. His wife knew that she was expected to have dinner on the table for the family by 6 every evening, no exceptions. This week was easier for her than usual because his parents were in Europe for two weeks.

"She is probably working late," thought Antonio to himself. "Well, she cannot work too late because she has to pick up the kids from Maria's place by 6:30."

Antonio decided to take a shower and try to calm himself down. Whenever Brianna defied him like that, it truly made his blood boil. He and his parents had been nothing but kind and generous to her, giving her a better life than she had growing up. And this is how she repaid them?

After drying himself off with a towel, he walked into the closet to put on a change of clothes. And that is when he saw that her side of the closet was completely empty. His heart began to race as he came to the realization that she had left him. He ran to Ari's bedroom and discovered her clothes and most of her personal things were missing. Many items were missing from Eshan's room as well.

He went back to his bedroom, got dressed, took a deep breath, and called Brianna's mobile phone. It went straight to voicemail. "Brianna, this is your first and last warning. If you and the kids do not come home tonight, I will make your life a living hell forever. That is a promise!" said Antonio.

His next call was to his mother. Although it was nearly 1 a.m. in Italy, he knew that she would answer his call. "Mom, she left me and took the kids. What should I do?" he cried out.

Tina had spent more than ten years waiting for this day. "Oh, honey, I am so sorry to hear that. You need to call the police chief and report that your wife has kidnapped the children. In the meantime, I will call Charles and get our legal action started. The best defense is an offense. Don't worry, honey, we will have your children back before you know it," said Tina.

"But Mom, I want Brianna back, too. I love her!" said Antonio.

"I know you do, dear. But sometimes we must show a little tough love," said Tina.

Antonio spent the rest of the evening drowning his sorrows. He was unable to sleep, quietly hoping that she would come to her senses and return to him. Had she somehow found out about his cheating? He had only been unfaithful to her with three people throughout their twelve-year marriage. Two of those were one-night stands that meant nothing to him. Felisa was a different story altogether. He had been seeing her on and off since Eshan was born. Felisa understood him and gave him the attention that Brianna simply could not or would not after having two children. But there is no way that she found out about Felisa; they were much too careful.

Brianna was the woman he genuinely loved. Why didn't she understand that? Perhaps she questioned his love for her because he occasionally lost his temper and hit her. He thought it wasn't his fault. She always challenged him and never did as he commanded. He never broke a bone on her dainty little figure and her bruises were minor. She always managed to cover them with makeup. Most of their arguments were her fault. After all these years, she should have learned not to set off his triggers. He couldn't help it that he lost his temper; it was genetic.

He texted her over and over again throughout the night. Sixty-two text messages in total. But she did not respond.

When Saturday morning finally arrived and Brianna had not returned, Antonio called the police chief, a close friend of the family, and set an unfortunate series of events into motion.

On Saturday afternoon, there was a knock on the door. When Antonio opened the door, his daughter Ari and son Eshan were standing there in tears. "What's going on, Daddy? Why did you call the police on Mommy?" asked Ari.

"Your home is here. Mommy had no right to take you away from us like that. Don't worry; Daddy is going to fix everything," said Antonio. He continued, "Grandma is going to take care of you, and Auntie Rhonda is on her way over right now to play with you."

After he ushered the kids in the house, he noticed his phone had several text messages. "You bastard. How could you do that to me!" texted Brianna to Antonio.

"You had your chance. We will see you in court," texted Antonio.

The following week, Charles met with Antonio, Tina, and George to develop their legal strategy. They agreed to pursue full custody of the children and to make a case that Brianna was an unfit mother. At best, she would get to see the children during supervised visits once per month. Additionally, because Brianna had a healthy income at The F Place and Antonio (technically) had no income, they filed for maximum alimony and child support. They were well aware that they would not get everything they asked for, but they knew that fighting them in court would drain Brianna's financials and make her wish that she had never walked into their lives and ruined their marital plans for Antonio.

One day after school, Eshan was playing chess with Grandma Tina. "Grandma, I miss Mommy. When can I see her?" he asked.

"Oh, honey, I know you do. But your Mommy is too busy for you and loves her career more than she loves you and Daddy. That is why the courts have not let you see her this past month. It is much better for you both to continue living here in our home, where we are here for you day and night. Daddy, Grandma, and Grandpa will always be here for you," said Tina.

Antonio got great satisfaction out of dragging the divorce out for years. Every mediation or court hearing gave him an opportunity to see Brianna up close and personal. He had tried to spy on her at her house a couple of times, and then she went and bought a guard dog. At more than 100 pounds, that Doberman scared the living daylights out of him, so he resorted to watching her from afar. How was it possible to love someone and hate them at the very same time? He loved her so much that he would spend the rest of his life hating her for leaving him. After nearly three years and $200K of legal expenses, the court finally ordered joint custody. But, by that time, the children had been sufficiently brainwashed that they no longer wanted to live with their mother.

2017: My Fellow Associates

The Hamptons, New York

Eugene and Flora Wood's family spent the Christmas holiday season at their Hamptons estate every year since their sons, Alexander and Hamilton, were 12 and 10.

The family tradition continued after Alexander married Taylee in 1985. Their son and twin daughters loved that special holiday time with their grandparents and parents every year!

Hamilton's participation in the family tradition was inconsistent at best. Everyone knew that Hamilton only joined them when he literally had nowhere else to go or no one else to spend the holidays with. Nevertheless, the family welcomed his presence and did their best to show him grace, even though he was the most self-centered, entitled, and greedy person in their world.

The year 2016 had been another rough one for Hamilton as he had just gone through his third divorce. His older son from his first marriage had decided to spend the holiday with his mother's family. His younger son from his second marriage had been estranged from Hamilton ever since he had cheated on his mother and married his much younger third wife a few years prior. So, Hamilton decided to grace everyone with his presence to avoid spending the holiday in isolation.

Per usual, they all went to the Christmas Eve candlelight service and had planned to enjoy a delicious Christmas Eve dinner afterwards. Before eating, Eugene always said the most beautiful prayer of thanks, and this year was no exception. After the prayer was finished, everyone except for Hamilton enthusiastically said, "Amen."

"Hamilton, we are overjoyed that you could join us this year. I know things are hard right now, but always remember how much we love you," said Flora with warmth in her voice.

"Mom, can we please cut out the pleasantries? Your life is great, their lives are great and, well . . . my life sucks!" said Hamilton as he looked around the table at Alexander and his "perfect" family.

"Hamilton, it's Christmas Eve; please don't talk to Mom that way. You know how much it hurts her!" said Alexander forcefully.

"Who died and made you king? Get off my back," said Hamilton as he stared down Alexander.

"Hamilton, can we please stop? It's Christmas Eve. Let's all reflect upon the things that we are thankful for. OK? Dad, why don't you start?" said Alexander.

"Thank you, son. I am thankful to be 87 years old and married to the love of my life, Flora. I am thankful for my health and to be sitting here with all of you on this blessed night," said Eugene.

"That's beautiful, my darling. I am thankful for you, too! And I am most thankful to have both of my sons and three of my grandchildren here tonight. We have not all been together for several years! Hamilton, the only thing that could make it better would be to have your boys with us," said Flora.

"Thanks, Mom. Sorry I am always such a disappointment to you! I knew I should have just stayed home this weekend," said Hamilton. He was truly on edge because he had not been able to convince his kids to spend the holidays with him this year.

"That's enough, Hamilton! Cut it out right now. I may be old and frail, but I am still your father, and this is still my house!" said Eugene.

"There you go again, Dad, holding your money and power over my head. What else are you going to threaten me with next? My inheritance?" asked Hamilton.

"Hamilton, if you keep this up, you won't get an inheritance!" shouted Alexander as he stood up from the table.

"Again, I will ask, who died and made you king, Alexander? Just because you are the older son does not mean that you control their estate. I will get half of everything whether you like it or not!" said Hamilton.

Alexander looked at his parents and shook his head, silently imploring his father to let it go that night. "Just leave it. Let's try and have a civil family dinner. OK?" he pleaded.

Eugene ignored his older son's request, stood up and shouted, "Hamilton, while you were busy squandering your allowance away, Alexander helped me build and grow The A Place. While Alexander was building The F Place, you were gallivanting around, unwilling to lift a finger. You have lived off our hard-earned money for far too long. You are an ungrateful son, who only calls his mother twice a year at best. You can't keep a relationship for more than a couple of years, and your children hardly even know you. You should be ashamed of yourself!"

"I should be ashamed of myself? You have treated Alexander like the heir for my entire life. I have always been treated like the red-headed stepchild in this family. You and Mom loved him and tolerated me. Merry Christmas—all of you can go to hell!" said Hamilton as he grabbed his things and left the estate, presumably to go back to his apartment in the city.

Flora looked up at Eugene, wiped the tears from her eyes, and went up to her master suite, where she could be heard sobbing. Alexander and Eugene rejoined Alexander's family at the dining table. Everyone was still in shock and quietly served themselves. No one said a word; they just ate their dinner in silence.

By Christmas morning, Flora was back to her positive, energetic self, and Eugene was also coming around. While Hamilton had a way of upsetting them deeply, they were very intentional with their mindsets and knew that they had made the right decision.

Everyone enjoyed a morning of coffee, along with generous helpings of Flora's homemade pumpkin pie. There was Christmas music playing on the piano and a roaring fire in the fireplace as they exchanged gifts. When they were finished, the only gifts that remained under the tree were for Hamilton, and there was nothing from Hamilton for any of them.

Alexander's blood boiled when he realized that, yet again, Hamilton had not bothered to get gifts for anyone, not even his own mother and father. While he always expected the best gifts for himself, he rarely gave a gift to anyone else without an ulterior motive of some sort. Alexander was fairly certain that the nicest gift his brother had ever given his parents was a set of bath towels! "How pathetic." thought Alexander. "After everything that our parents have done for him, this is how he treats them," he fumed.

All in all, the family enjoyed their quality time together on Christmas day, relaxing, eating, playing games, and watching TV. Alexander was grateful for his parents and strived to do everything possible to help his parents enjoy their golden years to the greatest extent possible.

The next day, they packed their bags and loaded the car to go home. Alexander had some business to attend to in the city the next day. Taylee and the kids hugged his parents tightly and told them how much they loved them.

"I love you, Mom. I am so sorry for how Hamilton treats you. I wish I could change things, but please know that I will always be here for you. And thank you for a wonderful Christmas. We'll see you and Dad again end of January to celebrate his birthday," said Alexander to his mother, Flora, as he gave her a big bear hug.

"Son, I am the luckiest mother and grandmother in the world because of you. You have always been my special gift from God. Thank you for everything," said Flora with tears in her eyes.

"Dad, I love you so much. Hamilton's issues are not your fault. He is a grown man, and his life is a direct reflection of his decisions. You have been the best dad that a son could ever hope for. You are my hero, and I am so thankful for you. Despite the blowup, we all had a nice Christmas. I'll see you again at the end of January to celebrate your birthday. I love you!" said Alexander, giving his Dad a big embrace.

"I love you, too, son. And I am prouder of you than you will ever know. You are an amazing husband, father, son, and business leader. You amaze me with your generosity every single day. That work that you and Taylee are doing with the orphanage in Africa is phenomenal. Just imagine what you will be able to give back—in time and money—when you retire one day. You have already given back far more than I ever did, and I couldn't be prouder!" said Eugene.

Saying goodbye was always a lengthy process with the Wood family. Eventually everyone said their last goodbyes. Then, Alexander and the family drove away.

Just as they were pulling into Manhattan, Alexander got a call on his mobile phone. "Hello, Mom, did we forget something?" Everyone in the car could hear the call because it was connected via Bluetooth.

Flora was sobbing and crying so loudly that it was difficult to understand what she was saying.

"Mom, what happened? Are you OK? I'm having trouble understanding you!" said Alexander as he pulled over to the side of the road.

"Your father is dead, Alexander! Please come back. I need you!" said Flora.

"What? That can't be! What happened, Mom?" said Alexander.

"One minute he was standing in the kitchen, and the next minute he collapsed to the ground. I called 911 and the paramedics arrived a few minutes ago. They said that it was likely a stroke. Oh, Alexander, please come back!" cried Flora.

The following days were a blur for Alexander as he took care of all the funeral arrangements for his father. His mother was completely devasted. She was lost without his father. He and Taylee were so busy planning everything that he did not have time to truly process his own feelings until New Year's Eve, which was the day after his father's funeral. To add insult to injury, his brother Hamilton chose not to attend their father's funeral and spent the rest of his life ashamed for the last words he had said to his very own father, words that he could never take back.

Since Alexander and his family were still at the Hamptons estate for New Year's Eve, they watched the New York City New Year's Eve special from the comfort of Flora's living room. As they watched the ball drop, Alexander declared to Taylee, his children, and his mother, "Life is short. Too short. I have achieved incredible success in my life, and now I want to retire and spend the rest of my life helping the orphans of this world. Taylee, we are going live and give like no one else! It's what Dad would have wanted. I just know it."

Alexander got up from the couch and grabbed his glass of champagne. He cleared his throat and looked around wistfully, thinking of how his father would always make the toasts at their family gatherings. "I'd like to make a toast to my dear dad as he's looking down on each of us. A toast to each and every one of you in this wonderful family and to the new year. May the new year of 2017 be our best year ever, and may we make Dad proud always as we carry out his dream of making the world a better place!" said Alexander.

When Alexander arrived at The F Place on January 2, his first course of action was to meet with his HR leader, Pat Pierson. He informed Pat about the sudden death of his father and then calmly shared his revised retirement plan.

"Pat, you and I have been working on my succession plan for quite some time. I know that we had not planned for my retirement until 2020 or 2021 at the earliest, but I am accelerating that plan. I have decided to retire this year, and we need to make this a smooth transition. How do you believe we can do this, Pat?" asked Alexander.

"Are you absolutely sure, Alexander? The F Place is your legacy, built on the foundation of The A Place founded by your father! Are you really ready to walk away so soon? Just like that? I know that you are shaken up about the loss of your father, but Alexander, your father trusted you with his vision," said Pat.

"I know, Pat, and I am not going to walk away completely. I will keep my majority shareholder position and serve as Chairman of the Board. And I will, of course, coach and mentor our next CEO, along with the handful of executives that I am mentoring today at The F Place," said Alexander.

"Both David Church and Michael Vitali have been groomed well, and they are both capable of assuming your CEO responsibilities. David has consistently exceeded sales targets, and Michael continues to deliver exceptional operational performance. However, I have heard a few unsubstantiated concerns with the interns. My gut tells me it is just watercooler talk, but I'll get to the bottom of it ASAP, given this turn of events," said Pat.

"Indeed, David and Michael are both capable. And now, we need to decide which of them is most ready to take the reins within the next six months. Although I believe they could both fulfill the duties of the CEO, we need a fair and impartial assessment before we decide," said Alexander.

"I agree, Alexander. I will start the confidential executive background checks as well as Board of Directors and key customer interviews. We should have everything we need to make a recommendation to the Board by the beginning of February," said Pat.

TO: All F Place Associates
FROM: Alexander Wood, President and Chief Executive Officer
SUBJECT: Time to Pass the Baton
DATE: February 27, 2017

My Fellow F Place Associates,

Since the day we opened the doors of The F Place for business in 2001, it has been my honor and esteemed pleasure to work with you to provide solutions that improve the mental health and lives of patients everywhere.

The progress we have made together has truly made a difference in this world, and I am so grateful for each and every one of you. Thus, it is bittersweet for me to share with you that I will be stepping down as your CEO effective July 1, 2017. While I will continue to serve you as Chairman of the Board, my retirement will allow me to pursue another burning passion in my heart, which is to provide education, food, shelter, and love to impoverished orphans around the world. You can follow my journey on social media HERE.

While we have many talented and capable leaders here at The F Place, the Board of Directors and I have decided to appoint Michael Vitali as your next CEO. For those of you who don't know Michael, he graduated valedictorian of his class at the United States Naval Academy and later successfully completed his MBA from Harvard Business School. He has held a variety of leadership positions at The F Place since its inception in 2001, most recently serving as our Chief Operating Officer.

Please take a few minutes to watch <u>this video</u> where Michael and I explain how we will work together over the coming months to pass the "CEO baton" smoothly and efficiently. I am confident that Michael is the right leader to take The F Place into the FUTURE!

I would also like to thank David Church, who has led our Sales & Marketing function since he joined the company in 2001, most recently serving as our Chief Commercial Officer. Effective immediately, David has decided to leave the company to pursue other opportunities. We plan to conduct a comprehensive executive search, internally and externally, for our new Commercial leader. In the interim, the regional sales leaders will report to Michael.

In closing, I want to thank each of you for your contributions to The F Place. We would not be who we are without you! Please kindly give Michael the same level of support, commitment, and trust that you have shown me these past sixteen years!

Michael shut the door to his office, closed his eyes, and savored the moment. The day had finally come when he was appointed CEO of The F Place! Although he was thirteen years behind his father, he had still accomplished what most people could only dream of. He had truly arrived and was going to be CEO of the number-three global pharmaceutical company in the world! And, with Michael's superior leadership, he was sure that they would become number one by 2020 at the latest. He poured himself a large glass of whiskey on the rocks and settled himself on the leather couch in his office. He grabbed the remote control to the television in his office and watched the CEO transition video several times before going home that night. He had finally achieved his goal of becoming CEO at The F Place, and he couldn't be happier.

Over the next several months, Michael endured his transition period with Alexander and longed for the day when he would finally retire so that Michael could rule The F Place the "right" way and with his own circle of leaders. Michael used the transition period wisely and carefully assessed who on the Executive Team had been loyal to him and who would be inclined to push back on his vision for the company.

Edward Ferris, his 51-year-old chief products officer, was on the top of his list. No matter what Michael asked of him, Edward consistently delivered for Michael. He was instrumental in the accelerated FDA approval and early product launch of HappyVITA. Edward, his good and loyal soldier, was a keeper.

Next in line was 35-year-old Tom Peterson, his right-hand man in Operations. Michael had hired him in 2004 and had groomed him for years. With his dark skin and blue eyes, Tom was a looker and had decided long ago that he would rather remain a bachelor than settle down, get married, and have a family. This worked well for Michael because Tom was willing and able to travel or move on a moment's notice. In fact, over the past seven years alone, Tom had moved and lived in Germany, Mexico, Brazil, and China to clean up and optimize the manufacturing facilities. Michael was especially pleased with Tom's diligence in setting up the company's manufacturing hub in China. Tom had a way of exerting powerful influence to get things done, and China was no exception. The growing "miscellaneous" fund in Tom's budget was probably used for bribes, but Michael never asked. He preferred to maintain "plausible deniability" in the event that something went awry. There was no question in Michael's mind that Tom would succeed him as chief operating officer of The F Place!

Michael then reflected on Dr. Torsten Schmidt, the 55-year-old Chief Medical Officer who was originally from Frankfurt, Germany. Torsten had most certainly leveraged his wife's family connections with the FDA to get HappyVITA approved. Michael appreciated the fact that it was not easy to find a Medical Officer who could be so easily controlled. However, he found himself constantly irritated that Torsten simply could not or would not enact basic hygiene and personal care practices. In the twenty-first century, how hard was it to use deodorant? With the money that Torsten was making, why didn't he get his clothes dry-cleaned like the rest of the civilized world? Instead, he continued to show up for work in wrinkled clothes with sweat rings under his armpits, and on more than one occasion, Torsten had unknowingly left his fly down. Nevertheless, Michael decided to keep Torsten in the lineup because he was a really good puppet and would do whatever Michael wanted him to do.

Michaels' thoughts shifted to 48-year-old Albert Weinstein, the infamous Chief Strategy Officer, and he could feel his blood pressure rising. Albert wore his intelligence like a badge of honor and claimed to have an IQ of 160. Albert was quick to assess people and, if he didn't like someone or thought their intelligence was lacking, he would use bigger words and talk down to them like a small child. From the day he met Albert, Michael detested him. How many times had Albert questioned and poked holes in his strategies? Albert had this way of making Michael feel small, dumb, and unworthy. But Michael kept his true feelings about Albert to himself all these years because Albert was Alexander's "golden boy." Michael had a special plan to punish Albert for everything that he had done to belittle Michael all these years.

Speaking of punishment, Michael was thrilled at the thought of pushing out the ever-optimistic 50-year-old Pat Pierson, Chief People Officer. Michael knew that Pat would never support his vision; nor would he ever be as loyal to Michael as he was to Alexander. Pat's fatal flaw was that he over-invested in relationships and cared far too much for the people of The F Place. Back in 2008, Pat had even convinced Alexander to reduce executive compensation rather than lay off employees during the downturn. No . . . Pat would never support Michael's plans! Michael needed an HR leader who would embrace his vision and help him to create a new company culture, one that would make him filthy rich and far more successful than his father had ever been. Michael knew that right man for this job was actually a woman, which would help his diversity metrics, too! His longtime "friend with benefits," Frita Fernandez, was a 61-year-old retired HR executive who would jump at the opportunity to work side-by-side with Michael. Twenty years ago, that Cuban woman was flaming hot and made him long to be single. Even now, when she had her hair and makeup done well, she looked ten years younger. Given their personal history together, Michael knew that Frita would be the perfect partner in crime at The F Place! He smiled at the thought that he'd also be able to have a little fun with her at the office. Frita knew exactly how to turn him on and was always eager to please him. His attraction to Frita was hard to explain; she simply reminded him of one of his early crushes.

As Michael's thoughts drifted to his growing bank account, he pondered what he was going to do about 50-year-old Barbara Kunkel, who had been Alexander's Chief Financial

Officer from day one. There was no doubt about it, Barbara was an excellent CFO, and her financial strategies had helped them grow the company exponentially. However, Barbara was simply too buttoned up, too black-and-white for the future of The F Place. Michael needed someone with a little more accounting creativity and willingness to push the boundaries. Besides, there was that one time when Barbara had declined to support Michael's footprint expansion project in Venezuela. That had really pissed him off. "Bye-bye, Barbara. Don't let the door hit you on your way out!" he thought to himself. He would leave the CFO position open in the short term, and he was confident that Frita would help him find the right finance executive. Frita had an extensive network in the industry and was seemingly able to recruit premier talent.

The second woman in the C-suite was Nicolette Dean, Alexander's Chief Legal Officer. At more than 70 years old, Nicolette was plain looking and older than dirt, and she had begun working for Alexander back at The A Place. Nicolette had challenged him several times while they were launching HappyVITA, always raising the legal risks of launching products prematurely to the marketplace. Well, Michael was going to launch her career straight into retirement! In Nicolette's place, Michael knew exactly who he wanted as his Chief Legal Officer. He and Kathleen Kane had graduated from Harvard together, and he had hired Kathleen as his personal attorney ten years ago. It would make his life so much simpler to have one attorney for his personal and business affairs at The F Place. Besides, Kathleen's superpower was being the ultimate spin master. No matter the subject, she could spin it in their favor. The icing on the cake was the fact that she was drop-dead gorgeous and reminded him of a famous actress.

Michael smiled as he thought about kicking the "high

and mighty" 57-year-old John Browning to the curb. John had been Alexander's choice in 2001 for Chief Information Officer despite Michael's prodding for him to hire his buddy from MIT. John constantly challenged Michael's plans and was unafraid to go against the entire Executive Team if he believed a different technology course of action was in the best interest of the company and its people. While Alexander welcomed that kind of independent thinking, Michael hated it. As the CIO, John had the keys to all the systems and data at The F Place, which made him a little too powerful. So, Michael decided to push John into an early retirement and hire Isaac Davis, who was a Silicon Valley prodigy. Isaac's experience with cybersecurity was second to none. In fact, he had sold his cybersecurity firm in 2016 to become a multi-millionaire before the age of 30.

Lastly, Michael mulled for about thirty seconds over what he would do about his Executive Assistant. Dorothy Chambers had served Alexander for decades, starting back at The A Place. How many times had she made his life more difficult? She was a glorified secretary, and her job was to assist, but she served Alexander alone while treating everyone else in the company like a minion whenever Alexander wasn't around. Michael could bring his current assistant with him, but she did not light his fire the way a true Executive Assistant should. So, he decided to terminate both women and bring in a beautiful, young assistant whose sole focus would be to serve his every whim, personal and professional. He also wanted to hire a Chief of Staff to help him run the place. He was certain that Frita could help him make things happen quickly.

True to form, Frita did not disappoint. By the end of July, she had helped Michael to hire three women to the team. Michael's new Executive Assistant was a 31-year-old beauty named Jean Lundberg. While Jean had no business experience, she had won Miss America in 2007 and had a successful career as a fashion model until the age of 28, when she was deemed too old. Michael's new Chief of Staff was 29-year-old Lizzy Brown. Many people questioned the power that she wielded in that ill-defined role, and the halls were filled with rumors about their alleged relationship.

Frita's first strategic recommendation to Michael was to create the new Chief Diversity Officer role. Given the high number of leadership changes, Michael needed to be careful about optics. While this role would report to Michael on paper, it had no power and took all its direction from Frita. After a couple of interviews, 47-year-old Shanice Brown was hired into the role.

The F Place Executive Leadership Team—Organization Structure 2017

Below are the key executive leadership team members and roles.

2017

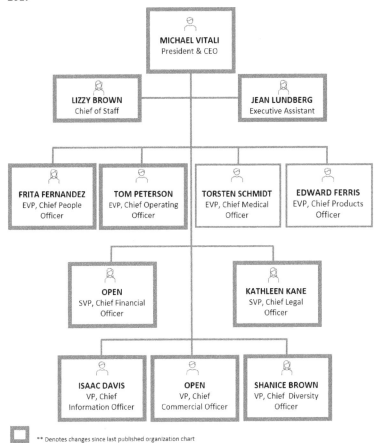

** Denotes changes since last published organization chart

CHAPTER 3

2020 Vision for the Future

December 2019

"It is never too late to be what you might have been."

—George Eliot

A S THE LAST week in December approached, Brianna began to consider the year coming to an end and all the highs and lows, all the milestones she had reached, and all that she wished she would have done. She found it soothing to look through her journal and her agenda. The memories would bring around thoughts of whether the time she spent this past year with her family, her friends, and her colleagues had really had an impact. Was she a good mother, daughter, partner to Justin? Was she a good friend? Was she living up to her life's purpose? Did her colleagues respect her? What did she want to accomplish in the new year? What lofty goals did she have for herself? Did she feel sad; was she happy? There were too many questions swirling through her mind. Christmas had passed, and the house was empty. As she started the process of cleaning and packing away the elaborate decorations, she ruminated on all that had come to pass. She contemplated the highs and the lows and everything in between.

Brianna admitted to herself that 2019 had been a pretty good year. It was a record-breaking year with The F Place. She had much to be proud of there. She had exceeded all her goals and was set for a prime bonus to show for it. But she missed having her beloved children with her. She longed to see and touch her daughter Ari. The holidays were unbearable for Brianna. She ached to be a family again with her beautiful children. She could not bear the thought of spending a holiday without them. Her son Eshan was such a love. It was so hard for her to believe that the kids were so hurt and lost that they did not want to be with her. Brianna had accomplished so much, and so many people in her life admired her, but not her own children. They were wounded, and it made Brianna feel lost and helpless. How could she have given birth to these two amazing people only to be rejected by them? It was unbearable. It was unfair. It was going to change; it had to change. This is going to be the last holiday and the last year that they were apart as a family, she resolved. Any time she had a moment like this at home to herself, she could not help but get consumed by these thoughts. This overwhelming sadness would sweep over her. It would make her feel as though she were spiraling out of control.

As Brianna started packing the ornaments, she lovingly held the beautiful portraits of her children in her hand. Tears kept streaming down her face, and she could not stop crying. "Oh, how I long to be up close to my babies' faces and look into their eyes and tell them how much I miss them and love them," she thought. "I need to send a text and tell them how much I love them." She picked up her phone and took a picture of the ornaments and sent it to Ari with the caption, "Love you, baby girl." She wanted to send Eshan a text, but he had blocked her.

Who knew if he ever got any of her endless texts or emails and voicemails? It made her feel awful. She decided to make herself a cup of tea. While the water was boiling, she carried the boxes containing the ornaments up to the storage room. There was so much in this room that she had not unpacked. It was hard for her to deal with. There were so many boxes of decorations, albums, kids' sporting gear, and sundry memories. It was all too much. She was determined to get it put away before she went back to work in the New Year.

Then it sank in. "I am actually off through the first week of the New Year. When was the last time I did that, take this kind of time off and actually shut off from work?" Brianna thought to herself. Well, all the numbers were in, and there was no need for her to chase down any of her customers for a last-minute close. The office was closed until January 5, and she was not traveling for New Year's. "I am getting this done!" she proclaimed to herself. Her eyes went to the wall around the right corner and she saw an upright box that said "vision boards." She immediately went towards it and managed to get it out of the massive pile of boxes that held precious family portraits and artwork. She wondered how this vision board had managed to get into this pile. The movers this time around had really done a wacky job of mixing up these kinds of things. How did all this stuff end up with the basement items, she wondered? She looked for a pair of scissors and, of course, did not have them nearby, so she decided to take her precious vision board box down with her to the kitchen.

Brianna had started to create these vision boards for herself every year for the last ten years or so. She and her longtime friend Kate had begun this tradition many years ago where at the start of the year they would sit down and set goals for themselves. Taking a large piece of posterboard, she would cut out images from old magazines that would represent her goals for the year to create a vision board that she could look at each and every day. As she came down the curved staircase she stopped halfway. The view of Central Park from her 20-foot living room windows always took her breath away. She thought to herself, "I am so very lucky to have this beautiful place to call home. If only my kids could be here to share this amazing place that I call home now. "

The F Place was not all that bad. There were some perks. They had relocated her to NYC in August of 2018 immediately following her promotion to Chief Commercial Officer. She remembered that she had included on her vision board that she would be Chief Commercial Officer of the company in 2018 after David Church had left. She had to see it with her own eyes. As she wandered into the kitchen, she took a knife and carefully opened the box. There it was—her precious vision board that she had made at the beginning of 2018. The previous year had been tough for her with the kids choosing to live with their dad full time.

Her phone rang and startled her. She saw that it was Michael Vitali, CEO of The F Place. What did he want? Wasn't he in Mexico with his latest girlfriend Tanya? She answered, "Hey, Michael, how's Mexico treating you?"

"It is fabulous! Brianna, you and Justin really need to come down here for a long weekend." Michael entertained Brianna with some more small talk. Then, "Brianna, can you meet me in the office on Monday? I've asked Frita to join us as well. I was thinking, since the sales conclave meeting is only a couple of weeks away, we should do some planning, and I've got some great ideas to run by you. Does that work for you?"

Brianna thought to herself, "This is corporate high-stakes politics, so of course I'm going to have to go into the office." She knew it was too good to be true to have ten days of peace and quiet from The F Place. Oh, well, she certainly knew what she had signed up for, and she enthusiastically replied, "Of course, Michael, that sounds like a great idea, and I would be happy to share my plans for our annual sales conclave meeting with the top sales leaders of The F Place."

As she put down her phone, she could not resist feeling a little uneasy about why he would invite Frita Fernandez, of all people. What value could she possibly add? She always tore apart everything Brianna proposed, especially in meetings like this. Brianna knew that Michael had a thing for pretty young women, but Frita? It could not be. She had to be 60-something, and while she looked younger than she was, she still looked a bit weathered. Frita was a short, plump woman who was extremely loud and boisterous. She had a pretty face, with bright blue eyes and platinum blonde hair. But one could see the sun damage on her skin that probably came from years of careless tanning. She told herself there was nothing between Frita and Michael other than the fact that Michael was a poor judge of character for bringing in Frita as the Chief People Officer of The F Place.

"That was not the case with me," thought Brianna. Michael knew what Brianna brought to The F Place. She basically saved The F Place by bringing in several multi-year contracts that were significant. This had enabled them to exceed their projected revenue goals—in fact, almost doubling them since she was promoted to Chief Commercial Officer. She was pretty proud of herself, and they needed her wisdom to bring this Transformation to a glorious finale.

Brianna could tell that Frita had a thing for Michael. Her tone always changed with him. Brianna had to admit, Michael was a very good-looking guy. He had rugged looks and that old-world Italian charm. He dressed extremely well and had all his suits hand tailored. He always managed to find himself on the Top 100 list of CEOs worldwide. It was his power, confidence, and good looks, combined with just a hint of that northern Italian accent, that made him attractive to women—especially Frita, who practically undressed him with her eyes every time she laid eyes on him. Brianna laughed at herself because she realized that she had mentally started to characterize Michael and Frita as soap opera characters.

Eventually she sat down on a stool at the end of her sleek granite counter. She inhaled her soothing peppermint tea and sipped on it. She picked up her 2018 vision board and placed it on the countertop in front of her. She started looking at all the categories. She had one for self-development, her health, her relationship with her kids, her relationship with Justin, and, lastly, her career. She stopped at the box with her career. There it was in black and white. She just could not believe her eyes. She had put down the following: "Continue to travel the world and meet with all Tier 1 customers and employees at our Top 20 sites. Become Chief Commercial Officer. Bring home a seven-figure income. Successfully operationalize the commercial Transformation plan and exceed revenue targets by 25 percent. Mentor and coach three up-and-coming associates."

When she had formulated these goals, she had been concerned that they were too ambitious. She reasoned to herself that the only way she would reach her aspirations would be to set the stakes and hold herself accountable. She had checked off all the boxes that year on her professional goals, but she wondered how she could pull that off and yet continue to be unable to fix the strained and practically non-existent relationship with her kids. She had been pretty unsparing in writing out her vision there as well: family dinners, moments of joy, laughter and love, show unconditional love to her children, spend most of the major holidays with the kids, be a role model to them, and so on. Yet, she had not been able to accomplish any of it.

She was sure that there was something magical in creating these vision boards. How could it have worked so perfectly for professional goals, but not effect any progress on her relationship with her kids? She started comparing how she had written the categories out. What she realized was that, whenever she thought about her professional goals, they always seem to be SMART—Specific, Measurable, Attainable, Relevant, and Time-Bound. Without such specificity in her vision, there was no way could she have come up with a salary of $3.1M and actually hit it on the dot. What were the chances of that happening? Yet it did. She had added on the .1M for fun, thinking, "Let's see what the universe can deliver." As she had continued to reference her vision board that year, she realized that she would often start with her career and give it a lot of energy. It was her way of avoiding the pain of having to deal with the kids picking Antonio over her. She felt like she had come to a real breakthrough, perhaps even discovering a path to materializing her dreams. She could not wait to tell Kate.

She grabbed her phone and texted Kate: "2020 is going to be our best year yet, and don't let me forget to tell you about my vision board idea." The phone rang again, and it was Justin. This was the fourth time he was calling today. She quickly contemplated whether or not to take his call. She was pretty sure that he would get upset with her for once again crying because she missed her babies. In every other part of their relationship, Justin was her perfect partner. But the continued drama with her kids had become a huge pain point in their relationship.

She knew that Justin loved her very much, but she was trying so hard not to let him see how inadequate she felt not having her children in her life. She knew he would worry if he did not hear back from her, so she finally picked up after the fifth ring. Then there it was—his deep, sexy voice on the other end. "Hey honey, what are you thinking for dinner?" His voice always made her feel like she had butterflies in her stomach.

Brianna quickly wondered if she should tell him how she was feeling. She reminded herself that she always thought that it was always better to be transparent with him. She told him she was having a rough day, putting away stuff as it kept reminding her of her kids, and she started crying. Instead of being his usual sweet and caring self, he got upset and irritated. He almost shouted out, "You let those kids ruin everything and steal all the joy out of our lives. If you want to sulk then go ahead; I want no part of that. You have so much to be grateful for, and you let them ruin our lives. We need to continue this conversation over dinner tonight. I have to get back to work."

She glanced at her phone; it was already five-thirty. Justin was coming over for dinner at seven. Hopefully, he would be on time. He had been so busy at the hospital lately. It was good that he was. Sometimes Brianna wondered how he put up with her traveling all the time and spending sixteen-hour days at the office. He was annoyed that he had taken the morning off to be with her and then she went into the office. He would never say that to her, but Brianna knew. She would make it up by making him a glorious dinner. He loved it when she cooked for him. What could she make tonight that would blow him away? She decided she would go with raclette. It was a perfect romantic meal because it would allow them both to linger, which meant closeness and bonding over a romantic dinner. Justin had bought her a raclette set shortly after their first visit to Lucerne. He knew how much Brianna loved to cook, and it always made him happy to add another fun gadget to her kitchen that would remind her of him.

Justin also did not mind being vegetarian for her on these date nights, and that was an added bonus for her. He appreciated her going through the effort, and he always let her know that. Brianna could see him smiling at her while they waited for their mouthwatering gooey cheese to melt before they poured it over their fresh French bread, asparagus, and jacket potatoes. She was excited about the thought of them lingering over their food and drinking a special bottle of the Umathum wine that they had brought back from Austria during one of their many visits there.

Brianna knew that it would be a perfect night to help them get over their tension. Brianna quickly waved to her building doorman Octavio; he was such a sweet man. He had worked at this fifteen-story historic building since he was 20. He had shared with her that he had taken over the job just a year and a half ago from his father. Brianna adored Octavio. She could not help but smile when she remembered Kate's daughter Sarah coming over recently and asking her, "Auntie Brianna, do you think Octavio is in college?" Sarah reminded Brianna of her own daughter Ari. All signs pointed to the fact that Sarah had a huge crush on Octavio.

As Brianna stepped out into the street, she thought about how much she loved her place in New York. It was a prime location and offered great views that overlooked the sailboat pond in Central Park, and it was conveniently located next to all the luxuries that she was getting accustomed to. Who would have thought she would land herself a penthouse right in the middle of NYC in her thirties? Justin loved it, too, even though he kept saying it was too big for her. Brianna did not care. She wanted a place where Ari and Eshan could move right in and call their home. She knew that as they got a little bit older and able to really think for themselves, they would come back to her. Justin did not get there until almost 9:30 p.m., but they still managed to have a wonderful dinner.

Justin suggested they have a dinner party for New Year's Eve.

Brianna did not really feel like another party or celebration, but she reluctantly agreed. It would be good to have their friends over, especially Kate. She was so happy that she and Kate somehow ended up living in the same city. Finally!

Tuesday, December 31, 2019

Tuesday finally rolled around. Justin had spent the night at Brianna's. It was sweet to wake up to his scent. She had to admit, he was the best lover she had ever had. They had a late breakfast, and then Brianna started to get the place ready for dinner. She laid out the china, put out fresh flowers, lit up candles all over the penthouse, and turned on some music for ambience. It was amazing how flowers, candles, and music could transform a place and make it feel so special. She started to think about the impact she had made at The F Place over the years. She truly had started to build a culture in her own way. She knew her team respected her and looked up to her. They loved their team meetings and retreats where they would work hard and then have time to bond. She was proud of the work family that she had built within her organization at The F Place. She really did have a gift for Transformation.

The phone started to ring, and Octavio announced that guests were on their way up. Brianna yelled to Justin, who was watching TV, "Our guests are here; did you check the bar and put the champagne in the ice bucket?"

Justin waltzed over and grabbed Brianna in a big hug and whispered, "Don't worry, honey. I've checked everything. It all looks great, and everyone loves your parties. You do an amazing job, always."

Brianna thought it was so considerate the way he always made her feel so great about herself; she could always be herself around him. There was not the pressure to be Brianna Grimaldi, the executive. All he wanted from her was her unconditional love. It always amazed her at how simple he made things. Justin answered the door and ushered their guests in. There were hugs and kisses all around. Guests nibbled on a beautiful charcuterie plate. The guys started talking sports and went into the library to play cards, while Brianna, Kate, Sandra, and Bela got comfortable on the oversized couches in her great room. They had so much to catch up on.

They started talking about what their goals and aspirations were for the upcoming year. Kate said she had been doing a word of the year for a few years now. The others asked what that was. Kate explained that it is an anchor word that inspires you and grounds you throughout the year. Brianna already knew that Kate would bring this up, as last year Kate's word was "balance," and she had wanted Brianna to be her promise partner and hold her to it. She was proud of her bestie for truly achieving personal and professional balance. After all, Kate had been through a lot, especially with the loss of her boy, Max. In so many ways, Kate was her guide, but when it came to Max, Kate turned to Brianna for answers that Brianna could not always give her.

Sandra went next and said, "Mine is accountability. I want to hold myself accountable for my word." Bela said she wanted to grow in the coming year by getting her APICS certification and becoming a certified yoga instructor. Kate chose "best" as her 2020 word. She then explained that she wanted to build on 2019, her year of "balance." She had achieved the personal and professional balance, and now it was time to take it up a notch and truly live her best life.

Brianna was in deep thought, as she really wanted her word to be meaningful. She recalled the deep conversation she and Kate had had on having the right mindset. It was just a few weeks ago when Brianna was confiding in Kate how much not having the kids with her at Diwali, the Indian festival of lights, was upsetting her. It was one of the most important holidays in the Indian calendar, and both the kids looked forward to it every year. Kate had reminded Brianna not to look at the situation as if the kids had left her. Even though Kate was sitting in front of her talking to Bela, she could hear Kate's voice in her head reminding her, "Your mindset can dictate how you view yourself and the world around you. Brianna, with your kids, Justin is right. You are creating self-imposed limitations within yourself and your own belief system." Brianna was not sure if it was the second glass of bubbly or finally coming to the realization that, after all, her word of the year "believe" would help her to reinforce a meaningful mindset about the outcome she desired with her children.

As the light bulb went on in her head, Brianna blurted out, "My word is 'believe,'" Her friends looked back at her and said in unison, "Ooh, that's good." Of course, they were waiting for her to explain herself. Brianna thought about how it was Ari's favorite word for a while. For Ari, it was because she was infatuated with Justin Bieber in her early teen years. It was so cute when she was crushing on him. She used to listen to his song "Believe" repeatedly on her iPod. Brianna did not go with that explanation; instead, she decided to be vulnerable. She knew something was up at The F Place, and she wanted to believe that everything she and her team were doing was going to make a difference and be accepted by Michael and the others on the executive leadership team. She also wanted to believe, really believe, that 2020 would be the year that her children and she would rekindle their relationship.

It was almost 9 p.m., and everyone was getting hungry for dinner. Brianna asked Kate to help her get the food to the dining room.

"Brianna, 2020 is going to be an awesome year, and the launch of a new decade, and I believe that we can be the best versions of ourselves. This is our year to do a true Transformation, a 360," said Kate.

Brianna was in full agreement. "Kate, let's take some time before we go back to work and plan this out."

"Let's take a day for ourselves this week and we'll go to our usual spot and just spend time working on our vision boards," suggested Kate.

"Yes, and we are going to do our vision boards for 2020!" exclaimed Brianna.

Justin was right—it was great to have their friends over as they watched the ball drop promptly at midnight. It was OK that they weren't at Times Square; it turned out to be a wonderful night. It was low key but a great way to welcome in the New Year. Brianna went to bed that night with a feeling like this was definitely going to be her year. And she had a trusted accountability partner in Kate, who would be by her side.

CHAPTER 4

The Fountainhead of Fear

January 2020

"It is how we embrace the uncertainty of our lives that leads to the greatest Transformations of our souls."

—*Brandon A. Trean*

Wednesday, January 1, 2020

JANUARY 1 ARRIVED, and Brianna and Justin spent a better part of the day doing FaceTime calls with their families, wishing all a happy 2020. Brianna felt sad about not being able to FaceTime the kids. She decided in that moment that this year was going to be different. She went up to the kids' rooms and did a video for each to tell them how much she loved and adored them and could not wait for them to come to their new home in New York. Brianna had moved all their furniture from the old house and found a place big enough where they could each have their own rooms as well as room for family and friends.

Friday, January 3, 2020

Brianna could not wait for Friday to finally arrive. Kate had suggested they do their 2020 vision planning that day. Brianna and Kate decided they would start the day by meeting for breakfast at the Plaza. It offered a beautiful dining room and an amazing menu. They got right into it with launching their vision for 2020 and the decade ahead. They were like two schoolgirls who could not contain their excitement. Between bites of savory crepes, they started to sketch out what the year would be like for each of them. They started their groupings by clusters: health, kids, career, family, etc. As they were going through the details of each category, they promised each other that they would help one another stay accountable and continue being each other's promise partner. Brianna felt so grateful to have Kate's friendship. They had so much in common with the way their careers were blossoming, the way that they embraced learning new things, how they always tried to be of service to others, the way they gave to those in need, and the fact that they always had an optimistic outlook in life.

Once they settled their bill, they headed to business lounge and, as luck would have it, they were able to get a private conference room. They pulled out their laptops and got to work. Kate had set the tone. She chirped, "We need to dream big and set a grand vision for ourselves and what we can achieve." Together, they white-boarded their ideas and dreamed about starting their own business in the future, perhaps a nonprofit. The games and politics at The F Place were just getting to be too much! While Kate didn't have to deal with the politics as badly as Brianna did, she was overworked at her company and always said that if she was going to work that hard that she wanted to do it for herself.

Both Kate and Brianna had always wanted to write a book.

Kate had wanted to write a mystery, and Brianna had wanted to write about her life and being able to make an impact on others. Both agreed that whatever they wrote about had to have purpose, be meaningful and inspiring, and be able to help others. Writing a book sounded like a great idea, but they knew they would have to work their way to it.

Kate suggested they start with a weekly blog. "We can get a page written each week, can't we? Maybe we can choose a topic each week and just write about our experience and then some tips and tricks that we used to maneuver through that experience. What do you think, Brianna?" Brianna loved that idea. She could easily do that. She so enjoyed journaling every day. That was her few minutes for herself where she took the time to pen out the major events in her life and the things that she was grateful for. It really made a difference for her to be able to have this ritual.

The day was going by quickly. It was 4 p.m. already, and Brianna looked at Kate. "We need to hurry to the spa for our massages." They quickly packed up and went down to the beautiful Ayurveda spa at the hotel. As soon as they stepped in, it felt as though they were in a different world. Brianna took a deep inhale of the jasmine fragrance wafting through the entryway. She reflected that Kate was always so good about taking care of herself. She always made time for doing these types of treatments and getaways. Brianna could use a ritual or two like this to pamper herself. Well, today she was, and she was proud of herself for carving out this day to build out her future.

Soon they were each greeted by their masseur. They took them to the waiting room and asked if they would like to relax with a glass of bubbly while they prepared their room. The answer was yes. As they sipped on their champagne, Kate asked Brianna how things were going with her and Justin. Brianna's eyes started to moisten, and she looked down. "They're going well, but I just wish the kids, Justin, and I could all be together as a family," she said.

Kate got up and gave her friend a hug. "Don't worry, Brianna; remember, this is going to be our year and our decade. Your kids are going to realize what an amazing mother you are, and they will find their way back to you! You need to believe."

Brianna heard someone call her name. She followed her masseur Joe into the dimly lit hallway. He instructed her to lie facedown and asked what she hoped to accomplish today during the next ninety minutes. She thought about that and wanted to blurt out, "Can you take away all my problems, please?" Instead she asked if he could do a relaxation massage and focus on her head, neck, and shoulders.

As Joe started to knead, he reminded her gently to relax and breathe. "Just breathe," he would whisper. Brianna had such a hard time breathing deeply. It was not like she had asthma or some kind of breathing problem. She would get lost in her stress, and it was unbearable to think about her kids. She always worried endlessly if they were OK. Were they happy? Did they miss her? And then inevitably she would end up in the same place. They had rejected her and chosen Antonio, their father, over her. They did not need her. They did not need their mom. She would always end up with the conclusion that they did not need their mother, and they were fine without her in their lives.

How could any mother breathe with that to deal with? Somehow, she managed to remind herself of the promise she and Kate had made to one another: 2020 was going to be different. This was the year that Brianna was going to get a better handle on her life and her destiny, and her kids were on the top of that list. She started to visualize what it would feel like to see Ari and squeeze her. She imagined the reaction on Ari's face as she would enter Brianna's penthouse. Ari loved nice things, just like her mother. Before she knew it, Brianna was sound asleep. Joe's voice broke that deep sleep. "Ms. Grimaldi, whenever you're ready, I'll be waiting outside with a glass of water for you. Just take your time getting up." Just like that, it was over, but Brianna felt so relaxed and refreshed. It is amazing what a massage can do for your mind and body.

Kate was back in the lounge with a glass of champagne in hand. Brianna asked for another as well. They got back to finalizing plans for how they would continue to bring their 2020 vision into focus this year. They agreed that they would meet on the last Friday of each month and set aside quality time to brainstorm and work on their blog. Brianna noticed the time and realized that she was going to be late if she did not scurry. Justin hated it when she kept him waiting. He was always so punctual—another quality she admired about him.

Monday, January 6, 2020

As Brianna hit the button on the elevator to take her up to her office, she thought again about why Michael had invited Frita to this meeting. She dropped off her coat and bag to her office. She did some quick emails and prepared to go to Michael's office.

Just as she was about to grab her laptop, she heard that annoying voice as she popped into her office. "Hi, sweet pea! All set to meet our fearless Mikey!? Now tell me, what have you got lined up for us? Let's grab some coffee while you tell me all about your big plans." So typical of Frita, Brianna thought, always needing to get the scoop beforehand so that she could claim it as her own. Brianna grudgingly told Frita she would meet her by the coffee lounge in ten minutes.

As Frita walked back to her office to get her belongings, she quickly stopped in the ladies' room to give herself a quick look and to spray on a little extra perfume before their meeting with

Michael. As she glanced at herself in the mirror, she admired herself and thought about how beautiful she was. Yes, she had put on a few pounds, but her face still looked lean and youthful. "It's amazing what a little Botox can do for a girl." She gave herself a wink in the mirror and then heard her mother's words ring in her head: "All you have are your looks, so you better take care of yourself." Often when Frita went in front of a mirror, she was haunted by memories of her childhood in Havana, Cuba. Almost as if in a trance, Frita slowly made her way to the luxurious sitting area and sat down to compose her thoughts before her first meeting of the year with Michael. However, she could not get the thoughts of her mother out of her mind.

Her mother was a beautiful woman with dark brown eyes the color of molasses. She had a sultry Cuban accent and an amazing hourglass figure. Today Frita was reminded of the time that her mother came home early in the morning after a night out with her latest boyfriend. Frita often woke up by herself as her mother wouldn't come home until the wee hours of the morning. In this memory, Frita was only 12 years old, and she had already seen way too much for a child her age. It always seemed to Frita as though her mother had a new man every week. Frita always longed to meet her father, but she never had the chance. Her mother had told her that he died before she was born.

Frita's eyes misted with tears as she remembered asking her mother, "Mama, why are you always out all night with men instead of home with me? I get so lonely here all by myself." She still recalled that conversation so vividly. Her eyes had teared up when she was a child, too, and even then, she did her best not to cry in front of her mother.

Her mother had responded, "Baby, you know I love you, don't you? Ever since your father died, I have been looking for the perfect husband who can take care of both of us and give us the life that we deserve. And sweet pea, he will be tall, dark, handsome . . . and rich!" Frita could hear her mother's giggle ringing in her head. It was bubbly and full of life.

"I know, Mama, you tell me that all the time. But why do we need a man to give us a better life? Why can't we just work and do it ourselves?" asked Frita as she leaned in to embrace her mother.

Frita's mother went from giggly to furious. "Now, Frita. If I've told you once, I've told you a thousand times! We were born dirt poor here in Havana, but also smart and beautiful. You and I, we are just girls living in a man's world. If you want to get ahead in life, you need a rich man. It's not right, but that's just the way the world works. And, at 30 years old, I am not getting any younger! That's why I am spending so much time with these men. I promise you on my mama's grave that I will find Mr. Right and he will rescue us from this gutter. We might even get to live in the United States of America one day! Do you trust me, sweet pea? Everything I do, I do for you, baby. I'm doing this for us."

Frita's mother died when Frita was 16, and she never found her Mr. Right. Frita followed in her mother's footsteps and learned to use her beauty with men to get ahead in life. Frita thought, "Now I've found my next rich man, and it's going to be Michael. He's powerful, wealthy, good-looking, and soon he's going to be all mine." Just then the door to the ladies' room swung open and in marched Brianna. Frita stood up, quickly composed herself, and told Brianna that she was headed to grab some coffee before their meeting with Michael.

"Good morning, ladies, and a very Happy New Year!! This is going to be our year. Frita, what do you think about Brianna's plan for the Sales Leadership Conclave?" asked Michael.

Frita leeringly looked at Michael and chirped, "Happy New Year to you, Michael! Well, Brianna shared the highlights of her plan with me just prior to our meeting with you this morning. Quite frankly, it is a tad bit dull for that audience. No offense, Brianna. I just call it like I see it."

"Thanks for that, Frita. Given your vast experience leading a global Commercial organization, I should clearly defer to your infinite wisdom, right? Yeah, I don't think so," said Brianna.

"Cool down, Brianna. We're all professionals here. You need to learn to take constructive feedback a little better. I'd like to hear more about Frita's perspective, and then you can share your view. Sound good?" said Michael.

Frita glared at Brianna. "Thank you, Michael. As I was saying, if the theme is 'Accelerate to Innovate,' I would expect to see some accelerated focus on BalanceVITA sales. Brianna does not plan to have her team begin selling BalanceVITA until Q4. As we have discussed countless times, that is simply too late," said Frita.

Michael looked at Brianna, who sat there with a stone-cold face. "Oh, is it my turn to speak now, Michael?" Brianna asked with disdain in her voice.

Michael looked at Brianna with his bright green eyes and nodded his head. "Yes, please go ahead."

"The theme of acceleration is focused on accelerating the growth of our existing product portfolio so that the development team can properly finish the BalanceVITA clinical trials. We must make sure that we don't sacrifice quality and innovation for speed," said Brianna.

"Brianna, we need to accelerate growth *and* innovate. The two are not mutually exclusive. I need you to get on board with this strategy and lead by example with your team at the conclave. Is that something you can do?" asked Michael.

Brianna straightened her posture further and pulled her shoulders back for effect. She hated it when Michael used "stylistic latitude" as an operation mechanism. While Brianna was fully aware of him being the CEO, it drove her crazy when he used his formal power and position to reinforce his authority.

Instead, Brianna challenged Michael with a firm response. "Since we're taking the gloves off, let me just say this, Michael. Frita is adding absolutely no value to this conversation whatsoever." Brianna turned to Frita and leaned in to ask, "Frankly, I am not even sure why you are involved in this conversation, Frita." Brianna could not understand why Frita kept interjecting herself into her business. She wondered why Michael kept inviting Frita to all these conversations. It made Brianna upset because Frita was really starting to have a negative impact on Michael's decision making.

That said, Brianna was not intimidated by Frita one bit and firmly continued, "I am the Chief Commercial Officer, and I would like to see Frita spend a bit more time focusing on her own HR sandbox for a change and worrying about doing her job well." Brianna pursed her lips as she was incredibly frustrated by this point but wanted to nip this in the bud before it got out of hand. She continued, "Secondly, I cannot in good conscience promote a product prematurely. This is my Sales Leadership Conclave, and we are going to do it my way!"

Michael looked angry with Brianna and immediately his nostrils started flaring. Brianna started doubting herself and thought that dropping in her title may have been a bit much. She wondered why Michael was getting so upset, as she believed that he too should want the Conclave to be successful. He knew full well that "Accelerate to Innovate" did not imply that they were ready to launch products prematurely.

As if Michael heard her thoughts, he interrupted them by saying, "That's where you're wrong, Brianna. I did not want to do this, but you leave me no choice. I am going to pull rank here. You will promote BalanceVITA at the Sales Leadership

Conclave or there won't be a conclave this year. And you will run all your material by Frita. If she approves it, then I approve it. End of story. You're excused, Brianna. I need to speak with Frita alone." Michael waved his hand at Brianna to motion her to leave. As Brianna left, Frita beamed at Michael and chirped, "Michael, The F Place is your kingdom, and you are the king. Brianna needs to remember that as CEO, you're in charge here." Michael flashed a quick smile at Frita and told her he would speak to her later.

Michael turned to look outside his window and thought about how much Frita reminded him of his mother. She had this way about her that made him feel invincible, just like his mother had. Michael was fond of his mother and knew how much she had done for him. He thought about his childhood and the summer of 1979 when he was only 10. Michael and his parents had just moved from Milan, Italy, to Manhattan. His father, Michael Vitali, Sr., was the European president for Moda di Lusso and newly appointed as CEO at the young age of 35 years. His then-29-year-old mother Giulia was a beautiful homemaker who had doted on Michael.

Fourth and fifth grades were incredibly difficult for Michael. His Italian accent was strong, and his English was weak. He was teased and bullied a lot. It all changed overnight when he met Jimmy Capone and became fast friends with him. Jimmy made sure that no one messed with Michael again.

Thereafter, with Jimmy as his protector, Michael began to excel in academics; after all, his parents would accept nothing less than the best. He was also outstanding in sports and loved playing soccer. Jimmy was an average student and had no interest in extracurricular activities. Rather, he preferred working in his father's business. Michael never understood why Jimmy was so interested in waste management.

Before Michael was sent off to boarding school in

Pennsylvania at the age of 14, his mother had a heart-to-heart talk with him. She told him that he was on his way to being just as successful as his father, and she was sure that he, too, would become a powerful CEO by the time he was 35. She reminded him that he came from a long line of successful Vitalis, and, as an only child, it was his duty to carry the torch into the next generation. After all, his mother would constantly remind him of the symbolism of his name and what it meant, which was "Who is like God?" She would make him feel like he was God himself, and he had no fear within him.

As Brianna left the office and got into her car, she was furious and started to replay everything that had transpired. She wondered, "What was wrong with Michael? He was so cold and sharp during their conversation. It is almost as if he was trying to put distance between us." Brianna continued to feel uneasy about the way things had unfolded and pressed herself to further ponder, "Did he not see that this was the wrong way to accelerate growth? There was no way they were going to be ready before Q4 with the new product launch for BalanceVITA." There was no way Brianna was going to get up on that stage in front of their top two hundred sales leaders and declare that they were putting this out in the marketplace by Q1. It was beyond ridiculous. She started to question Michael's motives. She thought how much he had changed ever since Frita came on board a few years ago.

She decided to call Kate, and they agreed to meet over coffee. Brianna was dying to unload all the details of what had been going on at The F Place. Kate always had a good sense of how to read into these things. Brianna saw Kate at the table by the far window in the café. She waved to her and made her way over. After exchanging hugs, Brianna dove right into it. She explained the bizarre and frustrating meeting with Michael and Frita. Kate was fascinated and perplexed at the same time.

She wondered aloud, saying, "I think Frita is trying to take you down."

Brianna looked at Kate straight on and said, "You just confirmed my hypothesis." Her eyes clouded over as she wondered aloud, "Why would she want to do that, though, Kate? Why? I just do not understand it! I have stayed out of her way and have gone over and above to give her support on her initiatives, even when I haven't wanted to. Why would she possibly want to take me down? What did I do to her?"

Kate sighed. She knew she had to change Brianna's energy. One sure way to do this was to make Brianna laugh. Kate always thought that Brianna had the best laugh ever. So, Kate started, "Brianna, I want you to close your eyes for just a moment. Can you see it now? You're at The F Place in your boardroom. The door is open, and everyone is seated and ready to start. You can all hear Frita thumping down the hall. Just as she is about to turn the corner, can you imagine her taking a slip and fall as she's walking on those nicely polished floors on her way into the boardroom? Whoops! That's too bad, because it happens right as she goes to make a beeline for Michael. Just think, she falls on her bottom and goes flying with her big stainless-steel cup of soda in hand. I can just see it now! Just imagine the look on Frita's face as she is sprawled on the boardroom floor when she takes herself down. You won't even have to lift a finger, Brianna, as she makes a complete fool of herself."

Brianna bust out into hysterical laughs with Kate. The visuals that crossed her mind as she started imaging this scene were just too much. When she finally caught her breath, she said, "In all seriousness, I cannot afford to have Frita and Michael ruin everything my team and I have built this past year. I am not going to go along with this ridiculous plan of theirs."

Kate was always so great at listening to Brianna's problems

and being able to look at these things with a clear head. Brianna was grateful for her friend.

"OK, enough about The F Place," Kate said. "Let's catch up on how we're progressing on our 2020 vision. I want to talk about what the new decade holds for us, Brianna." They spent the next hour catching up and eventually said their goodbyes.

As Brianna was making her way back home, suddenly, she heard a loud siren coming up behind her. It startled her, and she quickly looked for a place to pull over. Brianna let out a sigh of relief as the ambulance accelerated and passed her by. This was the thing about living in New York: It was so congested at all hours. If you failed to take charge and command your own, you would get trampled over in a heartbeat, Brianna realized. With The F Place still on her mind, she decided that she would remain determined to carefully manage the commercial launch of BalanceVITA. She told herself, "This is what is in the best interest of The F Place and our customers, period. End of story. If Michael does not like it, too bad."

Meanwhile from late January onwards, the world was in turmoil. Public health agencies in the U.S.A. had detected fourteen cases of coronavirus disease 2019 (COVID-19), all of which were related to travel from China. Brianna had just traveled to China in mid-December to meet with one of their customers. It scared her to think that she may have caught the disease. It was a pandemic in the making as the disease was spreading so quickly. She thought it was only a matter of time before it started to spread here in the United States. Everyone at work was speculating about how their colleagues in China were exaggerating about the virus as they had shut down the factories for the next few weeks in order to contain the disease. No one at The F Place was taking it seriously despite the President's nationwide travel ban from China that went into effect on January 31.

Brianna had a different perspective altogether from Justin. He would tell her every day that this was a serious thing, and it was only a matter of time before it was going to get out of control here in the United States. Justin had a close friend who worked at MIT medical and kept him updated on the situation as they were monitoring it so closely. Every day it seemed as though there was new evidence to indicate there were more and more people who had become infected with coronavirus. There were endless warnings of how the disease could become contagious before one even noticed the symptoms. Justin urged her every day to postpone any travel that Brianna had, but Brianna knew that it was going to be a tough quarter, and she needed to do everything in her power so that she could keep business on track.

CHAPTER 5

Love Is in the February Air

February 2020

"What can you do to promote world peace? Go home and love your family."

—*Mother Teresa*

Tuesday, February 4, 2020

FEBRUARY WAS UNUSUALLY cold in NYC. As Brianna stepped out onto the street, the cold wind hit her face like a sharp needle piercing through her. It had not even been a minute since she left the lobby of her warm building. What was she thinking, wanting to walk to the subway instead of driving to the office as she normally did? She decided to walk a little more quickly and went down the steps to catch the next train. As she settled into her seat, she remembered that she had vaguely heard the sound of a Snapchat coming in. She was too tired to look. It was probably one of the silly team chats announcing that soon it would be the day of love. She decided to look through and open it anyway. Her heart raced as she noticed it was actually from Ari.

She had not heard from Ari in months. Was she OK? What did she need? As Brianna started to read the text, she could not believe her eyes. The message read, "Mom, can you talk?" Of all the times for Brianna not to have reached for her phone last night, how could she have been that lazy to have missed this text from Ari? She started panicking—what if it was too late and Ari had changed her mind about talking? Should she call her now? No, of course she could not; it was barely 6:15 a.m., and for Ari it would be only 5:15. She thought, "I better wait to call, but at least I can send a snap back now." She quickly typed a message to Ari: "Hi, darling—sorry I missed your snap. I was so exhausted from work last night that I crashed and did not see your message until now. Call me when you wake up. I miss you and love you so much." That was easy enough.

Brianna hoped that she would hear back from Ari later in the day. A snap popped back up instantaneously. "What do you put in your banana bread?" Brianna started typing back all the ingredients and the order of how to mix them. She asked, "Why are you up so early making banana bread? Did you just get back from a night out @ Red Lion—lol?"

Brianna could see that Ari was typing something, and then she paused before, finally, the answer came: "Yeah, I went with my sorority sis." Wow, thought Brianna. My daughter is talking to me via text. They continued back and forth for a little bit. Brianna realized that she had arrived at her stop. As she quickly got off the train, another message came from Ari, who asked if she could talk to her. Brianna called Ari, but Ari did not answer. Brianna got worried and wondered what in the world was going on with her daughter.

Then the phone rang and on the other side was Ari's sweet voice. "Mom?"

"Hi, darling, how are you?" asked Brianna.

"I am fine," Ari said. "I was wondering if I could come see you this weekend? Will you send me a ticket, Mom?"

"Is everything OK, Ari?" Brianna could hear in her voice that she had been crying, and she also sounded a little buzzed.

"Yeah, it's fine. I just miss you," she answered.

Brianna was elated to hear from Ari. "That's good to hear," she said. "Of course, sweetheart—of course I'll get you a ticket. You just tell me exactly when you want to come."

Brianna arrived at the lobby of her office. She quickly badged herself in and made her way up the elevator to her office. She was always the first to make it to work. Somehow, she still had not figured out how to turn on the lights in the main hallway. She made her way to her office and flipped on the lights. Despite all the craziness with the Sales Leadership Conclave preparations, Brianna was determined to be in good spirits. Things were looking up. Her daughter just asked to come visit her!! Brianna could not believe it. "My baby is finally coming home!" Brianna said to herself.

Brianna started to look through her calendar. Another day with back-to-back meetings. She was so excited about her call with Ari that when the phone rang it startled her. She quickly glanced at the caller ID and saw that it was Frita. Brianna wondered, "What did she want and how was she here so early?" Brianna answered brightly, "Good morning, Frita; how are you?"

Frita asked if Brianna would come to her office to talk about the product launch for BalanceVITA. Brianna wondered why Frita needed to get her nose into every major project in this company.

As Brianna grabbed her notebook, she noticed an email pop up on her screen. It was a meeting request from Karen, their CFO. Brianna quickly opened it and wondered why

Karen wanted to meet with her. Was it about the upcoming Conclave or the headcount reductions that Frita was hounding Karen about? She quickly accepted. The meeting was not for a few more days, and right now she needed to clear her head to prepare to meet the witch, Frita.

As she came down the corridor, she noticed that Tracy, Frita's executive assistant, was not there. She was always like a guard dog and watched over Frita's calendar and office. In some ways, Tracy reminded her of Conan, Brianna's Doberman. Brianna heard Frita's muffled voice followed by a man saying he would meet her at the club at 6:45 p.m. Frita giggled and replied, "You know it, boyfriend."

A few seconds later Michael came out of Frita's office and awkwardly cleared his throat and said, "Um, morning Brianna."

Brianna was taken aback. Did Frita just address Michael as her boyfriend? "She is so disgusting," thought Brianna. What 64-year-old people officer spoke to her CEO like that? She was so dreading what the next few minutes would hold.

"Well, hello there, sweet pea. Have a seat at the table there and I'll be right with you," said Frita.

Brianna began to assess Frita quietly. She had a smirk on her face like she had hit the jackpot. Why did Frita speak to her with such derision? One could see that back in the day, Frita must have been a real stunner with her looks. She had high cheekbones and perfectly tanned skin. Now, though, she had several excess pounds on her petite frame. Her haircut looked dated. Brianna was not one to be critical of other people's looks, especially when it came to women. It was an unspoken rule with her, but as she looked at Frita, she could not help but think that the half bun that Frita wore every day had been out of style for at least a decade.

Brianna prided herself on being diplomatic and being able to get on with everyone at The F Place. But Frita was just unbearable, and everything about her turned Brianna off. She always spoke down to everyone except Michael and the Board members. How Michael could turn a blind eye to Frita's behavior was unconceivable to Brianna. Brianna wondered if there was anything going on with Michael and Frita outside the office.

Just then Brianna had to shift her attention back to Frita as she made her way to the conference table, with a staggering and exaggerated walk, hand on hip. "Well, how are you, missy girl? I hear you have been quite the busy body with this Balance-a-jig project. Which idiot produced that name for that product, anyways? Tell me all about it. I want to understand exactly how and when you are going to start selling it. How many customers do we have queued up? You know, that sort of thing," said Frita.

Brianna reminded herself to smile and take a deep breath. "Well, Frita, we have this topic on the agenda for the upcoming Executive Team meeting. You will get a chance to get the full scoop there."

Frita quickly responded, "Yes, but my team needs to be prepared for any new hires that we are going to be doing. If we are going to launch in the next two months, that does not give us enough time to get the right talent to support. I need my team to get started on this right away."

Brianna was dumbfounded. Was Frita really that dumb, or was she just in denial about the promotion and launch? Either way, Frita should know that at best it may happen at the end of the year, but that was a long shot.

Frita looked down at her phone and did that coy smirk again. Then she quickly had this dark look come over her and tersely said, "Brianna, I need to understand everything that's happening with this project—everything! I really need you tell me roughly what kind of headcount we'll need to ramp up the sales team."

Brianna debated whether she should inform Frita again about the delay in the launch. She replied, "We're not in a position to estimate that at this point, Frita; we need to know that this drug is going to be viable first."

"Yes, yes but once you work all those details out, how many headcount additions will you need on your team—fifteen? More? Thirty? Fifty? How many, Brianna?" insisted Frita.

Brianna answered, "For a product of this nature, the better approach would be to leverage our existing team and put our best and brightest on it, along with some external resources that have a proven track record of new pharmaceutical product launches. I will let you know as we get closer to that milestone."

Tracy knocked on the door and placed a message in front of Frita. Frita quickly looked at it and said, "Brianna, I'll have to end this now. Michael needs me to do something urgent for him. Please send me all you have on this, especially the timeline of launch."

The rest of the day was filled with endless meetings. As Brianna often did, she skipped lunch and finally heard her belly growl. She glanced at her Omega and realized it was almost 6 p.m. Her beautiful Omega watch—Justin had gotten her that watch for her 35th birthday. He was so thoughtful.

Enough of that. She needed to find someone to accompany her to the club tonight. The Executive Club was a membership-only place that was located within a few blocks of The F Place. Brianna occasionally went there for either a breakfast or lunch meeting. She would also sometimes host an event or two for her team. For the hefty membership price, she paid, it was a shame she did not use it more often. Justin however, enjoyed the golf privileges it afforded them. It was a lovely place that overlooked Manhattan. In the summer months the terrace was extremely popular. It often got crowded with the rich 20-somethings who were looking for a sophisticated, hip place that offered live music.

She thought, "Who can I call that will meet me there on such notice?" She decided she'd reach out to Karen Goldman, the new Chief Financial Officer of The F Place. Yes, Karen had sent her a meeting invite earlier in the day, but she'd had been practically begging Brianna to go out for a drink ever since she joined The F Place a few months ago. Brianna walked down the hall to Karen's office and was glad to see her there.

"Hey, Karen, it has been a long day, and I know you wanted to catch up. How about grabbing that drink we spoke of?" asked Brianna.

Karen smiled and said, "Yes, that sounds so great, Brianna! Where do you want to go?"

Brianna suggested they go to the Exec Club. Brianna went back to her office and decided she needed a change of scenery. So, she left the office and decided she would finish her work at the club.

Once there, she was immediately greeted by Paulina. "Ms. Grimaldi, so lovely to see you. Will you be joining Ms. Fernandez? She said she was expecting someone special and is already seated at the lovely alcove in the library."

Brianna smiled and said, "Thank you, Paulina. I am afraid I am not meeting Ms. Fernandez; I am meeting another guest. We are going to grab a drink in the lounge. You're always so helpful, Paulina!" Inside, Brianna was practically dying to find out who Frita was going to meet up with. If her hunch were true, it would explain so much! Just as she finished ordering her drink, she got a text from Karen saying she was delayed but would meet her shortly.

Brianna took a sip of her merlot and contemplated when she should walk by the library. She decided she would wait a little bit. It was almost 7:15 p.m., and she ordered another glass of wine. She took a big sip and decided she had enough liquid courage to investigate further. She'd be able to make it back before Karen got there. She walked down the corridor to the big mahogany doors that led to the library. Brianna paused for a second and then decided to go for it. She entered the magnificent room. She did not realize that they had added in new furniture. She thought, "I shouldn't be that surprised; I barely visit this place." It was such a rich room, with mahogany paneling throughout. There were several little tables in the middle of the huge room, along with a couple of card tables. It looked as though they had a jazz trio tonight.

She noticed that they had put in several booths all along the right side. Paulina mentioned that Frita had asked for the special alcove booth. She decided to take a few steps to see if she could find Frita and Michael together. As she headed in that direction, she was quickly intercepted by a staff member. "Um Ms. Florence, is it? May I help you get seated and offer you this complimentary glass of champagne?"

Brianna quickly responded that she was just in to check out the music, but she was waiting for a friend to arrive in the lounge. The waiter bowed and suggested Brianna sit down and try a few sips of the featured champagne. She could sense that he was so eager for her to taste it and listen to a little music. Brianna told him she had a call to take. He waved around and told her to pick any seat she desired and waltzed away. She thought that he must be new because he called her by the wrong name. She was grateful for that mishap. Brianna made her way to the alcove and saw that the booth next to it was empty and quietly slid in. As she sat down, she was thankful for the half-round velvet high-backed sofa booths, as they allowed for privacy.

All of a sudden, she heard that unmistakable squeal. "Oh, Michael, you naughty boy." Brianna gasped and moved over to the other side of the booth so she could hear a little better. Her heart started pounding so loudly that she was sure that Frita and Michael would hear it. She quickly took a couple of gulps of the gold bubbly, and it instantly calmed her nerves. Why was Michael talking in such a low voice? It was almost as if he was trying to be seductive. No, not almost—he was being seductive. He went on to tell Frita that he would tell his assistant he needed her for the trip to Los Angeles and that he would ask Karen to cancel at the last minute so that the two of them could do the flight alone. Brianna could not believe what she had just overheard. Her phone buzzed and looked down at a text from Karen that she was waiting in the lounge. She quickly ducked out of the library and headed back to the lounge.

Brianna waved to Karen, who had already seated herself. Karen apologized to Brianna for running late and explained that she was working on some last-minute financials for the upcoming investor call. They made some small talk for a bit and Karen started sharing her own personal story about her awful divorce. Brianna felt so bad for Karen. She thought she had it bad with Antonio, but Karen's ex sounded like a real loser. Brianna felt vulnerable and shared a little bit about what she and the kids were going through. It felt good to tell someone else what a difficult period this was for her with her children, and things had not been that easy for her. They decided to order dinner as it was starting to get a little late.

As Brianna started to dig into her saffron risotto, Karen inquired about Frita. She had a series of questions for Brianna, including what Brianna thought of Frita. Brianna sensed that, for some reason, Karen seemed to have a distaste for Frita. Brianna could hardly blame her. Karen was complaining how she had never worked at a company before where the Chief People Officer had this much power. Karen expressed to Brianna how frustrated she was with the fact that she had to review what she was going to present to the investors with Frita. Brianna could not believe that Frita was interjecting herself in the preparations for the investor call and thought to herself, "It's not like Frita could even spell finance." But Brianna was wise to keep most of her true thoughts to herself concerning Frita.

Brianna advised Karen to prepare as she normally would and disregard Frita's nosiness. "Treat her as you would any other member of the executive leadership team. She gets the presentation the same time as the rest of us. You do not need her blessing," said Brianna. Meanwhile, Brianna was thinking to herself that Frita has no business getting involved with this incredibly important investor call.

Karen gave Brianna a nervous smile and told Brianna she was so glad to have finally had the chance to share how she was feeling about Frita with her. She confided to Brianna, "Oftentimes it feels lonely at the top." Even though they were just a couple women in the leadership team, Frita confided in Brianna that she did not feel close to any of them. She again thanked Brianna for being so understanding. They walked out of the club and went their separate ways.

While Brianna was waiting in the lobby for the valet to bring her car, she saw a red Ferrari 488 Pista pull up. There was no mistaking that was Michael's car. She thought to herself, "That man sure has a need for speed." She stood there and watched as Michael slipped behind the wheel. Just then Brianna saw her red Range Rover and walked out quickly. She thought about knocking on Michael's window to say a quick hello but went straight to her car instead. It had been a long day, and it was 9:30 p.m. Brianna needed to get home as there was still so much left to do before the day was truly over. As Brianna was getting situated in her car, she noticed Frita walking out. "Oh, God," thought Brianna, "please don't let her see me." To her astonishment, Frita got in with Michael. "Where are they off to?" she wondered.

Brianna could not believe she had actually come close to sleeping with Michael. It was several years ago when she and Justin had taken a break in their relationship, when Michael had made advances at Brianna. They were at a company retreat, and everyone had overindulged in the amazing wine that night, including Brianna. Michael had insisted he walk Brianna back to her villa. He was so charming, powerful, and strong. The dimples when he smiled made Brianna melt. But most of all he seemed to adore Brianna. Brianna was in a vulnerable state that night, and she gave in to his advances. They had spent a few hours making out in the living room of her villa, and then she realized she did not want to be one of those corporate sluts who worked her way up, so she had asked Michael to leave. For many months after, he had tried to take her out, but Brianna had resisted, knowing full well that it would complicate things, and she wanted to leave things simple between them. She loved her job too much to risk it all. As Brianna brought her thoughts back, she felt like it was a lifetime ago when it had all happened.

Later, as she finally started to settle in for the night and got her pillows tucked behind her perfectly, she grabbed her journal from her nightstand and started to write down all the things she was grateful for that day. When she finally turned off the lights and closed her eyes, she thought to herself the events of the day were a little bizarre, but she was feeling pretty great because her daughter was finally coming to visit her the next weekend. As she mentally started to plan the epic weekend with Ari, she thought about what they would eat and where Ari might want to go shop and what she needed to do to ensure a completely successful weekend with her precious daughter.

Friday, February 14, 2020

Friday finally arrived. Ari was flying in late in the afternoon, and it was almost time to head to the airport. Brianna replayed the conversation in her head that she'd had with Justin about Ari coming to visit this weekend. She thought he might be upset, especially given that he thought that her kids were being unfair towards Brianna and downright mean. The reaction was not what Brianna expected. Instead, he was thrilled for Brianna, and it was yet another reminder to her that Justin was so incredibly considerate and understanding, as well as quite the planner. He had called in a favor with his chief of staff to get them third-row tickets to see Josh Groban's concert at the Barclays Center for Valentine's night. He made a joke out of it and said, "You will enjoy the concert much more with Ari than me. You know I don't enjoy loud places that much anyway."

Brianna and Justin had ended up having their Valentine's celebration the night before. Justin had taken her to Eleven Madison Park for an unforgettable dinner. They had talked about visiting the restaurant, which was in the Flatiron District of Manhattan. He was so passionate about food and always managed to take her to the finest restaurants. She was still amazed at how he managed to get reservations to a Michelin restaurant on such short notice. She knew the answer to that; being one of the top cardio-thoracic surgeons in New York City had its benefits.

Justin had ordered them a ten-course dinner with a wine pairing. The restaurant even managed to prepare a special menu to accommodate Brianna's vegetarian diet. Justin had attended to every detail to ensure that their evening out was special. Their table presented them with a view that overlooked Madison Square Park. Justin thought it was one of the most beautiful parks in Manhattan. He loved to surprise Brianna with these romantic dinners, and because it was going to be their five-year anniversary tomorrow, he had gotten Brianna a special present. As soon as they were done finalizing their order, he put a beautiful velvet box in front of Brianna. He loved gifting her with jewelry. "Open it, darling. I hope you like it; I had your mom help me get it."

Brianna slowly opened the box, and it was a beautiful, chunky 22-karat gold bracelet with several charms on it. Justin quickly explained to her that each charm had a special meaning in their relationship. As he went through each one, he explained why he had carefully chosen it. The butterfly, he said, was a reminder that she was constantly transforming; the heart engraved with "Brianna" on one side and "Justin" on the other was to remind her that they would be together forever. Then there was the diamond-studded locket charm. Justin asked her to open the charm and inside was a beautiful picture of Brianna, Justin, Ari, and Eshan. It was from their trip to Petra, Jordan. They looked like the perfect family, and all of them had beautiful smiles.

Brianna's eyes started to well up with tears. Justin took Brianna's hand and squeezed it. "Honey, I know how important being a family is to you. I want you to know that I love you, and I want us to be that happy family you always dream of. I told you your kids will come around, and they are. You are an amazing mother. I don't want you to worry so much. Everything is going to work out. You will see, and whenever you doubt it, just look at this locket." He turned the locket over and in beautiful script it was inscribed with her word of the year, "Believe." After all that she had been through with her ex-husband Antonio, Brianna still could not believe that she had found this amazing man sitting across from her.

As Brianna shifted her thoughts back to the day ahead, she mentally prepared herself for the meeting with one of their largest customers, Healthy Aid Pharmacy. She visualized herself being confident and straightforward, and making sure they knew that the launch for BalanceVITA would be delayed. One thing Brianna never compromised on was her integrity. Brianna believed in treating her clients in the same way that she would like to be treated, which was with respect and honesty.

Once at The F Place, Brianna was thankful that it was Friday. Most worked from home on Fridays, and it was usually pretty quiet at the office. She still had an hour before her meeting with Healthy Aid; they were coming to meet with her at the office. Brianna popped in to see Lizzy. She had requested that Michael join this important meeting and back her up in case there was an issue with the product launch for BalanceVITA. After repeated requests, Brianna still had not been able to confirm Michael's availability. Brianna knocked on Lizzy's door and went in. Lizzy seemed startled but greeted Brianna in her cheery manner. Brianna liked Lizzy and thought highly of her. Michael had brought Lizzy in not only as his Chief of Staff, but Lizzy also played a key role in the program management of the company's enterprise initiatives.

Lizzy was a bright young lady. When she first started at The F Place, she made a lot of improvements, especially in operationalizing Michael's vision to transform The F Place into an agile and competitive player in the pharmaceutical industry. Over the last couple months, though, Brianna could not help noticing that Lizzy always seemed a little timid and unsure of herself, especially around Michael and Frita.

Brianna asked Lizzy about the meeting with Healthy Aid and whether or not Michael was planning on being there. Lizzy said she had spoken with Michael yesterday, and yes, he was planning on joining but would be there for only the first half-hour. Brianna was relieved that Michael would be attending; he needed to share with Healthy Aid that the delay in launching BalanceVITA was to ensure that the drug was safe and that The F Place was just taking all the necessary precautions needed in order to be able get final FDA approval. As of now they were looking at a launch date of November 2020. Brianna knew Healthy Aid would understand. Brianna had a great relationship with their CEO, Buck Thornton. Buck and Brianna shared the same alma mater, Northwestern University.

Brianna arrived a few minutes early at the boardroom. She noticed the sign on the door said "In Use." Brianna looked down at her Omega watch and it was 8:45 a.m. Her meeting was to start at 9 a.m. Her assistant had reserved the room from 8:30-10:30 a.m. to ensure she had time to get settled in.

She quickly walked over to Michael's assistant, who oversaw the boardroom reservations. "Hi, Cheryl. I have a meeting with Healthy Aid at 9 a.m., and I had reserved the boardroom starting at 8:30 a.m. I see that there is a meeting in progress. Who is it? Will they be out in time?"

Cheryl replied, "I am sorry, Brianna—no, Frita is in there now, and she won't be finished until 10 a.m."

Brianna looked at her dumbfounded. "But Cheryl, I reserved the boardroom weeks ago, and this is one of our largest customers, for crying out loud."

Cheryl looked at Brianna with confusion. "Frita came to me yesterday and said she needed the boardroom, and, when I told her you had it reserved, she told me to cancel it and you'd be OK with it because she and Michael were meeting with one of the Board members this morning."

Brianna quickly thanked Cheryl and told her Frita had never approached her. Brianna was beyond furious, but right now, she needed to figure out where to take her clients. It was almost

9 a.m., and the receptionist rang Brianna. Brianna went down to greet Buck. Thankfully, it was just him and his Supply Chain head.

Brianna greeted them. "Good morning, gentlemen! I am delighted to have you with me this morning. Buck, you look great! Are you still fond of Nespresso?"

Buck smiled at her and said, "You always had such a good memory, Brianna. I cannot remember the last time you and I had a coffee, yet you still manage to know my favorite."

Brianna flashed a smile at Buck and Sameet. She suggested they have their meeting in her office as the only Nespresso machine on this floor just happened to be there.

Inside her office, Brianna asked the gentlemen to take a seat at the sofa to be more comfortable. As Brianna was making the last coffee for herself, Michael walked in unannounced.

"Buck, good morning; it is good to see you." They exchanged pleasantries, and Michael continued on. "I don't know why Brianna brought you here; we should have had our meeting in our new customer showcase room. We just had it built; everything in there is state of the art. As you know we are about to launch BalanceVITA, and they tell me we've now got the packaging finalized as well. Next time you guys come down, we will entertain you guys there. Listen, I hate to do this, especially since you took the time to visit us today. I have to catch a flight to LA shortly, but I wanted to come in and just reassure you that all is well with BalanceVITA, and we are on schedule for a mid-year launch."

Buck let out a huge sigh of relief. Brianna was pissed. How dare Michael come in and blatantly lie to Buck like this? He damn well knew that in the pre-clinical trials, the FDA had specifically refused to let The F Place proceed past Phase 3 studies to the pre-NDA period because they were still not satisfied with the findings. There is no way that they could pull this off by mid-year, even if they accelerated approval provisions.

Michael ended up staying for the full hour. Brianna decided that this was not the time to call Michael out. Instead, she politely walked Sameet and Buck out to the lobby. As soon as she got back to her office, she texted Buck and asked if he could give her a call back when he had a few minutes.

Brianna had a bad feeling that Michael was up to something. She decided to put whatever she had on the back burner because she had promised herself that when she got to the airport, she was going to be completely focused on her daughter.

On her way to the parking garage her phone rang, and it was Buck. She was so relieved that he had called her back, and she shared with him why she had wanted the face-to-face meeting with him. She said that she did not think that they could go to market with BalanceVITA until end of the year at the earliest. She told him she could share all the details, but if he really wanted, he should insist on receiving the FDA report. Brianna promised Buck that she would follow up with him over the next two weeks and keep him updated on the situation. She was so grateful to set the record straight with him.

Over the next few weeks, in addition to her already loaded schedule, Brianna would have to deal with co-leading COVID-19 meetings with Frita. It was unbearable. She wondered how that woman had made her way to becoming the Chief People Officer of a company like The F Place. What was Michael thinking when he brought Frita in? She had come from a mid-sized company in a completely different industry. Brianna recalled when Jolie, the Communications Director, had confided in Brianna that she had to make up details to make Frita's organization announcement look suitable. Michael even persuaded Alexander and the Board that Frita was the right candidate for the job, even though the Board was not convinced.

Brianna could not help but think that there was something not right with Frita. For being the Chief People Officer, she never supported anything that put the employee concerns first. She could not believe that despite the rise in COVID-19 cases in Europe, Frita fought the rest of their colleagues to keep all their factories open in Europe. Sure, Brianna understood that they were considered an essential business, but forcing employees to work their regular shifts seemed so irresponsible.

It was typical traffic for New York City. Brianna took a couple of deep breaths and brought herself back to the present moment. She was profoundly grateful that she was on her way to the airport to finally pick up her daughter. Right now, she needed to shift her thoughts to Ari. Brianna still couldn't believe that Ari was actually coming to see her. Her heart was so full today. Brianna was relieved that she got to Terminal Eight just in time.

As she was looking for a safe spot to pull into, her phone rang and it was Ari. Brianna quickly shared her location and stepped onto the island anxiously looking for any signs of her daughter! She should have gotten here a little earlier so that she could have gone into the airport to find her. It was such a pain to park at the airport. Just then, finally she spotted her stepping out of the sliding doors. It was surreal watching Ari come out. Brianna noticed how her hair had grown longer. It was silky straight and shiny as always, and she looked stunning.

Brianna was taken aback at the sight of her daughter. She realized that she had stood there for a few seconds frozen at the sight of Ari. As she started walking towards her, she reflected, "Ari is a beautiful girl, and not just because she's my daughter, but because everyone that meets her feels the same way." Ari was tall and slim and had a way about her that drew people in. Neither she nor Antonio were very tall, but there were uncles on both sides of the family who were. Brianna's grandfather and her brother Grayson were pretty tall.

Ari immediately saw Brianna and waved. Brianna ran to her and engulfed her in the biggest hug ever. Tears streamed down Brianna's face as they walked towards the car. Brianna held on tightly to Ari's arm and helped her with her suitcase. The airport security woman told Brianna to hurry up. Brianna just smiled at her and said, "My daughter is finally here to visit me." She reached over and gave Ari another hug and then got her luggage tucked into the trunk. Brianna pulled out of their spot and quickly got them on their way back to the city.

Brianna started gushing about how excited she was to see Ari, and in between smiles and tears she reached over and grabbed Ari's hand. Ari looked at her mom and said, "Stop crying, Mom; I'm here, already. It's fine." Little did Ari realize that her mother's tears were bittersweet for her. While Brianna was beyond grateful to finally see her daughter, she could not help but miss her son and wonder if he was OK.

Brianna brought herself back to the present and reminded herself that one of her wishes had finally come true, and it was a day to celebrate her daughter and their reunion. She had to pinch herself because she could not believe that her Ari was with her at last. Even though Ari had come for the weekend, Brianna knew that she had finally gotten her daughter back.

Brianna and Ari savored every moment of the Josh Groban concert on Friday evening. Ari felt like a celebrity getting all dressed up and riding to the concert in a limousine. After the concert, Brianna surprised Ari with an evening limousine tour of New York City! There was more laughter that evening than the prior ten years combined. That night as Ari went to sleep, she felt an overwhelming sense of guilt over how she had treated her mom through the years. She had forgotten how much fun her mom was. Despite all the letters, calls, and text messages that Ari had ignored, her mom never gave up on her. Ari fell asleep that night with an ache in her heart, realizing that she had almost given up on her mom, and she determined to not live another day without her mom in her life. She also decided that she was going to talk to her brother, Eshan, because he too had had a big void in his life.

Together in that short forty-eight hours during Ari's visit, Brianna had made sure that it was fully packed with just the both of them bonding, laughing, eating, walking all over the city, and of course shopping. Ari was in love with the shopping that only NYC could offer. That Sunday when Ari had left for Chicago, she had promised Brianna that she would come visit her once a month. Brianna knew in that moment that Ari meant it, and that they were on their way to rebuilding their relationship.

CHAPTER 6
The Flashpoint of Chaos

March 2020

"Chaos is a friend of mine."

—*Bob Dylan*

THE NEXT FEW weeks ended up being so bizarre and chaotic. The World Health Organization had declared that there was a pandemic underway, and it had made its way to the United States. There was a travel ban that the President of the United States had put into place. It banned travel from twenty-six European countries, and the United States had declared a national emergency. Justin had urged Brianna to cancel her flight to see a customer. Brianna had brought it up to Frita and the leadership to see what the company policy was going to be on travel. After weeks of discussion, it was only because the government was putting a travel ban in place here in the United States that Frita conceded to stop travel abroad.

Things continued to get tense at The F Place. They had put into place a working committee to start strategizing about how to deal with the impact of the pandemic on their business. Brianna was extremely grateful that Frita had not called on her to be part of the group. Brianna was trying hard to keep her customers calm as they were already anticipating delays in shipments due to the fact that all their factories in France, Italy, and Spain were shut down because of a high number of COVID cases with their employees. There was so much uncertainty with their sales forecasts, but Brianna had a great relationship with all their Tier One customers, and they trusted her.

Friday, March 13, 2020

As Brianna's flight back from North Carolina touched ground and landed at JFK airport, she felt butterflies in her stomach. She thought back to when Ari had come to visit a few weeks ago; they'd had such a wonderful time. Ari had promised Brianna that she would come to see her once a month. Given everything that was going on, Brianna was not sure whether Ari was going to be able to fly. Then as if her prayers had been answered, she received a text message from Ari that her flight was on time and that she was excited to see Brianna in just a few hours. Brianna's eyes welled up with tears as she thought about the fact that her daughter was going to be landing at the same airport later that night to come back for a second visit, just as she had promised. Even though it was just for the weekend, Brianna was grateful that she had her daughter back in her life.

The limousine dropped Brianna off in front of her building. Octavio immediately came to help her with her bag and inquired about her trip. As he opened the door he said, "Oh and Ms. Grimaldi, Dr. Mehra just arrived a few minutes before you and was smiling from cheek to cheek." Justin!

"Oh, is that so Octavio? I wonder what that's all about." Brianna gave him a warm smile and told him she would take her bag up herself. As Brianna walked into her penthouse, she could not believe her eyes. There were bouquets of lavender-colored balloons throughout the family room and kitchen. She looked at the kitchen table and there was a big sign that said, "Welcome Home, Ari," surrounded by a dozen cupcakes from Sprinkles.

Justin greeted her with his arms open and said, "What do you think, darling? Do you like?" Brianna ran into his arms and held him tight. She knew in that moment things would work out with her kids and Justin and they would all be a family. Brianna was so touched by what Justin had done for Ari.

When Ari had come home last month, as much as Brianna had begged Justin to come by and say hello to Ari, he had insisted that it would not be a good idea. He told Brianna it was important that it was just Brianna and Ari reconnecting. He had reassured her that there would be plenty of opportunities again in the future for him to talk to Ari.

At the time, Brianna felt hurt and sad that Justin had not even called her to see how their visit was going. Brianna had talked to Kate about all of this and told her that she questioned whether Justin wanted a relationship with her kids. Kate had sided with Justin and pointed out all the things Justin did for Brianna to strengthen her relationship with her kids. Brianna started smiling as she recalled how Kate had practically yelled at Brianna during their conversation and said, "Brianna, wake up. What is it going to take for you to realize that Justin worships you and the ground that you walk on? He loves you with all his heart. You must stop thinking this way about him. He is coming from a good place. Trust me, Brianna." Brianna was grateful to Kate, as she always knew how to remove her doubts and fears.

After all that and now this gesture that Justin had done to welcome Ari home, it was crystal clear to Brianna that he really was thinking of her best interests. Justin asked Brianna if she wanted him to come to the airport to pick up Brianna. Brianna eagerly nodded yes. He asked her to go relax until it was time to go to the airport, and Brianna did just that all while thanking her lucky stars.

Brianna realized they still had almost ninety minutes before they were going to leave for the airport. She decided to take a quick bath to relieve herself of the stress of the day so that she could truly enjoy her time with her daughter. As she dipped her toes in the water, she couldn't help but wonder how she and Antonio had managed to end up in this situation with their kids being separated. She knew the answer, but she couldn't help but be saddened by their story. She thought about the love they once had. It was so very special, and then, of course, their kids were special, too.

Brianna was so grateful that despite all that had transpired, she had Ariana and Eshan. She remembered how supportive Antonio had been in choosing the children's names despite Tina's interference. Brianna and Antonio both believed in blending their Indian and Italian traditions and heritage. Hindus believe in selecting their child's name based on his or her birth star. More specifically in northern India, which is where Brianna's family was from, as was Tina's, they used Rashi to name the children. Rashi is the sign in which the moon was placed at the time of your birth. It is commonly referred to as the moon sign, and also one of the most important points in selecting your baby name if you were to follow this Indian tradition.

Brianna's mother Sonia had contacted their family astrologer to confirm the sign. Both children's names were of Sanskrit origin. Based on the Rashi, they had named Ariana and lovingly nicknamed her Ari for short. Ariana meant the "holy one." Eshan meant "a god and guardian." Brianna recalled how easy it was for Antonio and her to come up with names for their children. They were both very spiritual and had a strong faith in God. With all that had happened with Brianna and Antonio, she was thankful that she still had some of the fond memories to look back to. After her bath, she quickly got herself ready to go pick up her daughter.

Brianna went into the airport to get Ari since Justin was waiting in the car. Ari actually squealed in delight when she saw Brianna. "Hi, Mom!" Brianna engulfed her in a huge hug and kissed Ari on both cheeks. It was surreal again that her daughter was back.

"Here, let me help you with your bag, Ari," Brianna said. Nervously she told Brianna that Justin was outside waiting for them in the car. Waiting for a dramatic reaction, Ari just shrugged and said, "Oh, cool," and proceeded to tell Brianna all about the weird couple sitting across from her on the plane.

Once they got to the car, Justin greeted Ari with a smile and said, "Hey, Ari, are you excited to be back home with your mom?"

Ari smiled back at him and nodded. Brianna let out a sigh of relief and thought to herself, "Well, that was not too awkward."

Once they were home, Justin got dinner going. He had made a gorgeous cheese fondue for them. He knew it was one of Ari's favorite dishes, and he was an expert at making it. Ari was so excited, and she gushed, "Oh, my God, Mommy, the food at the school cafeteria is so awful."

Even though there were cupcakes for dessert, Brianna prepared a nice chocolate fondue for them. Ari loved her fondue, and Brianna loved making her kids their favorites to eat. As they sat there, the three of them dipping their strawberries and pound cake into the warm molten chocolate, in the background there was breaking news on TV. Justin wandered over to see what it was, and it was an announcement that the coronavirus had claimed its first death in New York State. It was an elderly woman in her eighties who also had emphysema and had died at a Brooklyn hospital.

By mid-March there were over 20,000 reported cases in NYC, and there was a stay-in-place order, which mandated that everyone stay at home. The governor of New York had urged anyone leaving their homes to practice social distancing and remain at least six feet away from others. The order allowed businesses that provided essential services to remain open, but they would also need to implement rules to facilitate social distancing.

Friday, March 20, 2020

Justin was working around the clock at the hospital. Ari ended up staying well past the weekend as travel was not safe. There were lots of stories in the media about NYC going into lockdown, and sure enough, the governor put into effect on March 20 a stay-in-place order for NYC residents. This meant except for essential services, all New Yorkers were ordered to stay indoors.

Luckily, Ari had planned to come to New York right as her spring break was starting. Brianna had offered to drive her back to Chicago because she did not want Antonio to be upset with Ari for staying longer than planned. Ari insisted it was not safe to travel because of the stay-in-place order. Deep down Brianna knew it was because she really did not want to go back to Chicago. Brianna worried about Eshan and how he was faring with all this and not being able to travel with his sister to Italy for spring break as had originally been planned for both.

Meanwhile, The F Place was considered "essential" because it was in the business of manufacturing pharmaceuticals. The F Place COVID team had deemed all manufacturing plant workers as well as vice presidents and above to be classified as "essential" workers. Frita had insisted that they all continue to come into the office. There were no exceptions to this rule. She was insistent that this should be the protocol at all their global sites. What was unbelievable was that Michael supported her decision without any question.

Every day for the last couple of months, Brianna had been getting calls from employees and colleagues about how upset employees were at the lack of planning and communications regarding how The F Place was going to handle the crisis. At first Brianna tried to defend the leadership team, but it was now at a point where she herself was beyond disgusted and in complete disagreement with how matters were being handled. It was very apparent across the enterprise that there was a lack of clarity on the process for informing employees when people got sick, which was now starting to create a climate of panic. Employees in Europe were starting to piece this information together. To make matters worse, The F Place HR team did not have a clear way to reach out to the factory workers, as many of them did not have internet access nor email addresses to which communications could be sent.

All of this was a perfect storm and created uncertainty, and Frita did not seem to care. Any time someone raised these issues before their leadership team, Frita would turn to Michael and reassure him that the work councils abroad were looking at this as an opportunity to negotiate an upper hand. Michael bought it. It upset Brianna that there was not much she could do, and she truly came to hate how careless Frita was. Brianna knew that aside from her, Jolie, the Communications Director, had approached Frita several times about sending out some sort of company-wide communication to reassure employees that The F Place had their best interests at heart.

Despite all these warnings, no communications had been

sent out. Frita continued about her day-to-day and would walk around the entire office without a mask. Finally, due to local city decisions in NYC, Frita had no choice but to send out guidance on a remote work policy.

TO: All Vice Presidents and above
FROM: Frita Fernandez, EVP and Chief People Officer
SUBJECT: New Work from Home Policy
DATE: March 20, 2020

Effective March 20, 2020, our new "Work from Home" policy will go into effect. Please review and acknowledge the policy HERE before Monday morning.

As senior leaders in our organization, you are "essential" to the *FUTURE* of our company. We are counting on you to be *FLEXIBLE* and lead by example. As such, although your non-manufacturing team members will be working remotely, we expect you to show up *FOCUSED* every day at the office so that we can be *FIRST* and *FAST* in the market.

Lastly, we have received numerous questions about the new employee monitoring software. Please review the Leadership Training HERE and contact the IT Helpdesk if you need assistance.

Everyone else at the NYC headquarters was given only twenty-four hours' notice that they would be working from home indefinitely. There was a sense of relief amongst employees that at least they could continue their jobs from home.

This meant that Brianna would continue to have to come to

the office as she was part of the executive leadership team. Once the memo had gone out, Brianna was fielding calls and emails from her team members all day long.

Wednesday, March 25, 2020

Brianna received a text from Kate informing her that she had been infected with COVID-19. Brianna quickly called her, and Kate told her she had been feeling extremely tired the last few days. She had a high fever and her body ached uncontrollably. Brianna felt so bad for Kate; she sounded so fatigued. Kate didn't have any family around to take care of her. She only had her 14-year-old daughter Sarah.

Apparently, Sarah had also tested positive for the virus. Brianna was the closest family that Kate had in NYC.

"Kate, what about Sarah? How is she? Who's cooking for you? Do you need anything? Can I drop anything off?" inquired Brianna.

Kate reassured Brianna that she and Sarah were going to be OK and had everything they needed in the house. She shared that even though Sarah had tested positive, she didn't seem to have any symptoms of the virus, except for a loss of smell. Brianna felt a little better and promised Kate that she would call to check in on her a few times a day. Brianna hoped that they could control the pandemic quickly, as it was really like a wildfire taking over the world. It just felt like there was more chaos and uncertainty in the world with each passing day.

CHAPTER 7

Death on Two Fronts

April 2020

"No one really knows why they are alive until they know what they'd die for."

—*Martin Luther King, Jr.*

Thursday, April 9, 2020

A s usual, Brianna's alarm clock woke her up way too early at 4:30 a.m. She loved the way the sound of the silk chimes would awaken her every morning. As she put her feet on the ground, she thought to herself, "While most of the world sleeps, I have a job that requires me to wake up at zero dark-thirty. After all, the early bird gets the worm."

Brianna really did love the morning hours and especially the start of a new week. This was yet another Monday morning. Today was going to be a tough day, and she needed to prepare herself for what lay ahead. She allowed herself an extra five minutes in her hot shower. She then turned the knob to cold and finished off the last minute with icy-cold water. This always gave her the kick she needed to give her brain a nice wake-up before The F Place marathon resumed. While getting ready for work, Brianna typically listened to leadership podcasts. Today was EntreLeadership with Daniel Tardy and Dave Ramsey. They shared helpful insights for business owners about how they should not fear but instead should stick to their core values. Brianna thought to herself, "I needed to hear this today! Bravery is being afraid of something and doing it anyway. I am determined to be brave today, even though my soul is filled with trepidation."

Brianna's mind was saturated with thoughts of everything in front of her that day. Endless meetings, a video recording for the upcoming regional sales conference (now virtual), a Zoom lunch meeting with the Asian American Diversity Council, and so on.

She made a mental note to remember to get on Amazon to order the school supplies that Ari had requested. Ari held Brianna's heart in her hands. She was smart, funny, and at times even a little bossy. She had inherited all that from Brianna. Brianna was so proud of her daughter; she really was born to dream, and she worked fearlessly to achieve her goals.

She still could not believe that Ari had decided to stay with her. The university had requested the kids to not come back after spring break because they were afraid that the virus would spread like wildfire on campus. It was sad to say, but Brianna thought were it not for the virus, she may have not gotten her daughter to move back in with her. She also started to have more hope that Eshan would follow her sister's lead and consider coming back. Her mind turned quickly to all the to-do's she had. So many things to do, and she continued to sift through them one by one, all while playing out in her mind how her day would unfold.

It probably would be faster to take the subway, but with the hours Brianna worked, she did not want to wait for a train so late in the evenings. Therefore, she always took the forty-five-minute commute each day by car and usually drove to the office. It was not that far in distance to the office, but it was normally the NYC traffic that created the long drive. Also, given the current climate with the pandemic, she was not going to use any public transportation any time soon. With the stay-in-place order, traffic had thankfully changed and lightened up significantly. She arrived at the office and parked in her usual spot. Brianna thought to herself and smiled. "Since I am almost always the first one in, I get to choose my spot, and everyone knows it." Even though she had access to the executive parking, she always parked in the same area as the other employees.

She turned off the engine and closed her eyes for a few seconds. She took a deep breath in and let it all out slowly. Brianna then said to herself loudly and with a laugh, "Let's do this!" As Brianna came off the elevator at about 6:30 a.m., the office was still dark. She had one hour to review the materials (again) and finish preparing before the monthly operations review in the boardroom. Q1 2020 was simply a nightmare. Between the global pandemic, the economic meltdown, and the quality concerns with BalanceVITA, Brianna's commercial team were unable to hit their financial targets. Despite pulling out all the stops, they fell short by 16 percent. And in The F Place, if you do not hit your numbers, no matter what is going on in the world, there will be hell to pay!

Her cellphone buzzed, and Brianna saw that it was her mom calling. She quickly decided to answer. "Good morning, Mom. I am about to go to an important meeting; can I call you back tonight?"

Sonia, Brianna's mom, replied, "Honey, I heard some news from Auntie Kimberly." Auntie Kimberly was one of Sonia's best friends and had been a part of Brianna's life since she was only 3 years old.

"Mom, what is it? Is she OK?" asked Brianna.

"Yes, Auntie Kimberly is OK. It is George, Brianna. Kimberly said that Ari's grandfather has got this coronavirus," replied Sonia cautiously. She knew that Brianna would be upset upon hearing this news.

Brianna was stunned. "Are you sure, Mom? I mean that is horrible; he already has so many issues with his heart and diabetes. She must be mistaken."

Brianna's mom softly said, "No, Brianna, she works at Advocate Hospital, and she was on the shift when your ex-husband brought him in. Didn't Antonio tell you? What about Ari? She must have told you? This happened two days ago."

Brianna knew Ari had been a little sad these past couple days, and Brianna had tried to talk to her about it, but Ari had gotten upset with her so Brianna had backed off so she would not distress her any further. Brianna was really trying to give Ari all the space she needed. Intuitively, she knew that her father was probably making the poor girl's life hell because she had chosen to come and stay with her.

"Antonio will have to deal with it," thought Brianna. She wished him well, but that man had created hell for her. She was also so hurt by the events that had unfolded over the years. Brianna promised her mom that she would call her later and told her to keep her updated if she had learned anything else about her ex-father-in-law's condition.

As Brianna arrived in the boardroom, the IT technician wished her a good morning. If time allowed, Brianna almost always got to these kinds of meetings early. She did a mental run-through of what she would say, how she would say it, and how she would reassure the leadership team that they would turn this ship around. Over the next few minutes, the rest of her peers started to trickle into the boardroom. Besides Brianna, Karen was the only other person with a mask on. It appalled Brianna that hardly anyone in the office was following safety measures despite the dire situation that the city of New York was in with COVID cases climbing out of control.

Michael walked in five minutes late and sat in his spot at the head of the table. "Good morning, everyone, and apologies for being a few minutes late," he said. "I was on the phone with one of our customers. We will get into that a little later. For now, let's get started. We have a lot to discuss."

He always filled the room with his energy. Today he seemed to be in a relatively good mood . . . for now. His Chief of Staff, Lizzy Brown, sat next to him (six feet away) to take notes and do whatever Michael wanted her to do. Lizzy always looked as if she had just consumed a meal that consisted of foul-tasting fish. Brianna felt bad for Lizzy; the poor girl looked worn out all the time. Brianna also sensed that she tended to get more fidgety around Michael as of late. Michael was easy enough to work with, but over the last year he was starting to get short with a lot of folks.

Brianna kicked off the meeting with a review of the Q1 financial bookings. "While we delivered well over plan in January and February, the disastrous month of March wreaked havoc on our quarter. Thus, we were 16 percent below plan for the quarter," said Brianna. She continued to share details of the mitigation plan that she and her leadership team had developed. They had personally contacted each one of their key accounts by video call and reassured them that The F Place was open for business and here to help them through these challenging times. Given the quality issues with BalanceVITA, they stayed away from that and focused on the other products and solutions in the portfolio. Although BalanceVITA has an incredibly high profit margin, Brianna was simply unwilling to sell something that conflicted with her personal values. And she most certainly would not ask her team to do something that she was unwilling to do.

Edward jumped in and questioned the booking numbers by each product. He continued to press, asking why there were no bookings in Q1 for BalanceVITA. In many ways, Edward reminded Brianna a lot of Michael. After all, he was Michael's protégé. Knowing how unhappy Edward was, Brianna danced around the issue and explained that their customers were simply unwilling to take a risk on a new product during these uncertain times.

Karen chimed in and criticized the profitability figures, stressing that their Q1 targets included BalanceVITA, and the only way to hit the profit numbers was to get BalanceVITA launched in the marketplace. She knew that this was not Brianna's fault, but Frita had coached Karen before the meeting to make sure Karen went on record against Brianna. Karen had told Michael and Frita that they could think about extending the quarter. She had reminded them that there was nothing in SEC rules that says a company cannot have uneven quarters. They would simply have to ensure that they were consistent year to year. Michael seemed interested in the idea, but clearly, he was not on board because just then he stood up and pounded his fists on the table and startled everyone. It was so unlike him to behave so aggressively in front of a group.

"Unacceptable performance, Brianna. Because of you, we all missed the boat on Q1. This quarter, you will get to join Karen and me with the Board in LA and in the earnings call to answer for your incompetence!" Michael then nodded to Frita and said that it would be necessary to enact the downturn planning scenario. He further maintained that this would include a 20 percent workforce reduction. Everyone in the room was astounded upon hearing this news. They knew things were bad, but to enact a double-digit reduction in workforce was going to hurt them all around.

Brianna wondered if Michael meant what he was saying. How could they possibly have the Board meeting in person when so many Americans were under lockdown? She had just heard on the news that as of this morning a majority of states had now issued stay-at-home orders.

Brianna tried to calm Michael down and pleaded, "Michael, I understand your frustration. I really do. However, you know as well as I do that our people are our greatest assets. Rather than jumping straight to a workforce reduction, I propose that we look at other options first. We say that we always put our people first, and I know you are a leader who believes that, but this is not what it means to be an employee-focused company!"

Frita did not miss a beat. She jumped right in and in a condescending tone chirped, "Brianna, we have a lot of fat in this organization. I mean, look at your Commercial Transformation team. What is it that they really do, anyway? Karen and I have already run the numbers, and I am confident that we can reduce the workforce by 20 percent and barely feel the impact."

Brianna clenched her Mont Blanc pen in pure frustration and turned her chair towards Frita's direction. She wished that her pen was a dart that she could aim at Frita's mouth so that she could get that smug look off her face.

"Frita, are you kidding me? In your role as Chief People Officer, aren't you supposed to be the champion of our people? Give me a break. Those of us around this room make more money in one year than most of our employees will ever earn in their lifetime. You know they count on us for their livelihood, their families, their homes. How can we just drop them the moment we miss our numbers one quarter while there is so much uncertainty and fear in the marketplace? We should be better than this. This company has weathered so many storms, and this is one more. You are jumping the gun here and making a huge mistake!" argued Brianna.

As soon as she blurted out those words, she knew that Frita would make sure that Brianna would pay for her frankness in a big way. Brianna did not care, though; she was not intimidated by Frita, and she was not going to back down. Brianna took their company's values seriously, and she made it a point to live by them.

"Brianna, this is not up for debate. The matter is settled. We are going with Frita's downturn plan," stated Michael.

Brianna looked at Michael and locked eyes. She pleaded, "Michael, with all due respect, this should be an executive leadership decision, not a unilateral one. I strongly recommend that we explore other options. As for me, I am willing to forego my bonus, stock grants, and 50 percent of my salary to preserve jobs while we ride out this storm."

Brianna then turned to the rest of her peers and asked, "Come on, everyone, what do the rest of you think? We cannot just go to such an extremity without looking at other options. How will your teams react to this news?"

"Brianna, while your heart is in the right place, your recommendation is just not practical. Besides, Frita has shared that most of the employees that we will be letting go of are considered 'at will' employees. There is practically no liability here at stake for us," said Karen, as she sat there clothed in her three thousand dollar Chanel suit. She pointed her perfectly manicured fingers at Brianna, and Brianna could not help but notice her big oyster pearl Rolex, the 10-plus-carat diamond, and half-dozen or so gold bracelets on her hand.

Brianna thought to herself, every single person in this room had so much financial security and yet no compassion. They were all so greedy and selfish. All they cared about was adding another zero at the end of their compensation.

Brianna's head started pounding, and one by one they just kept going at it. Next it was Edward chiming in. "I agree with Karen. Besides, I have earned my seat at the table and all the rewards that go along with that. Why would I give that up? Don't we get paid to make these decisions? Michael and Frita, I am in complete agreement with you. It is time for us to downsize."

Brianna glanced at Michael again, hoping that he would see that this was just not right. Instead, he looked absent and preoccupied and quickly responded, "Nice try, Brianna. But your proposal simply does not hold water. Frita, do you have the employee lists ready?"

"Yes, I have reviewed them with everyone except for Brianna. She has been a no-show at three of my meetings to discuss this very topic," said Frita, coyly flipping her platinum blond hair aside.

Brianna was livid at this point and could not contain herself any longer. "What the hell, Frita? I haven't had a single meeting request from you. What exactly are you implying? Better yet, what kind of games are you playing?" said Brianna.

"Calm down, Brianna. There is no need to get emotional here. You really do need to compose yourself, girlfriend. If your schedule will allow, we can review together right after this meeting concludes," said Frita petulantly.

Brianna quickly composed herself. She thought about what Kate would do if she were in her position. Fully knowing that she was in an impossible situation, she answered in a calm, cool, and collected voice, "Yes, let us do that, Frita. Until we have aligned, not even one of my employees will be included in the reduction in force action. Are we clear on that?"

Frita dismissively looked away from Brianna and leaned in to whisper something to Edward. Michael went on as if this outrageous conversation had never happened. "Great. It is settled then. Team, I count on each of you to lead by example and make this happen as smoothly as possible," said Michael.

Sometimes Brianna wondered how such a talented man like Michael could be so blind to what was happening at The F Place.

As they exited the boardroom, Brianna followed Frita to her office, ready to discuss the downturn plan. Frita shut the door and stood behind her large mahogany desk, fuming. Frita stared at Brianna and thought about how she could not stand Brianna. Brianna always had to challenge Frita every step of the way, and Frita could not stand how Michael's eyes would flicker appreciatively at the sight of Brianna. "Who did Brianna think she was anyways? Brianna may have the looks and the attention of most of the people in this office, but I am the one with the power here. It is time for me to remind little Miss Perfect," thought Frita.

She looked Brianna in the eye and started seething. "Brianna, you have double-crossed me in front of Michael and the Executive Team one too many times. You, missy girl, really are dead to me. Do I make myself clear? There will be no review of employee lists. You will find out about my plan when I decide to inform you. You can go cry to Michael, but he is also done with your drama. You should go ahead and pack your bags. It is time for you to leave. Bye-bye, sweet pea. Don't let the door hit you on the way out," said Frita.

Brianna walked back to her office and quietly closed the

door. She had to talk to Kate, who had finally recovered from COVID along with her daughter, Sarah. Kate did not answer, so she texted her to see if she would meet her for coffee. Luckily, Kate's office was only a few blocks from her. Brianna knew Kate would have some words of wisdom for her. Brianna's stomach was growling, and even though she knew that there was food that had been catered in for their meeting earlier, she could not bear the thought of going back into that boardroom any time soon.

She got in her car and the breaking news quickly got her attention. The broadcaster went on to say they suspected that NYC was about to get hit hard with the coronavirus. They went on to say that the woman in New York had encountered dozens of others while exhibiting these symptoms. Apparently, she had recently traveled to Iran and was now isolated in her Manhattan home.

Instead of picking up coffee, Brianna stopped at Bombay House, as Kate was working from her home office, and picked up lunch for them. Brianna was thankful that even though it was impossible to dine anywhere in the city, at least there were a few of their favorite neighborhood eateries that were still open for takeout and delivery.

Brianna was so thankful that Kate was able to shake off her virus. She had been bedridden for four days straight with diarrhea, fever, chills, and vomiting. She had also lost her taste buds for a few days. She said she had never felt so bad as she did when she had the virus. The poor girl had lost eight pounds in that short two weeks that she was sick. Now that Kate had her taste buds back, the least Brianna could do was pick up Kate's favorites before she unloaded on her. Kate fancied samosas and butter chicken, while Brianna preferred her palak paneer and naan bread. When Kate opened the door to greet Brianna, she became worried as Brianna was not her bubbly self. Once in Kate's house, Brianna took off her sunglasses, and Kate saw that her dear friend had a despondent look on her face. Kate helped Brianna with the takeout and then gave Brianna a tight hug. Kate urged Brianna to let it all out.

Brianna confided; she did not know where to begin. It all seemed so surreal. She thought about Tony Robbins' words from the podcast she had listened to the day before: "Identify your problems but give your power and energy to solutions."

As Brianna replayed the events of the morning with Kate, she started to have faith that together they would produce a plan to address the chaos happening at The F Place. It was moments like these that Brianna felt even more grateful to have Kate as a wonderful friend and a guide. Brianna told Kate that she had gotten quite emotional during the meeting and how Frita called her out on it in front of everyone. "She said, 'Calm down, girlfriend!' Can you believe that, Kate? She is the Chief People Officer of The F Place, and she continuously talks down to people, and no one, I mean no one, says anything. It is as if she walks on water. Do you remember when they fired Charlie over that simple comment?"

Kate reminded Brianna that one of her superpowers was her intuition and her ability to have empathy for others.

"Brianna, you know who you are. You are a genuine person with a heart of gold, all passion, courage, and strength. I know you cannot be stopped when you believe in something and set your heart on it. Now, you've faced nightmares that have been so bad, but nothing has broken you down. You are the best leader that I know, and your soul is filled with nothing but compassion and kindness. Frita doesn't see the world the way that you do, and that is going to be her downfall. She is going to dig her own grave and lie in it. You just watch."

Brianna knew Kate was right, but she really needed the

reminder today. Brianna thought to herself, "So what if I am right? What can I do about it?"

Throwing her hands up, she said to Kate, "You always have all the answers, my friend; tell me what can I do to stop them from going through with this RIF?" Kate advised her to let it go; there was nothing else left to do. She could not defy Michael.

"Brianna, start looking at how you can help your team members. I can take on a couple more in my company. I could use some more talent on our sales team. I know you think so highly of that fellow Christian; is he impacted?" asked Kate.

Brianna knew deep down that Kate was right; there was no changing Michael's mind at this point, as he was determined to allow Frita to continue with the cuts. She then told Kate about Frita's timing on all of this. It was just so unbelievable. They expected to implement the cuts over the next month.

Just then her phone started to ring, and it was Ari. She was crying hysterically. Between sobs, she got out, "Mom, Grandpa passed away."

Brianna herself started to cry. "I am so sorry, darling. I am on my way; I'll be home right away. I am so sorry, honey." Brianna told Kate what happened and ran out the door.

Brianna got home and consoled Ari as best as she could. Brianna's father-in-law had been a nice man. He had worked hard to provide a secure future for his family. Brianna had always had a soft spot for George. Why couldn't everyone else in that family have been more like her father-in-law? She wished that things could have been different between her and her ex-husband, Antonio.

Brianna thought about calling Antonio, but she knew he would just be nasty. Instead, she ended up sending a text message: "Antonio, I am truly sorry to hear about your father. He was a wonderful man. I cannot imagine what you and your family must be going through. Please know that you are in my thoughts and prayers."

Almost immediately, Antonio sent her a nasty text back calling her names and telling her to keep her sympathy to herself. Brianna just could not understand why he hated her so much. She had done nothing but love him unconditionally.

Brianna asked Ari if she wanted to go to the funeral, but they both knew that it would be a bad idea to travel to Chicago. Brianna knew why Antonio and his mother Tina were always against her as it had never been the plan for Antonio to marry Brianna. While Tina Grimaldi was not Brahmin, she came from a good Indian family and had created a successful enterprise in the United States. She remembered the early days shortly after she had given birth to Ariana. Brianna had come down to the kitchen when she had overheard the conversation between Tina and her longtime friend from Berkeley. They were having tea one afternoon. They were relishing in memories of their friendship. Ordinarily, Brianna would never eavesdrop, but knowing who Tina's friend was, she just couldn't help herself, and so she had quietly stood in the kitchen and taken in most of their conversation.

At first the women embraced and savored memories of their first moments together. Then Tina's voice changed, and she told her friend that she would make sure that they kept their promise. Bri knew she shouldn't be listening, but she couldn't move. She had a feeling that she was going to hear something about herself that she knew was going to be bad.

As if on cue, Tina obliged and told her friend, "I don't know what's gotten into Antonio, but I'm going to make sure that I straighten him out. I made a promise to you that Antonio would marry your beautiful daughter Adira, and I intend to keep it."

Tina continued, "I remember that day so perfectly when I walked into your beautiful nursery, which was fit for a princess. I remember telling you how perfect Adira was in every way. You and I made a promise that my Antonio and your Adira would marry one day and our families will be united forever! We've worked so hard to create two perfect families. And as for that sassy, sorry girl that Antonio has brought around, now that Antonio has his two children, he has no use for her. I promise you, he'll be leaving her in no time."

Brianna had gone quietly back to her room and sobbed for hours. She brought herself back to the present and felt sorry for Tina and Antonio. They were a sorry bunch. Brianna still couldn't understand how people like Tina could be so obsessed with money and power. Then there was more bad news the next day. As if the news of her father-in-law was not bad enough, the next day Grayson, Brianna's younger brother, called. "Brianna, it's Dad," Grayson said in a grave voice. "We think he has the coronavirus, Brianna. He was admitted to Swedish Covenant Hospital this morning, and they won't let any of us in to see him."

Brianna's heart pounded in her chest and she struggled to take a breath. Her dad had struggled with Type 1 diabetes for practically his whole life. Given this pre-existing condition, she knew that his chances for survival were not good.

"Let me make some phone calls and see what I can find out. I will call you back as soon as I can," Brianna said to Grayson. She immediately called Dr. David Buxley, a friend of hers from university, who worked at Swedish Covenant Hospital. David promised to check in on her dad before his shift started.

About 3 p.m. that afternoon, David called Brianna back and confirmed the worst. Her dad was on a ventilator and struggling to survive. They were doing everything they could for him, but the odds were not in his favor. David promised Brianna that he would check on him again when his shift ended.

Justin began preparing Brianna for the worst. "Brianna, darling, it just doesn't look good for your father." Brianna was angry at him for suggesting the worst was going to happen, even though deep down inside, she knew he was right.

Monday, April 13, 2020

Every day, Justin came home from the hospital with bleak news. Today, he explained how nine out of ten patients who were on ventilators at his hospital died. While those with diabetes were more likely to have received invasive mechanical ventilation or care in the ICU, it still did not promise a positive outcome.

Justin had always urged Brianna to have a good relationship with her father. Brianna's dad had remarried after he and his mother had divorced. His second wife was much younger, spoiled, and only cared about her dad's money. She never reached out to Brianna or Grayson. Her daughter was the only thing she cared about. She felt sorry for her stepmother. She relied on her dad for everything.

Brianna thought about her mother Sonia. Her mother had never stopped loving her dad. She vowed she would never get remarried after he left her for a younger woman. Brianna's mom was such a beautiful soul. She sacrificed so much for both her and Grayson. Brianna thought about the day that she found out about her parents' divorce. It was Valentine's Day. Brianna's parents, Sonia and Milan, had taken both their children out for dinner. Brianna recalled how nervous her mother seemed. She had gently pulled both Brianna and Grayson towards her in the cozy booth. Brianna still remembered how shaky her mother's voice had been when she inquired, "Brianna and Grayson, you know how much your dad and I love you, don't you?" Brianna had exclaimed back, "Yes, Mommy. I do! I do!" Grayson, who was only 2 ½ back then, had also shouted excitedly, "Me, too!"

Brianna still recalled how sad Sonia and Milan looked when they had locked their eyes. As they always did, Sonia had given a nod to Milan to continue. Brianna remembered her dad trying to be positive as he had said, "Yes, we love you both so much! And even though your mommy and I love each other, too, we have been arguing a lot lately, right?"

Brianna was always first to respond and had said, "Yes, you guys fight more than any other adults that I know. Maybe you need a timeout!"

Milan had responded, "That's right, Brianna. You are such a smart young lady. Your mommy and I do need a timeout! So, I am going to move into a different house down the street. But don't worry; you will still get to see both of us every day."

Brianna was always quick to grasp things. She realized quickly that her baby brother Grayson didn't really understand what was going on and looked confused. Brianna didn't miss a beat and quickly picked up on what was happening. She recalled how she was trying desperately in that moment to hold back her tears, "You're moving out of our house, Daddy? Why?"

"Daddy is going to move into the Smiths' old house down the street. Remember that they moved to a new home last month? Well, Daddy is going to buy their house so we will both be here for you every day. And by living in different houses, we won't fight anymore. Do you understand?" asked Sonia with tears in her eyes.

"Will we still be a family?" cried Brianna as she looked back and forth to her parents.

"Yes, sweetheart, we will always be a family, even if your father and I aren't married anymore," said Sonia as she tried to smile through her tears.

"You and Mommy aren't going to be married anymore?" Brianna had sobbed.

"No, my love. But we will always be your daddy and mommy. No matter what, OK? We both love you more than anything. That is what matters the most. Isn't that right, Mommy?" Milan had said tenderly.

"Yes, your father is right. You are the most important people in our lives, and we will always love you," said Sonia.

Brianna knew that her parents loved her and Grayson more than anything. Grayson was getting impatient and asked, "Um, can I have ice cream for dessert?"

Brianna felt better once they ordered dessert. She went on and inquired, "Will Grayson and I get to have a bedroom at your house, too, Daddy?"

"Of course, my princess. Whereas most kids only have one bedroom, you both will have two!" said Milan, trying desperately to be positive.

Sonia and Milan handled their divorce well and never spoke ill of one another. They decided to put their children first and to co-parent well no matter what. With Milan living down the street, the children grew up with both of their parents active in their lives. They even celebrated birthdays and most holidays together.

Later that same year, Milan had married Valerie in a quiet ceremony, just a few short months after his divorce from Sonia was finalized. Sonia kept her head held high and decided not to be nasty despite Milan's affair and marriage to a much younger woman.

Throughout the years, Brianna tried to get her mother to explain why her parents got divorced, but Sonia refused to talk about it and never said a negative word about her ex-husband to her children.

Brianna thought, although not perfect, her father Milan was truly kind and generous. It hurt Brianna so much to think of her parents' divorce. They were a match made in heaven, and her Dad had thrown it all away for an affair with her now-stepmother.

As forgiving as her mother was, Sonia could not tolerate infidelity. That's another thing Brianna had in common with her mother. Antonio, too, had cheated on Brianna. He had an affair while they were married. Brianna did not find out until they were separated, and at that point, she did not care.

She was just so hurt with everything he did to try to get full custody of their children. Brianna just wanted out from the nightmare, so she ended up agreeing to joint custody. Their divorce had dragged on for years, and it had drained Brianna financially. She just did not have the kind of financial resources that Antonio's family had. Brianna reminded herself that this was all in the past. Just this year Brianna finally had some real savings accumulated and felt like she was becoming financially secure. Justin had been wonderful at helping her figure out how to invest her money.

Wednesday, April 15, 2020

A few days later she received the dreaded call from Grayson at 2 a.m. Her dad had died. Brianna was heartbroken. She thought back to the last time she had gone to visit him. They'd had such a wonderful time. Even though Grayson had not been there, she and her Dad had some great laughs. She remembered him telling her how enormously proud he was of her and all that she had accomplished.

Her father Milan had come to the states from India with

forty dollars in his pocket and worked his way up to become an executive at a manufacturing company. Brianna always admired her father for his work ethic. She wished so badly that Grayson would see the best in her father. Grayson was never able to forgive him for leaving their mother.

Brianna told Grayson she would hop on the next flight, but Grayson talked her out of it. "Brianna, they're not going to let either of us see his body. What is the point of your risking getting corona to fly here? At some point, I will take his ashes to India as he wished and do my duty as his son. I will sprinkle them on the Ganges as he wanted. If you are able, maybe we could do the trip together?"

Brianna broke out in tears again. Her poor father was dead, and she could not even say goodbye to him. Brianna promised Grayson that she would go to India with him. She worried so much about Grayson. Ever since he had gotten married to Samantha, he was so distant from her. They had always been close growing up. Brianna idolized her little brother, even though he was not so little. She felt close to him now as they only had each other to deal with this loss.

"Grayson, you need to check in on Mom. Promise me you will go see her today? She's not going to handle this well. She's going to be heartbroken. I wish I could be there, Grayson— with you and Mom. This is so unfair," Brianna sobbed. Grayson tried to console her, but Brianna continued to weep. As she finally ended the call with her brother, it dawned on her again that she was not going to be able to go to her own father's funeral.

She continued to check in on her mother regularly to see how she was coping. Brianna had also reached out to her stepmother, Valerie. After the first call, Valerie did not bother to answer any more calls from either Grayson or Brianna. Brianna knew this had to be hard for Valerie. She was a gold digger, but she did care for Milan. Brianna was appalled when Valerie had brought up the will during their phone conversation. Brianna thought Valerie was showing her true colors. Milan had not even been gone for twenty-four hours, and Valerie was already questioning Brianna about her father's will. Brianna was so upset at Valerie that she had hung up on her after that. Brianna knew, though, that Valerie would eventually reach out to Brianna when she found out that Milan had left half of his estate to Brianna and Grayson.

The weeks that followed were exceedingly difficult for Brianna. She reached out to Kate often to console her. Every time Brianna thought about Kate's own tragedy of losing her son, Max, at such a young age, Brianna reminded herself to be strong. That did not stop Brianna from mourning the loss of her father, and in many ways, she thought to herself, it was a blessing to be so busy with work. Even though she was not traveling anywhere, she was extremely busy.

Friday, April 24, 2020

Brianna thought about how things continued to be so tense at The F Place. In a million years, she never thought she would dread working there. To make matters worse, the earnings announcement that was released today created chaos with their investors. Brianna's phone was getting bombarded with calls from customers inquiring about the status of BalanceVITA and when The F Place was expecting to get FDA approval for the drug.

The F Place Reports Q1 2020 Results

New York City, New York—April 24, 2020—Today, The F Place announced financial results for the first quarter ending March 31, 2020.

- First-quarter worldwide sales of $4.2 billion decreased 15.9 percent year over year

- Due to uncertainties regarding the impact and duration of COVID-19, The F Place is suspending its previously announced annual guidance for 2020

"We remain *FOCUSED* on our vision to become the global leader in pharmaceuticals, and we are taking *FAST* action to adjust our cost structure in response to the market decline. We are optimistic that our BalanceVITA clinical trials will be wildly successful and we will receive FDA approval soon. Early results are incredibly promising," said Michael Vitali, President & CEO.

[Read More]

Brianna was still disturbed about what was going to happen next week. Of course, she knew about the reduction in force that would happen on Thursday, April 30. Despite multiple efforts, she had been unable to get any information about the people in her team. Rumors were flying, though, and she had gotten a few names of impacted employees from her colleagues. Yet again, she found herself questioning the company she had spent her career working for. It was simply beyond belief that she was an officer of the company and yet she had no official access to the reduction in force information, let alone a voice in the process. She was determined to either change the company culture or leave The F Place.

Monday, April 27, 2020

As usual, Brianna arrived in the office before 6:30 a.m. This morning, instead of listening to something inspirational on the way to the office, Brianna had to take a call with China. As she got the rundown from Ming on a recent customer meeting, she was saddened that Ming may be impacted by the RIF this week. Ming had been such a great addition to the supply chain team in Asia. She was young and bright and had a great rapport with customers. Brianna was profoundly grateful that she had such a competent team to work with.

Brianna had been told that several directors in Asia were going to be let go due to the RIF. It was horrible to face the fact that The F Place was about to let go of such talent. As she wrapped up her call, she realized she was already pulling into the parking garage.

Due to COVID shelter-in-place for most people, traffic was incredibly light. Brianna reflected on the fact that the one bright side to COVID was the traffic . . . her commute time to the office had never been this short.

Dressed in a smart dark pantsuit, as always, Brianna arrived early in the boardroom. Brianna always dressed impeccably. Today she needed an extra lift, so she had a green silk blouse under her jacket for effect. The one thing that Brianna never compromised on was self-care. While she and Antonio were going through their divorce, Kate had insisted that Brianna add yoga to her exercise regimen. Brianna alternated between cardio and yoga. Yoga had really helped her with her breathing and was a great stress reliever.

Brianna could tell that the witch was coming down the hallway. Without any greeting, Frita came in next and had her assistant set up her computer for the session. All the while, she tapped her fingers on the glossy boardroom table.

Brianna thought to herself how most people assume that Frita does not even know how to use technology. There were so many dumb-blonde jokes floating around about Frita's understanding and consumption threshold of technology. It would not surprise Brianna one bit if Frita had a slide rule hidden in her office somewhere.

Brianna looked Frita straight in the eye and gave her the most confident smile. Frita looked straight through Brianna and literally pretended that she did not exist. Brianna had expected nothing else from Frita. "Oh, yeah, what a true professional and a really inspirational People Officer," she thought.

Once everyone arrived, Frita kicked off the session. She handed each leader a leadership briefing packet for this week's RIF. She stood right in front of Brianna and dropped the packet on top of her phone. She then looked at Brianna in the eyes and smiled in such a sinister way that Brianna truly believed she could be the devil herself. Frita continued her briefing, but Brianna did not hear another word that was said.

As Brianna opened her packet, she stared in disbelief. There it was in black and white. She saw that the best and brightest leaders and team members from her organization were on the RIF list. It was all her top salespeople. She was stunned and shocked and could not believe the names she was looking at. She had known it was going to be a blood bath, but Brianna did not realize that most of it would be targeted towards her organization.

She blinked several times and thought, "They're going to

be gone. My Commercial Transformation team is going to be gone. What kind of organization will I have left standing, and how will we be able to deliver results for The F Place?"

She quickly did the math and realized that this plan would reduce her team in the U.S. by 35 percent and in EMA by 15 percent. Her blood was starting to boil, and she could not think straight. She implored, how could Michael have approved something this disastrous . . . not only for the people, but for the company? But she knew exactly what was happening. Frita was using this as an opportunity to bring her down because she refused to bow down to her highness.

Brianna tuned back in to hear Frita continue in her condescending voice. "Now boys and girls, your HR business partners will join you in all the leadership video calls to help your impacted employees through this process. You simply need to read your script. Let me remind you that it is important that you make sure your video is on and make sure you keep your emotions out of it. This is nothing to cry about."

Brianna was outraged at Frita's behavior. She took a deep breath, stood up, and picked up her packet. With all eyes turned on her now, Brianna walked over to Frita and threw the packet in front of her just as she had done to Brianna.

"Let me make myself crystal clear here, Frita. I refuse to play any part in this circus. The way that this is all being handled is unethical and unacceptable." Brianna paused and took another deep breath. "This whole thing is wrong on so many levels."

Then turning to Michael, Brianna firmly said, "Since you approved this plan, you can execute it yourself for the Commercial team. I am out of here." Brianna grabbed her belongings and decided she needed to leave. Brianna thought to herself, "I did not get too emotional; I am acting with integrity. Shame on Michael and Frita for behaving this way."

As she got in her car, Brianna looked at the text from Michael in disbelief. "Cool down, Brianna. Let's get you a few drinks and then you can make the calls to your team."

Brianna dialed Justin and told him what happened. He consoled her, and just as she would expect of him, Justin told her she did the right thing. He always knew what to say to her. She thought about how lucky she was to have him.

Brianna dialed Kate next and repeated the story. Kate was proud of her for standing up to Michael and Frita. She advised Brianna to work from home for the next few weeks so that she would cool off. Brianna knew right then and there that she was not going back into The F Place offices for the foreseeable future. In all honesty, she knew they could not make her.

Most people were working remotely anyway, so she decided to do the same thing. She cringed again at the thought of The F Place; it was so very toxic. Based upon this afternoon's events and all the political warfare, she really wanted to give up and throw in the towel and resign. She had talked it over extensively with Justin. They had weighted the pros and the cons. He could not bear the thought of her going through so much stress. He reminded her that Ari was back and how Brianna used to say that she would drop everything to just spend quality time with her kids. However, they both acknowledged that her executive contract was not up for renewal for another fourteen months. Thus, leaving early would cost her dearly, and she could not afford to do that just yet.

Brianna tried to put the events of Monday behind her and focus on the people in her team and her customers. She knew that she could not breathe a word to any of the associates that would be impacted by Thursday's RIF, so she did her best to avoid speaking with any of them. She told them she was working on a critical project for Michael. It was all too painful. Instead, she focused her extra energy on preparing recommendation letters for the leaders in her organization who were going to be let go. She had already started to provide stellar recommendations for them on LinkedIn. She promised herself that she would reach out to them individually on Thursday evening and Friday to make sure that they knew that she would be there for them and help them in any way possible to land their next role.

Thursday, April 30, 2020

Brianna woke up in tears looking at her poor dog Conan laying at her feet. Last night had been so rough. Ari was a mess when she saw Justin bring Conan back from the animal hospital. It was so hard dealing with the chaos at The F Place while their poor Conan had just suffered through a traumatic surgery. They would have to wait a whole week to get the pathology report back from the vet. They were hopeful that most of the cancer would be out, but Justin was not completely sure. Not only was Brianna hurting from feeling helpless as she watched Conan, but this week was becoming more and more unbearable for Brianna.

Later in the day at 4 p.m., Brianna received a text from Beverly Blessing with two short sentences: "All done. Your turn." Beverly was the only human resources (HR) business partner that Brianna trusted since Frita had taken over the group. Most people did not know that Brianna and Beverly had known each other since childhood. It was none of their business, anyway. Beverly and Brianna had become friends in grade school. There were a few years after college where they lost touch, but they always managed to find their way back. Several years ago, unknowingly, they were shocked to find out they had both ended up working for The F Place.

After things went down earlier in the week, Brianna reached out to Beverly to ask for a favor. Without skipping a beat, Beverly agreed to be Brianna's "eyes and ears" during the ludicrous RIF. Following Beverly's note, Brianna knew that it was safe for her to contact the people in her team that had been let go. Brianna was incredibly frustrated and angry about being put in this position. It was completely unnecessary, and she vowed that this would be temporary. She would figure out a way to hire every one of these good people back.

Brianna decided to get the hardest call out of the way first. She picked up her phone and facetimed Christian. She had known and worked with Christian for nearly ten years. Not only was Christian the most valuable team member that Brianna had, but he was a dear friend. They had been through so much over the years. Brianna thought so highly of him.

Christian was an exceptional servant leader, a dynamic salesperson, and the most loyal and trustworthy person she had ever known. Two years ago, she had lobbied to promote Christian to the Vice President of Commercial Transformation role, which would provide him with development opportunities and take his career to the next level. The plan was to ultimately have Christian succeed her as Chief Commercial Officer.

Christian and his team had delivered impressive results during the past two years, but their Transformation efforts put a spotlight on some ghosts of the past that a few executives would rather have buried for good. When faced with doing the "right thing" or the "politically correct" thing, Christian always chose the "right" path, and, unfortunately, he had suffered a few political setbacks as a result.

"Hello, Christian. Before you say a word, I just want to let you know how sorry I am. This was not how things should have ended. You deserved much more than this," said Brianna empathically.

"Brianna, thank you so much for your call. When I joined the video call today with Michael, I thought something was strange. But when Kyle from HR showed up, I knew it was not good. Anyway, I know that this was not your decision and that you would have prevented it if you could," said Christian.

"Christian, you are absolutely right. And I wanted to tell you that I will support you through the next chapter of your career. When you are ready, let's make time to discuss your options and plan next steps. I have also written a letter of recommendation that you can use on LinkedIn and anywhere else. Please know that I think the world of you. Christian, I am confident that you will land a great position, despite the craziness in the marketplace right now," said Brianna.

"Thanks, Brianna. I really do appreciate your continued support," said Christian.

"It's the least I can do, Christian. Also, I have a few leads for you, which I will send over tomorrow. Among those, you remember my dear friend Kate, don't you? She leads a phenomenally successful consulting practice, and she has asked that you give her a call to discuss the opportunity that she has in mind for you. I am just so sorry that this has to end this way, Christian," said Brianna gravely.

"Thanks, Brianna. I will always remember your kindness. Unlike some others at The F Place, you really do care about people. Do not worry about me. Since my wife and I completed Dave Ramsey's Financial Peace University four years ago, we have literally transformed our personal finances. As such, I will have plenty of time to stop, smell the roses, spend time with my family, and think about what I really want to do next. We have a healthy emergency fund. So, the severance really is gravy on top and actually gives me a lot of freedom to plan my next move," said Christian. He hated that Brianna had been put in this position. He knew that Brianna must have fought back to stop this. He also knew how much she valued him and their entire team. Brianna was an incredible leader, and frankly he thought she could and should replace Michael as the CEO.

Brianna put on a brave smile and said, "Nicely done, Christian. I am so happy for you and not surprised at all. No matter what path you take next, I have no doubt that you will succeed. Good luck, and let us please stay in touch. You know that I am here for you and will support you with whatever you may need. I really mean that!"

"One more thing, Brianna. There are a few things that I have discovered at The F Place recently. I really should have raised this to you sooner, but I was trying to complete my due diligence before bringing it to your attention. The ramifications of it are profoundly serious. Given the turn of events here, I need to share this information with you as soon as possible, but not over the phone. Would it be possible for us to meet tomorrow?" asked Christian.

Shocked yet curious by Christian's revelation, Brianna agreed to meet with Christian the next evening, which was a Friday night.

After wrapping up with Christian, Brianna called the other eight direct reports and thirteen next-level North American leaders who were impacted by the RIF. She would get up early in the morning and call the European leaders tomorrow. It was incredibly painful, but she decided to follow her heart and do what she believed was right. As she lay in bed that night, she could not help but think about what a backwards world this had become. The true customer-focused leaders were leaving The F Place, and the corporate politicians were left standing.

CHAPTER 8
Dr. George's F Bomb

May 2020

"The only thing necessary for the triumph of evil is for good men to do nothing."

—*Edmund Burke*

Friday, May 1, 2020

BRIANNA AND CHRISTIAN met in Central Park at 5 p.m. When Brianna arrived, Christian was already sitting at park bench by the water. Christian had obviously been to this part of the park before because it was very private and tucked away behind a big tree. With all the restrictions in the city and social distancing in place, there were no restaurants to go to. It was clever of Christian to suggest they meet here in the park as they managed to have a little privacy.

Christian smiled at Brianna as she came over and sat down next to him. He observed that Brianna had a N95 mask on even though they were outside. They exchanged pleasantries, and Christian inquired how she had managed to get such a mask. Brianna reminded him that Justin was a surgeon. Christian reached over and took out a bottle of red wine and two disposable coffee cups. He poured the wine quickly into the cups and handed one to Brianna. Brianna took it from him and thanked him. Christian gave her a nervous smile and quickly explained that his wife had packed it for them along with some cheese and crackers as she'd known that we wouldn't be able to go to a restaurant. Christian knew that Brianna would appreciate it once he explained to her the reason why it was so urgent for them to meet. He urged her to take a sip from her glass and then handed her a large manila envelope that was clearly packed with documents. "What is all of this, Christian?" Brianna asked.

Christian cleared his throat and lowered his voice. "Brianna, I fear that this information contains the real reason that I was let go yesterday."

Brianna blinked her eyes several times and inquired, "Christian, what exactly do you mean? What information are you talking about?"

"Brianna, what I am about to tell you is going to shock you. But you have to believe me that it is the truth. This envelope has everything you will need to validate what I am about to tell you. I don't know where to start, so I am just going to lay it out here for you. Brianna, I have uncovered some dark secrets that clearly someone at The F Place wanted to keep buried forever."

Brianna started to feel uneasy. Christian continued, "It all started when we launched the Voice of the Patient (VOP) last year."

Brianna thought back to the program, which had been The F Place's big Transformation initiative last year.

Christian went on. "I know that you will remember the unbelievable amount of resistance that we had from Michael,

Edward, and Frita on VOP. I remember coming to you for coaching on how to deal with the pushback. Despite everything that we did, I never understood why those three were resistant to the program until recently."

He turned toward Brianna and leaned in. "I know that you are not as familiar with all the details as I am, so if you don't mind me doing so, I am going to share a couple of critical data points. We conducted interviews with hundreds of patients who opted to participate in the VOP program. Many of them had also participated in the clinical trials," said Christian.

"Yes, of course I remember this program," Brianna said. "I fought hard for it with the Executive Team and made sure that we had the funding that we needed to proceed forward with the program. I recall your various briefings and action plans, all of which were very insightful and well structured. But Christian, in all fairness I do not recall anything remotely sinister. To be honest, I am a little confused. What is going on, Christian? What happened? Why am I just hearing about this now? Please tell me and spell it out. I mean, what exactly are you trying to tell me?"

Brianna could see the fear in Christian's eyes as he said to her, "Brianna, in hindsight, I know that I should have come to you earlier, but . . . I was afraid. The information that I discovered felt like the tip of an iceberg wrought with conspiracy. I was not sure what to do or whom to trust. I was so petrified of what I thought I had uncovered that I kept a lid on it until I could gather enough data to bring it to the authorities."

Brianna knew by the sound of Christian's voice and the look in his eyes that he was telling the truth. Brianna's mind was buzzing with a dozen thoughts. It was all beginning to make sense now. She instinctively felt protective of Christian. "Who else knows about this?" she asked.

"Jack, Cameron, and I were the only ones who knew about all this. You remember what happened to Jack last month, right? He was in that terrible car accident and is still in a coma. Cameron and his family all came down with COVID a few weeks ago. His wife is in the ICU and not doing well. I can pretty much guarantee that they aren't talking to anyone right now. So, I am pretty sure that it is just you and me," said Christian.

"Well, you have certainly piqued my interest, if what you are implying is true, and I have no doubts about what you're about to share. So, please go ahead and lay it on me. What on Earth did you find?" asked Brianna.

"Well, Brianna, back in February, I spent a week in Miami interviewing a number of patients. The third person that I met that week was Jose Fernandez. Just so you know, Jose does not speak English well, so he brought his 15-year-old daughter Malina with him to translate." Christian took a deep swig of his wine for liquid courage before he continued on. "Brianna, you are going to find this hard to believe, but here it goes. What I am about to tell you is his story."

Christian spent the next ten minutes unraveling the story for Brianna.

Jose, Maria, and their daughter Malina came to the U.S. in 2008 to create a better life for themselves. Jose's brother had lived in Miami for three years, so Jose decided to join him. Almost immediately after crossing the border and making their way to Miami, Jose started filling out paperwork so that their small family could become permanent residents.

They lived with Jose's brother and his family. I believe his name was Juan. Altogether, they were eight people living in a two-bedroom apartment. Jose worked odd construction jobs and Maria cleaned houses. They saved their money and dreamed of one day owning their own home and living the American dream.

After being in Miami for about three months, Maria became pregnant with their second child. While they were excited that the baby would be an American citizen, they were uneasy about their immigration status and what the government could do to them if they were discovered to be here illegally.

Maria never went to see a doctor during her pregnancy. They could not afford it and had no insurance, obviously. But she did find a local midwife, Camilla, who offered to assist with the birth in exchange for Jose's help with a few home improvements projects.

Fortunately for everyone, the birth went smoothly, and they became parents of a beautiful boy, whom they named Jose, Jr., or JJ for short. It was after this that Maria fell into a deep depression. She had always been a positive, optimistic person, but, according to Jose, she changed seemingly overnight. Maria was unable to function or care for the kids. This put a huge strain on the two families living together in the cramped apartment, not to mention the financial stress of losing Maria's income.

One day Maria's midwife Camilla came for a visit and spoke with Jose privately outside afterwards. She said that she could connect them with a big medical company that would provide them with medication and money. This all seemed too good to be true, but Jose was desperate. So, he asked Camilla to introduce them.

About two weeks later, Jose received a phone call from a woman who said she was with The F Place. The woman confirmed a few details and then arranged a location for Jose to meet the doctor.

On the appointed date and time, Jose made his way to the La Quinta Inn on Northwest 36th Street, Miami, for the meeting. He went to the front desk and provided the fake name he was given (Francisco Lopez). The clerk provided him with a room key, and he proceeded to the room.

Upon entering the room, Jose met a tall, Italian man who called himself Dr. George. The doctor spoke with Jose in Spanish and asked him many questions about himself, his wife, his children, his brother, and his friends. He then told Jose about a new drug called HappyVITA that could help his wife with her postpartum depression. If Jose could get ten people in his community to agree to take the drug HappyVITA, then the drug would not only be free, but The F Place would pay Jose ten thousand dollars for every person. Additionally, each person outside of Jose's immediate family who agreed to take the drug would get five thousand dollars. Dr. George also hinted that he may be able to pull a few strings and help Jose and his family get their green cards.

Jose quickly did the math. This would mean a hefty $100,000 for Jose and his family as well as $50,000 for Juan and his family. That was a small price to pay for taking one little pill every day, signing a non-disclosure agreement, and filling out some simple paperwork each week. The money would change their lives forever. They could finally buy their own home and give their children a better future. And, thanks to HappyVITA, Maria would become herself *again. He and Maria had met in Guadalajara, Mexico, when they were 10 and 12 years old. They were married at ages 16 and 18, respectively. They had their daughter Malina six months later.*

Without asking for more information from Dr. George, Jose committed Maria, Malina, and himself to the drug trial. He also agreed to convince his brother Juan and a few other friends to join, too.

Two days later, Jose, Maria, and Malina checked into the La Quinta Inn under the name of "Francisco Lopez" and went to their room. Dr. George was there along with a nurse, Miss Nancy. They did a physical exam and took blood from each of them. Jose was pretty embarrassed because Maria would not stop crying, which was normal for her these days. Then, they were each given a bottle of HappyVITA pills that they were to take each day. They were also provided a journal to write down their thoughts, feelings, and moods each day. They would meet each week for the next three months. Then, at the end of the three months, Dr. George would provide them a check for the money that they had earned. As a goodwill gesture, Dr. George handed Jose a thousand dollars in cash, which was more than he earned in a month. Jose was ecstatic and optimistic for their future.

After week one, Jose and Malina did not notice any side effects, except that they were hungrier than usual. Maria's crying seemed to be improving a little.

At the end of the first month, there were no changes for Jose or Malina, but Maria seemed to be getting better. She was no longer crying every hour of the day. Instead, she had grown quiet and seemed to be spending a lot of time alone in reflection. Jose had thought that maybe she was just working through her depression with a little help from HappyVITA.

A couple of weeks later, on Valentine's Day, Jose came home from work with some flowers to surprise Maria. Malina was out with friends and would be home later that evening. When Jose walked into their bedroom, he could not believe his eyes. There was blood everywhere—on all the bedsheets, the walls, the floor. His beautiful baby boy JJ was lying in his crib, lifeless, with puncture wounds in his neck. Maria was lifeless on the ground, her wrists slit and the knife by her side. Jose screamed at the top of his lungs and called his brother Juan, who arrived home approximately fifteen minutes later. Juan took care of everything, which was a good thing, because a big part of Jose died that day, too. The rest of the day was all a blur to him.

The next week, he went to La Quinta alone to meet Dr. George. By this time, he had figured out that HappyVITA must have been the reason that Maria had killed their infant son before killing herself. Dr. George listened intently, took a lot of notes, and showed empathy for Jose's situation. He promised to take this information back to The F Place and to compensate Jose for his trouble. Dr. George promised to have more information when they met next week.

One week later, Jose went to La Quinta to check in. The front desk clerk said that they had no reservation under the name of "Francisco Lopez" or "Dr. George."

He never saw Dr. George again. And he never received his $100,000 in compensation. His life and family were ruined because of HappyVITA and The F Place.

Brianna was taken aback and shocked to hear what Christian just shared. Christian refilled his glass and took another swig. His eyes looked haunted and distant as he continued. "Brianna, this is not one isolated incident. There are dozens of stories like this! And you know what, Brianna, they all have one thing in common, which is HappyVITA. I am really sorry to tell you, this but this is huge web that is tangled with conspiracy. One thing that I know for sure is that it is pretty significant, and I cannot even begin to imagine the lengths that powerful people will go to keep this quiet." Christian was shaking at this point, but there was no stopping him. "Brianna, a copy of all my research is in the packet that I just gave you. I want you to know that I plan to take it to the FBI on Monday, but given how close we are, I wanted you to be aware as well," said Christian.

Brianna was trying so hard to digest it all. She knew she needed to comfort Christian and reassure him that he had done the right thing. So, she took out some hand sanitizer from her purse and quickly rubbed it on her hands. She reached over and squeezed Christian's hand. "I am speechless, Christian. Thank you for trusting me with this information. You did the right thing by sharing this with me. I always knew you were a man of integrity and high morals. I absolutely agree with you in that you should take this to the FBI. When you do, promise me that you will let them know that I am willing to help with their investigation in any way that I can. Being on the inside could give us an upper hand and the element of surprise. If anyone can procure additional information on this, I can," said Brianna with all the courage that she could muster up.

She let out a deep sigh before continuing. "What is your hypothesis with all of this, Christian? You obviously have studied a lot of information and talked to hundreds of patients. This is all just so bizarre. What do you make of it?"

"While I don't have the data to connect all of the dots, I believe that HappyVITA clinical trials and the FDA approval was completed with falsified patient records. If that turns out to be true, The F Place could be facing a recall of HappyVITA, which would be the first in company history. And, if these suspicions are right, criminal charges could be filed, and, well you can predict the rest. Heads will surely roll," said Christian.

Brianna took a moment to digest what Christian was saying. It all started to make sense to her. Her jaw clenched and she took a deep breath. "If you are right, this could also explain why Michael and Edward keep pushing so hard to accelerate BalanceVITA. If our cash cow is on thin ice, we need a new cash cow, and we need it now. You know, Christian, as sad and difficult as it is for me to say, I think you may be right. Again, this place feels more like the Twilight Zone than a top-tier global pharmaceutical company," said Brianna.

Brianna's mind started to race, and then she started to worry about her dear friend and confidant. "Christian, have you told anyone else about this? Anyone, even your wife or best friend?" asked Brianna.

"No. Like I said, I was afraid and did not want to involve anyone else in this mess," said Christian.

Brianna let out a deep sigh of relief and smiled nervously at Christian. "Christian, you did the right thing. This is so very serious. I suggest you reach out to the FBI now rather than waiting for Monday," she said.

"I wish I could, but tomorrow is my son's birthday, and I need to be present for my family," Christian said. "You know that he's been having a tough time this year with school. I need to focus on my family right now. Brianna, they are taking my termination pretty hard. I was the breadwinner of not just our immediate family, but I've been supporting our parents and my brother's family ever since he lost his job earlier this year. So, bottom line, Brianna, what I mean to say is that I really think that this drama can wait a couple of days. It is all been burdensome for me, especially since my employment was recently terminated, too."

Brianna grabbed Christian's hand and squeezed it tight. "OK, Christian. I understand you need to wait, but please keep me posted. Most importantly, though, promise me that you will stay safe."

They finished their wine, cheese, and crackers while sharing a few lighthearted personal updates about their families. Brianna thanked Christian and told him that she would be in touch. They said their goodbyes and went in different directions to go home.

Sunday, May 3, 2020

Brianna, Ari, and Justin were all spread out on the couch at home watching Ari's favorite show, *Grey's Anatomy*. It was the perfect Sunday night. They had spent the entire day in their family room, relaxing and enjoying each other's company. Brianna was starting to doze off on the couch when her phone startled her as it rang out. She looked down and saw that it was Christian calling. It was 8:30 p.m. on Sunday night. It was not like Christian to call Brianna, as he knew Sundays were off limits for Brianna unless it was an emergency.

Brianna jumped off the sofa and answered. "Hello, Christian, how are you doing?"

Brianna was startled when she heard sobbing on the other end of the phone. "Is everything all right?" Brianna asked.

"Brianna, this is Sara, Christian's wife. I am calling to let you know that Christian was in a terrible car accident this afternoon." Sara was crying so hard. Brianna let Sara catch her breath. Sara continued, "Brianna, he is in the hospital in a coma. It is devastating, Brianna. They told me that his neck is broken. The doctors won't let me in to see him because of COVID."

Brianna knew that there was a chance that Christian could die if his neck was broken. Sara went on to say, "Brianna, I know that you and Christian were close. I know how much Christian trusted and respected you and that you had just met him on Friday. That's why I called you, because I wanted you to know." Sara paused and Brianna knew that there was more that Sara wanted to say. Brianna offered her sympathy and asked Sara what she could do.

Sara continued, "Brianna, I don't know how to ask this of you or if you are the right person. Even if you are not, I know you will know what to do. I need some help from you with our health insurance. Since Christian's last day of employment was Friday, the hospital is saying he isn't covered. I don't understand how all these benefits work. When Christian and I talked about our health insurance options last week he told me that we could not do anything until we received the COBRA packet from The F Place. Brianna, but we've been watching for it and we haven't received any information on COBRA yet. It is all such a mess." Sara started crying again. "I am scared for my husband, and now with this insurance issue, I don't know what to do. Is there any way that can you help us? Please, Brianna?" asked Sara.

Brianna tried to compose herself. Her mind was rapidly processing everything Sara was telling her, as well as her conversation with Christian on Friday. Brianna realized in horror that with the news Christian had dropped on her, having him get in a horrific car accident would be very convenient for someone if they knew he had uncovered such a horrific scandal.

Instead, Brianna quickly composed herself and said, "Sara, of course, I will make some calls now and see what we can do to help you and Christian with the health insurance. You leave it to me and focus on Christian. Is there anything else at all that I can do to help you right now?"

"Just your thoughts and prayers, Brianna. Right now, we need a miracle," said Sara through her tears. Sara shared the hospital details with Brianna and promised that she would call Brianna with updates on Christian's condition.

Monday, May 4, 2020

Brianna tried several times to reach Michael first thing the next morning. She needed to discuss the Christian situation with him and ask for his support with the health insurance. Normally, she should have been able to partner with Frita, but she knew that would be a non-starter. After three calls and two text messages, she decided to send an email to Michael directly.

"Michael, there is an urgent matter that I need to discuss with you immediately. When can we talk?" wrote Brianna.

"Brianna, as discussed, every single member of our Executive Team is considered an essential employee here at The F Place. We are all in the office. Where are you?" wrote Michael.

"I am working remotely after the RIF debacle last week. Can we please talk? It is a matter of life and death. Urgent!" wrote Brianna.

"If it is that urgent, then I suggest you join your peers and me in the office. Lead by example, Brianna," wrote Michael.

Brianna was beyond furious but had no other option but to go into the office and speak with Michael face to face.

One hour later, Brianna stepped off the elevator at The F Place and marched straight into Michael's office. She realized that she did not even stop to greet Jean. She wondered what was probably going through Jean's head because Brianna knew she looked pissed when she came in. Brianna did not care that Michael was on a phone call, instead she slammed the door shut and sat down at his conference table so that they could maintain their distance.

Brianna observed that Michael looked amused. Brianna knew he was probably thinking she looked good, in her fitted black jeans and black cashmere sweater. She had run out of the house so quickly that she had not bothered to change. Michael knew Brianna never wore jeans to the office. He finally finished his call and sat down at the other end of the table.

Michael spoke first. "Brianna, glad to see that you were able to make it into the office after all. Looks like you were in a hurry to get here."

The nerve of him, Brianna thought. She said, "Are you happy, Michael? I am here and we need to talk. Now!"

She continued. "Christian Boyd was in a terrible car accident yesterday. His neck is broken, and he is in a coma. His wife is having all kinds of issues with the hospital because of his health insurance. His last day of employment was Friday, but he hasn't received the COBRA paperwork yet. It is all a big mess. Is there anything we can do to adjust the date of his last day of employment? He hasn't signed the severance agreement yet. Perhaps we could revise it? I am looking for anything that we can do to make things easier on his family. It doesn't look good, Michael. Christian was an employee at The F Place for ten years! Surely, we can do something?"

"Slow down, Brianna. Why are you bringing an HR issue to me? You know who you need to speak to. What did Frita advise on this matter?" asked Michael

"I haven't spoken with her yet. I wanted to talk with you first," said Brianna.

"And why is that, Brianna?" asked Michael.

"Quite frankly, it's because she and I don't see eye to eye on many things," replied Brianna honestly.

"Please discuss this matter with Frita, and I will support whatever she recommends. Now, I really must get back to work," said Michael dismissively.

"In that case, we both know the answer already. But, sure, I will speak with her directly. Thanks for your time, Michael," replied Brianna before she walked out fuming.

Brianna stopped by Frita's office and popped her head in. "Frita, do you have five minutes to discuss an urgent matter?" asked Brianna, using the most calm and humble voice that she could muster with this woman.

"Well, hello there, sweet pea. A little birdie told me you might be stopping by to see me. Let me check my calendar. Yes, of course, let's do next Friday at 7 a.m. Does that work for you, dear?" said Frita

"No, Frita, it doesn't. I need to speak with you today. One of our employees, Christian Boyd, was in a terrible car accident yesterday. His neck is broken, and he is in a coma. Can we please adjust his employment end date from last Friday to this Friday? His wife is having all kinds of issues with the hospital since he has no health insurance but hasn't signed up for COBRA yet," said Brianna in her most reverent voice possible.

"For heaven's sake. That is terrible news. Unfortunately, my hands are tied on this one. You know how diligent my team is. As a matter of fact, earlier today at our staff meeting, they had given me an update on benefits for those impacted by the RIF. The legal documentation and processing are already in motion for everyone that was terminated. I sure wish I could help here, sweet pea. Please give my best regards to his family," said Frita. She flashed an evil smile.

Brianna was not going to give up that easily. "In that case, can we accelerate the COBRA signup for his family to make things a little easier for them?" inquired Brianna.

"Honey, we are processing a high volume of employee separation activities right now. My entire HR team is overloaded. It is simply not feasible to process an exception for one employee. After all, that would not be fair and equitable to all the others who lost their jobs last week. Would it?" said Frita.

"Thanks for nothing, Frita," said Brianna. Brianna could not believe that the Chief People Officer of this company hated people so much and had not an ounce of compassion for them.

Brianna went to her office to cool down. She had hit a dead end with The F Place, but she could still help. She wanted to help. She was not going to be a bystander in all of this! She called the hospital and spoke to the medical director. She explained the situation and informed him that she would cover all the family's out-of-pocket expenses and for the hospital to not say another word about it to Christian's family. The last thing they needed to worry about right now was financial stress. The medical director informed Brianna that he and his team would do their best, but she would have to work out the financial matters with their office manager. Brianna sighed and wondered how many others may be going through a similar situation. This was all so unfair, she thought.

Saturday, May 9, 2020

That Saturday, Kate and Roberta, Brianna's friend and personal attorney, arrived right on time at 7 p.m. for dinner. Brianna had invited them because she knew she could trust them with the information that had been weighing her down since she met with Christian more than a week ago.

Brianna offered them a drink, and they started with a nice bottle of merlot along with a fruit-and-cheese plate. Brianna wanted to warm them up before she dropped the news on them. It was so wonderful to have those two as her confidants. Brianna had stopped by and picked up a boxed Italian dinner from the delightful restaurant a few blocks away. Ari was craving angel hair with pesto sauce that night, and Brianna did not have enough time to prepare dinner that evening. It worked out perfectly. As the ladies finished with their meal, Brianna quickly cleared the table and then brought the folder of documents to the table.

She brought them up to speed on the whole RIF situation, the political battle with Frita, and her meeting with Christian less than forty-eight hours before his horrible car accident. Lastly, she shared the story of Jose and HappyVITA and they each read some of the materials within the packet.

"Wow. This is really heavy, Brianna. I cannot believe that you have had to get yourself involved in this fiasco. I mean, you just cannot make this stuff up," said Kate, still in disbelief.

Brianna turned to Roberta to see what she had to say. "This is a full-blown criminal conspiracy, Brianna. I know you understand already that there will be people that you personally know that will go to jail for this. What we need to do right now is to put together a plan that will keep you safe . . . physically, professionally, and financially."

Roberta frowned, then continued. "I hate to say it, but I think The F Place is going down. I know you have worked there your entire career, Brianna, but the environment is toxic, and look at how many leaders are criminals, based on the little information that you are sharing with us. The real question for me is how high and far does the criminal activity go? Do you think Michael is in on it?"

"Well, HappyVITA is his baby. Under his leadership, we completed the clinical trial and FDA approval at an accelerated rate, for sure. Normally, the whole process takes about twelve years. HappyVITA was only nine years from concept in 2001 to launch in 2010," said Brianna.

"We need to assume that Michael is part of the conspiracy. Who else on the Executive Team might be wrapped up in this?" asked Roberta.

"Roberta is right. We need to get clarity of who may be involved and then prepare your plan of defense," said Kate.

After discussing timelines, leadership roles, and stakeholder mindsets and motivations, Brianna prepared a list of possible F-Place leaders who could be involved in the conspiracy. One way or another, Brianna knew that she would need to be incredibly careful in her engagements with them until the situation was resolved.

Roberta then offered to arrange a meeting between Brianna and Nathan Price, one of her trusted associates who worked for the FBI. Brianna felt a sense of relief for not only sharing all this with someone besides Justin but for the fact that Roberta knew exactly what to do. While Justin had advised Brianna to go the FBI from the get-go, Brianna wanted to be sure that she had a clear plan and could confirm that the evidence she possessed was enough for the FBI to move forward. Now that Roberta and Kate had confirmed this for her, she knew what her next right move would be.

Friday, May 15, 2020

Days later, Brianna met Nathan Price at a local park on Friday afternoon. In that first meeting Brianna did not know what to expect. For that matter she did not even know who to look for or how an FBI agent looked. She had, however, brought along a copy of the HappyVITA materials to give to him and kept a copy for her records.

Brianna saw a young man dressed in a light jacket, dark shades, and jeans. He waved to her. Brianna started to walk towards him, and he greeted her. "You must be Brianna." Brianna nodded yes.

Nathan sensed that Brianna was nervous as she was looking around. After all, they were out in broad daylight. Nathan often got this type of a reaction when potential witnesses would first meet him outside of the office. He smiled at Brianna and reassured her that they would be OK.

Nathan pointed over to a dark black Cadillac that was parked just twenty feet from them. He told her that his partner was there as backup if needed. Brianna could not believe what she was getting herself into. She knew that she had no choice but to move forward. So, she provided Nathan with an overview of the events that had transpired. She told him in detail about her conversation a few weeks ago with Christian and offered him her list of suspected leaders at The F Place who may be involved.

Nathan's body language was difficult to read. Brianna could not tell if he believed her and the story or thought she was full of it. He simply listened, asked a lot of questions, and took notes. He was very matter-of-fact with her, she thought.

"These are some serious allegations, Brianna. Thanks for reporting this and providing me with this documentation. It will certainly jump-start our investigation. I have to warn you, please do not try to contact me unless it is an emergency. I will reach out to you if and when we need to talk. The extent of criminal acts will need to be determined. Either way, there are certainly major ethical issues that have been raised here that we'll need to consider. My advice to you is to keep your head down and stay clear of these guys. In all honesty, Brianna. If possible, try to work remotely, will you?" said Nathan.

As they rose to go, Nathan added, "One last thing before we go. Can you tell me how Christian Boyd is doing?"

Brianna was starting to doubt herself and wondering if she should have gotten herself involved in this case. As soon as she realized what she was doing, she snapped herself back into the conversation at hand. "Unfortunately, as far as I know he is still in a coma. His wife Sara has been giving me daily updates. She tells me that his brain activity is low. Sara and their family cannot even visit him due to COVID. It's a nightmare, Nathan," said Brianna, her eyes brimming with tears.

"I'm really sorry to hear that. I will see if I can get any more information about his condition and the circumstances behind his accident as I investigate the case," said Nathan.

"Thank you, Nathan. I deeply appreciate your help. I am glad that Roberta introduced us. I know she thinks so highly of you," said Brianna with a faint smile.

As they left, Brianna noticed the other man in the black Cadillac—Nathan's partner. She could not help but feel a little frightened at the thought of getting herself involved with the FBI. Once she slipped behind the wheel of her Range Rover, she quickly called Justin and told him that the meeting went well and that she would fill him in when he came home later that night. Justin had been working long hours, and she worried about him. He was now starting to see patients who had COVID-19. He worried that recovery for his patients who had COVID-19 was posing a whole new set of challenges that they had never seen. That, combined with the overcrowding of patients coming into the hospital and the shortage of staff, was taking a toll on everyone, both patients and physicians alike.

Brianna then thought about how Justin had promised Brianna that after the pandemic, they would finally have their beautiful wedding and be a happy family. He would rent out his apartment and move in with Brianna. Brianna had told Justin that she needed Eshan back with them before that would happen. He had reassured her that just as Ari had found her way back to Brianna, so would her son. Brianna wondered how all this would affect her personal life. What was she getting herself into with the FBI, she wondered?

Meanwhile, upon leaving his meeting with Brianna, Nathan debriefed his partner on the way back to their office. They both agreed that they would need to move on this quickly. Once back at their office, Nathan officially opened an investigation into The F Place. After submitting all the paperwork needed to officially kick off the case, he received a call from his superior. Nathan quickly learned that the FBI had already had their eye on The F place for the past year. What Nathan found out, though, was that it was due to potential corporate fraud, insider trading, and sexual harassment. This was a different picture than the one that Brianna had laid out for him.

Nathan had started with the Federal Bureau of Investigation a few years after college. He had done his three years as an investigator at a private firm and quickly created a reputation for himself. The FBI had recruited him, which was not common. Nathan was no rookie, and he knew that this case was going to be a lot larger than anyone had ever suspected. He had a good feeling about this meeting with Brianna. She came across as polished, knowledgeable, and levelheaded. Nathan remarked on the fact that, for a corporate executive, she seemed emotionally vested and like she genuinely cared about the people and the future of The F Place. It would come be an advantage for the investigation to have someone like her on the inside. Nathan knew before he could do anything else, he would need to understand more about the current investigation that was underway.

So, Nathan decided to get the ball rolling and quickly reached out to Greg Butterfinger, who had been leading the corporate fraud investigation. Greg was quick to respond, and they agreed to connect as soon as possible.

Monday, May 18, 2020

On Monday, Nathan and Greg spent a good portion of the day sharing the details of their investigation. Greg was more than happy to have a partner because he felt that the investigation was going far too slowly. By joining forces, they could make a stronger case against The F Place. Intuitively, they both knew that criminal activity was afoot at that place, but they needed to run this one by the book because of the magnitude of potential crime.

Nathan walked Greg through the "Christian dossier," and Greg perked up several times as dots were finally being connected. Greg was extremely pleased with the concrete data and facts that Nathan had procured from Brianna. It was Greg's turn next. Page by page, Greg shared the details of his investigation to date. Nathan wondered how these people were still walking around freely, considering the growing pile of evidence. They knew that given the new findings Nathan had brought forward, they would be able to finally get some movement and additional resources on this case.

Greg shared that The F Place investigation started when Tim Knight, the former CFO of The F Place, had contacted the FBI to file a complaint. Tim reported fraudulent activity going on within the company. Tim was pushed out by Michael a few weeks later. It was still unclear to Nathan whether Michael was aware of the FBI investigation or not. Greg went on to say that the bureau had granted Tim full immunity in return for his cooperation and testimony.

The plot was starting to thicken as next Greg shared that Michael was being investigated for insider trading, tax evasion, and sexual harassment in the workplace. Nathan was not expecting to hear the details that Greg was about to share. Michael had a longstanding friendship with Jeffrey Epstein. Greg had photographic evidence that Michael had visited Little Saint James Island twice between 2015 and 2019. With this news, Nathan nearly fell out of his chair. Greg looked at Nathan in amusement and said, "Dude, hold your horses! Wait for it, because I am telling you, man, this thing is messed up. It's going to get even more convoluted."

"Who else on their Executive Team do you think we are investigating? Who else do you think is going to be sent to the slammer for insider trading and sexual harassment in the workplace?" asked Greg.

"I have no idea. Edward Ferris or Tom Peterson?" asked Nathan. He continued, "And don't forget, I haven't been in this thing as long as you have. I am just now getting the lay of the land".

"I know, man. But no, you are wrong about the other two guys. It is their Chief People Officer, that lady Frita Fernandez! Can you believe it? And here I am going to throw you another bone since you are salivating. Interestingly enough, this Frita character also had a longstanding friendship with Jeffrey Epstein. I'll just give it to you, man; our working hypothesis is that this is how she and Michael met many years prior to her joining The F Place," said Greg.

Nathan could not believe what he was hearing. "But wait, there's more!" said Greg, with a note of humor in his voice.

"Oh man, please don't tell me anyone in this story is mixed up with that movie mogul who was in the news for multiple cases of sexual assault of young actresses?" inquired Nathan.

"Nope, we have not found any connections there. But we may have a possible connection with an Italian crime family," said Greg.

"Say what? Who?" asked Nathan curiously. Nathan could not believe how complex this was all getting. He thought to himself that this was not ordinary white-collar crime they were looking at.

"Jimmy Capone is being investigated for sex trafficking and conspiracy to commit murder," said Greg.

Puzzled, Nathan asked, "Who the hell is Jimmy?"

"Jimmy is Michael's 'fixer,' and basically he goes around and cleans up his messes. But like all criminals, Jimmy boy made a few mistakes," said Greg.

"Please tell me that's the end of the list of alleged criminals at The F Place." said Nathan.

"Almost. We are keeping our eye on Kathleen Kane. Did you know that Kathleen was Michael's personal attorney before he brought her into The F Place? She and Michael go back to their time at Harvard. Apparently, Michael thought it wise to keep his personal and professional legal affairs covered by someone he could really trust," said Greg.

Nathan and Greg continued to discuss the details of the cases, and both came to the hypothesis that Michael Vitali must be the ringleader. However, his motive was not fully clear.

Nathan inquired about Brianna and whether Greg had found any evidence to link her to any of these crimes that they had discussed. Nathan was relieved to hear that Greg had confirmed that Brianna was the only one so far that they had nothing on.

After discussing several potential paths, they devised a plan to send in an undercover agent to The F Place. His undercover name would be Toby Townsend. They would have Toby apply for a position at The F Place. They did a quick search on all potential openings that were currently available at The F Place. For having just laid off so many people, they were surprised that they had several options to choose from. They both agreed that Toby should apply for the opening in Frita's organization, which was an HR Business Partner role. After looking through Greg's information they were able to figure out that the position was several layers down in Frita's organization. They knew it would work.

They spent the next couple of days reviewing countless candidates and finally decided to have Donald Clooney be the undercover agent. Donald had the perfect profile to be able to lure Frita in. He had good height at 6 feet, 3 inches, and was a West Point graduate. He possessed a photographic memory. He taught CrossFit and had an incredible sex appeal. All of this combined with his Southern drawl made him seem that much sexier, and it seemed to be enough to make many women swoon in his presence. Greg and Nathan were sure that he would get in with Frita on his looks alone, but they made sure his CV was dapper as well so that the rest of the team could embrace him, too.

By the end of the week, they had created "Toby's" digital fingerprint, and he applied for the position in the HR organization, where he would report to Beverly. To sweeten his chances of getting the job, "Toby" made a short introduction video of himself (being sure to accentuate his physique) and sent it to Beverly with Frita on copy.

When Frita got the email, she was intrigued. She watched the video at least half a dozen times before she called Beverly. "Beverly, who's this hunk Toby on this video and where did you find him?" she inquired. After getting the highlights from Beverly, Frita insisted she wanted to be included in the interview process and asked Beverly to arrange it ASAP. Later that same day, Donald was able to secure a virtual interview in the afternoon.

Unsurprisingly, the very next day, "Toby" was offered the position with a start date of June first.

As planned, Toby eagerly accepted the position. Not one hour later, Frita invited Toby to meet with her on Friday, May 29, for lunch at the Exec Club as her way of welcoming him to the team.

Friday, May 29, 2020

That Friday, Frita was like a little kid waiting to open a present. She checked her lipstick, sprayed a little extra perfume, and wore a navy dress with her Spanx body suit so that she could look curvier and slimmer. She decided she would head to the club a few minutes before Toby and asked for a vodka soda to be served in a tall water glass. She wanted to feel a little relaxed before she enjoyed her eye candy.

"Why not? I deserve it," said Frita to herself. Right at noon, Frita saw Paulina lead Toby towards her. When he walked through the dining room doors, Frita felt a warm feeling throughout her body. She started imagining what it would be like to have Toby up against her. Since she was already sitting at the table, she got to admire his swagger as well as he made his way over. Paulina greeted Frita and left the two of them at the back of the dining room in the discreet booth that Frita had specifically requested when she had her assistant make the reservation.

Without a doubt, Frita saw "Toby" as a sexual object, but she also wanted to be sure that she could trust him.

Frita batted her eyelashes and started. "Thank you so much for joining me for lunch today, Toby. I make it a point to meet one-on-one with all my high-potential talent from the start. This enables me to take them under my wing and mold them to be successful at this amazing company."

Toby flashed Frita a smile and purposely made sure she noticed his deep dimples. "Ms. Fernandez, the pleasure is all mine. I am honored to join your elite organization and serve under your courageous leadership," said Toby.

"Why, thank you, Toby. You can call me Frita," said Frita, blushing ever so softly. Frita did not know what was going on with her, but she decided that it was OK to let her guard down and have a little fun with her newest boy toy.

"Toby, have you had the chance to review our Five Fs yet? Our Core Values?" asked Frita.

"Why yes, ma'am, I mean Frita, I have," said Toby clearing his throat.

"Good. I want to talk with you about flexibility, because I need you to demonstrate your willingness to be flexible and discrete with your first assignment in my team," said Frita.

"Just say the word, Frita. Your wish is my command," said Toby, bowing his head and waving his hand for added effect.

Frita paused to take a drink of her second vodka tonic before continuing. She was getting a little flush and hoped Toby would not notice.

"Toby, as an HR Business Partner, you need to know the leaders at The F Place. I am confident that you will build trusting relationships with them over time. Well, I need to fill you in on my problem child, Brianna Grimaldi," said Frita.

She sighed in frustration.

"Brianna is the most incapable leader on the Executive Team and has been a thorn in my side from day one. I need you to do some digging and find out what skeletons she has in her closet so that we can cause her enough pain that she will want to leave the company. Are you catching my drift here, boyfriend?" asked Frita, batting her eyelashes again.

Toby was shocked at how much Frita had shared with him. It was highly unusual for someone to share that level of confidential information in a first meeting, especially with a subordinate so far down the ladder. There can only be three reasons why. One, she was dumb as a doornail. Two, she was desperate. Three, this was Frita's way of testing Toby to determine if she could trust him. Based upon what he knew about this woman, he was certain the answer was a combination of two and three. Just to test out his theory a little further, Toby said, "Is Brianna the one who thinks she runs the show and has that sexy hair?"

Frita almost spit out her salad. She was about to snap at Toby, but he was looking right through her with his gorgeous green eyes.

Toby knew she did not really want him to be an HR Business Partner on her team; rather, she wanted him to be an HR Business Spy. Toby gathered that this was Frita's strategy. She would collect any kind of dirt she could on a given person, and then at the right time pounce upon them and blackmail them into getting her way.

As they finished their lunch, Frita made a mental note to have her assistant find out where Brianna got her hair cut and book her an appointment ASAP. Just as they were wrapping up, Frita's face turned white while she answered her phone. She nodded into the phone and mumbled a few words. Toby gently reached over and grabbed Frita's hand, which was shaking, and inquired, "Is everything OK, Frita?"

Frita responded in almost a whisper, "No, Toby it certainly not. I just found out that Michael's Executive Assistant committed suicide a few days ago. I need to get back to my office as I need to make some calls urgently." Toby nodded with compassion. He could tell that Frita was shaken up by the news and told her that he would walk her back to her office.

On the way back, Frita started thinking about what a nightmare this was all going to be. Once safely in her office, she redialed the last number on her incoming call log. Through her trusted HR business associates, she came to find out that Jean had been suffering from depression for several years. She had jumped off the Brooklyn Bridge and taken her life. They had found a suicide note in her apartment. The note talked about how she couldn't take the isolation anymore. It had become unbearable for her to live, and the man that she had fallen in love with was a power-hungry bastard named Michael who only cared about himself.

Frita quickly went to Michael's office to share the news of Jean's untimely death. Michael didn't flinch when Frita told him what had happened. Instead, he inquired, "Did she say who the bastard was?"

Frita paused for a moment and decided to withhold the details that she had learned. She smiled at Michael and reassured him "According to my sources, there was no mention of any names in her suicide note." Michael seemed relieved. He quickly dismissed Frita and told her to find a replacement for Jean as soon as possible.

Earlier that morning, Brianna had arrived in her office about

6:30 a.m. Despite all the chaos underway, she was pleased that she had had a pretty productive week. Then she read the memo from her highness.

TO: All F Place Employees
FROM: Frita Fernandez, Chief People Officer
SUBJECT: Employee References
DATE: May 29, 2020

In order to protect our company brand and to continue building a culture *FOCUSED* on employees, we are revising some of our company policies.

Effective immediately, current employees of The F Place are prohibited from providing public references for former employees of The F Place. This includes social media platforms, such as Facebook, TikTok, and LinkedIn. Please read and acknowledge the policy HERE.

If you have any questions about this policy change, please contact your HR Business Partner.

"You have got to be kidding me. This is one company policy that I am going to ignore," said Brianna to herself. Brianna had written twenty-seven recommendations on LinkedIn, and taking them down was not an option. "What are they going to do, fire me?" she said under her breath.

At lunchtime, she decided to leave and work from home the rest of the day.

On her drive home, she got a call from Christian's phone. Hopeful that it might be Christian calling her, she quickly answered.

"Hello, Brianna, this is Sara again. I wanted to let you know that Christian died yesterday morning. I just thought that you would want to know. I don't know what we are going to do about a memorial service, but I will keep you posted," said Sara, who was crying into the phone.

Brianna gasped and felt her chest tighten. "Oh, Sara, I was so hoping that Christian would pull out of this. From the bottom of my heart, I am so deeply sorry. Please let me know if there is anything I can do to help you," said Brianna.

"Brianna, I hate to ask, but I need help with The F Place. Christian was never able to sign his severance agreement because his accident happened just two days after he was let go. In the meantime, his paychecks have stopped, and I am using our emergency fund to pay the bills right now. I know Christian had a big life insurance policy through The F Place, but I do not know where he kept any of that documentation. Could you please help me with this? And if you could find out what I need to do to get his severance payments directed to me, that would help us a lot," Sara asked, sobbing as she spoke.

"Sara, I will work these two issues, and you just take the time you need to focus on your family," said Brianna.

Just when you think you cannot handle one more thing, life throws more crap your way, Brianna thought. "How can I possibly get this situation resolved for Christian knowing that Frita doesn't give a rat's ass about our employees, whether current or former? I need to take some time to think about this and bounce a few ideas off Kate this weekend. You just cannot make this stuff up," Brianna thought to herself.

Sunday, May 31, 2020

That weekend, Kate and Brianna met at their favorite Indian restaurant for lunch to celebrate Kate's birthday, which was

Sunday. Instead of being able to eat at their usual table, Kate had gotten there first and had a big bag with their food ready to go. Brianna had packed a small picnic basket that held a bottle of chilled bubbly, some flowers, a picnic blanket, and silverware. They made their way with a short walk to Central Park. It was a beautiful day; the sun was out, and they found a nice spot to picnic at. They talked about how crazy it was that most of the city was still shut down due to the pandemic. They settled down on the blanket. While Kate popped open the champagne Brianna quickly plated out the masala papad, which was Kate's favorite Indian appetizer.

Brianna tried so hard to focus on Kate's birthday rather than her problems with The F Place. They spoke about the progress they had made towards their vision boards and how COVID had disrupted 2020 in such unexpected ways. Kate reflected on how much different her life looked right now than she had envisioned even last year at this time. Brianna shared with Kate that Jean had committed suicide. She told Kate about Michael's reaction when she had gone to offer her condolences. She told her about the new executive assistant, Denise, who had replaced Jean practically overnight. They spoke of others that had mental disease and were struggling during this difficult time. Kate seemed to get sad and gulped down her entire glass of bubbly, and then the conversation inevitably shifted to her son, Max.

"I can still remember the sound of his very first cry in the delivery room. It was the most beautiful sound I had ever heard. People always told me that there is something special about a mother and her son. Until Max was born, I did not understand this. Even now, eight years later, I can still close my eyes and see his beautiful, smiling face. I miss him so much, Brianna, especially on my birthday. He would be 12 years old now, in middle school," said Kate gently.

Brianna's thoughts drifted to that somber day eight years ago. She was in the Dubai airport on her way to India when she listened to the heartbreaking voicemail from Kate. Kate's little boy Max was gone. Brianna sat there in that crowded airport terminal and broke down crying amongst the sea of strangers.

She and Kate were living in different countries at the time, so she had not gotten to spend a lot of time getting to know Max. But that did not matter. She knew Kate, and her heart shattered into a million pieces for her. Every time she thought her crying spell was going to end, she would imagine Kate in the hospital holding Max in her arms as he took his last breath. What would the pain have felt like if it were Eshan? Thinking those thoughts caused her heart to explode, and she broke down all over again.

And then she had boarded her flight to Bangalore. As hard as she tried, she could not eat or drink anything on that flight. All she could do was sit there next to complete strangers for the entire four hours and cry. She mourned and cried for her good friend Kate, and she cried for all the moments that Max would never get to experience in this life. She cried for mothers everywhere who had lost their children. Parents should not have to bury their children.

Brianna suddenly snapped out of it and became present with Kate again. There were no words that she could use to comfort Kate. Instead, she just held her tight and told her how much she loved her and how amazing Max was. "He is your special angel, and he is waiting for you in heaven," she said.

Brianna decided to hold off talking with Kate about The F Place situation with Christian. While it was important, today was about Kate.

So, the two friends enjoyed a delectable chocolate mousse birthday cake that Brianna had made for Kate, and they cherished their eleven-year friendship while celebrating Kate's birthday. Life is short, and you need to savor these moments while you can. With a promise partner like Kate, Brianna knew that she could live to fight another day at The F Place.

CHAPTER 9
An FBI Guy Named Toby

June 2020

"Secret operations are essential in war; upon them the army relies to make its every move.

An army without secret agents is exactly like a man without eyes or ears."

—*Sun Tzu*, The Art of War

Monday, June 8, 2020

O<small>N HER DRIVE</small> into the office on Monday, Brianna reflected on the Christian dilemma. She decided to reach out to Beverly Blessing and see if she could get some inside HR support.

After explaining the sticky situation to Beverly, Brianna felt a small sense of relief and hope that she may be able to find a way to help Christian's family.

Beverly wanted to help Brianna; she really did. But Frita had been crystal clear in her People Leadership virtual town hall last month that she had zero tolerance for exceptions. Beverly had a flashback from that dreaded day.

"Exceptions create inefficiency, inequality and waste. We must remain FOCUSED and FAST if we want to be FIRST," declared Frita.

"How can we live our value of FLEXIBILITY if we have zero tolerance for exceptions, Frita?" asked LeeAnn, a new HR Manager on Beverly's team.

Frita's facial expression let everyone on the video call know that she was displeased that a mere HR Manager would ask the Chief People Officer such a question in front of such a large audience.

"LeeAnn, as a leader in this organization, you should know the difference between FLEXIBILITY and policy adherence. Quite frankly, I am disappointed that you wasted our time with such a rookie question. Think before you speak next time, girlfriend," said Frita with controlled anger.

After the town hall was over, Frita called Beverly directly. She was angry at Beverly for hiring someone like LeeAnn who would mock her in a public setting. "Beverly, how long has LeeAnn been with us?" Frita demanded.

"About three weeks, Frita," said Beverly. Beverly knew that Frita was upset and would eventually blame her for hiring LeeAnn.

"Good to know. Her ninety-day probation period is still underway. I am afraid that she is simply not a fit with the

culture we are creating at The F Place. You need to let her go immediately," said Frita.

"Frita, I understand that you are upset. But LeeAnn is incredibly talented. How was she supposed to know not to challenge you in a leadership meeting?" asked Beverly.

"That is your job, Beverly. I suggest you figure it out, because there will not be a next time for you! Do you understand what I'm saying to you?" said Frita with hostility as she hung up on Beverly.

Just then, Beverly's calendar alarm went off to signal that she needed to join the new employee orientation call to welcome her new employee, Toby Townsend. She sure hoped things worked out better for Toby than they had for his predecessor, LeeAnn.

When Beverly joined the virtual call, she was surprised to learn that there were thirty-one new employees in this week's session, and all but two were joining the HR organization. She wondered why there were so many new hires after that huge RIF late April.

Beverly completed her usual song and dance to welcome the new employees and gave them the company overview, lay of the land, and that sort of thing. She believed in investing in people and always lived by the mantra that "You never get a second chance to make a first impression." Thus, she always prioritized welcoming the new employees to The F Place, although she had to admit that it was becoming harder and harder to project an air of confidence and optimism about the company. There were days when she felt like a passenger on the *Titanic*, and she desperately wanted to find the nearest life raft and jump overboard.

After the employee orientation call was completed, Beverly reached out to Toby directly. As his direct manager, she wanted to get to know him a little more and get him started on the right path at The F Place.

Her intuition told her that something just was not right about the way Frita decided to hire Toby on the heels of his video interview call. After Frita made that decision, she also told Beverly to add Toby to the "essential" list because he needed to physically be in the office at least half of the time. "Why would Toby need to be in the office, when I, his manager, do not?" she pondered.

"Thanks so much for reaching out, Beverly. This has truly been a warm welcome to The F Place. I'm wondering where I can find the company org charts. As an HR Business Partner, I would like to review those charts to know who's who in the zoo before reaching out and building my new internal network. I am especially interested in connecting with the Commercial team first," said Toby.

"Toby, that's a great question. At The F Place, we only share the top-level organization chart, which was included in your new-employee orientation materials. Sharing any more than that becomes an administrative nightmare given that we tend to reorganize a lot around here. However, I can let you in on a little trick. If you go to the company email directory, you can search for an individual and then see their reporting line there. That is what I do, and it works most of the time. While our IT team is far from perfect, I have come to the realization that since they are the ones that provide and also take away employee network access, they seem to know exactly who is an active employee and who's not," said Beverly.

"Thanks for the tip, Beverly. Much appreciated, and I will do that. Is there anything else you need from me today?" asked Toby.

"No, I will leave you time to get settled, and we can talk tomorrow at staff meeting," said Beverly.

Later that evening, Beverly called Brianna after her day of meetings had concluded. She was dreading the thought of Brianna's reaction when she would give her the news. Inevitably, she picked up the phone and dialed Brianna's number. "Brianna, I wish I had good news, but I don't. Here is the situation. Christian's last day of employment with The F Place was May 1. He had thirty days to sign his separation agreement, thirty days to complete the COBRA documentation for health insurance continuity, and thirty days to transfer his life insurance policy. Unfortunately, because he had the accident on May 3, he was unable to complete any of these. The bottom line is that The F Place is not legally obligated to pay his severance because he never signed his separation agreement. The health insurance for his family will not continue through COBRA because he did not submit the paperwork. Lastly, The F Place life insurance policy will not pay out because its coverage ended when his employment ended. The only good news is that his 401(k) and vested company stock will go to his wife, Sara, because she was set up as his beneficiary," said Beverly.

"Beverly, this is a lot to process, here. Do you know approximately how much Christian has in his 401(k) and company stock all together?" asked Brianna.

"Around $700K," said Beverly.

"Well, that should provide some relief to Sara and the kids. However, it is not nearly what Christian earned after his ten years at The F Place. Thanks again for investigating this for me. Is there anything that we could do to create a different outcome for Christian's family?" asked Brianna.

"That's the thing that is really bothering me, Brianna. All it would take to make things significantly better for the family would be to change Christian's last day of employment from

May 1 (Friday) to May 4 (Monday). Doing so, his accident would have occurred while he was still an employee, so all the benefits would follow. Unfortunately, I asked about doing this and could not find a single HR or Legal team leader willing to even have the conversation because that kind of thing is not covered in any of our policies," said Beverly.

"Thanks for your help, Beverly. I cannot tell you how much I appreciate you. Talk to you later," said Brianna.

Brianna then decided to call Sara. "Sara, would you mind if I popped over to talk with you for a few minutes tonight? I am about fifteen minutes away," asked Brianna.

"Hello, Brianna. Sure, that's fine. I will talk to you soon," said Sara.

When Brianna arrived, she asked Sara how she was doing. She inquired about any other life insurance policies that Christian may have had. Sara confirmed that Christian had purchased a $1M life insurance policy with the help of Zander Insurance, as recommended by Dave Ramsey when they went through Financial Peace University a few years ago. Dave always warned about only having life insurance through your company. And Christian wanted to make sure that his family was taken care of.

In their discussion, Brianna learned that Christian and Sara had paid off all of their consumer debt four years ago, had built a six-month emergency fund, had been investing in 529 funds for their 6- and 8-year-old children, had been putting 15 percent of Christian's gross income into retirement, and had been on a diligent journey to pay off their mortgage in the next three years. They had only $200K of mortgage debt left, and then they would be completely debt free. Brianna also knew that the time that Christian was in the hospital, uninsured, had cost more than $200,000, which she had paid hoping that it would eventually be reimbursed by COBRA.

"Sara, I am so glad to hear that you guys had another life insurance policy. Unfortunately, the situation with The F Place benefits is not good," said Brianna. She then explained the dilemma as discussed with Beverly.

"Brianna, this may be legal, but it is wrong . . . simply wrong. How could they do this to Christian after all that he sacrificed for the company?" cried Sara.

"Sara, I agree with you. I do not know how or when, but I am going to make sure that every one of those bastards pays for this. In the meantime, please know that I will always be here for you and the kids. Is there anything you need right now?" asked Brianna.

"Thanks, Brianna. I cannot tell you how much it means to me that you are here with us. I can keep paying the bills using our emergency fund until the life insurance is paid out. After that, I will pay off our mortgage and finish funding the college funds. We can live off the rest, even though it is far less than Christian really earned all those years," said Sara.

Brianna murmured her agreement. She added, "Here is the contact info for my attorney, Roberta. She is wicked smart and may have some other legal ideas for you. Please reach out to her and keep me posted. I've got to go home now and take care of dinner for the family."

Brianna felt terrible for Sara. Right now, she had to get home, grab an early dinner with Justin and Ari, and then head to see Sam for a haircut. Bri hadn't had her hair cut since January. With the stay-in-place order finally lifted, she felt comfortable in going to see Sam. She had met Sam through Kate. Sam was one of the best stylists in all of New York City and very sought after. Lucky for Brianna, Kate and Sam had gone to high school together and were good friends. When Brianna had first moved to New York, Kate had insisted that she meet with Sam right away. She had half-jokingly said to

Brianna, "Anyone who is a somebody here in New York City has a celebrity stylist." Brianna had been taken aback at Kate's comment, but she trusted Kate implicitly and knew that if Kate made a recommendation, she should take her good advice and go for it! Brianna was so looking forward to seeing Sam. She needed it after the long week at The F Place. Besides, it had been months that she had seen her, and she couldn't wait to catch up with her!

Brianna was a few minutes late getting to Sam's salon. It was a few minutes after 7 p.m., and while the salon was closed, Sam was delighted to take care of Brianna after hours. The two of them had connected very well. Sam was always fascinated with the stories that Brianna would share about the corporate world, and Brianna was equally delighted hearing about celebrity gossip from Sam. It made for a perfect Friday night. There were only air hugs once Brianna got there as everyone was being extremely cautious due to COVID-19. Once Brianna settled into her chair, Sam immediately went and poured Brianna a glass of champagne. She squealed in delight when Brianna told her that Ari had moved in with her. They caught up about how the pandemic had impacted Sam's business. The salon had been closed for months, as it was not considered an essential business. They giggled over how every woman thought a good color job and haircut were essential.

Sam inquired about how the virus had impacted The F Place. Brianna started filling her in about how stressful things had been. She did not share all the details but gave Sam a quick rundown. Then suddenly out of the blue they heard, "Frita is a Cuban hamburger. Pronounced Fri-ta. The original Frita is a Cuban dish with a seasoned ground beef and pork patty on Cuban bread topped with shoestring potatoes."

Brianna and Sam both realized at the same time that it was Siri. Sam had just put her phone down after checking for a message. They both burst out in giggles as Brianna had just been talking about Frita from The F Place.

Siri responded again: "Hmm. . . . I don't have an answer for that. Is there something else I can help you with?" Brianna and Sam couldn't stop laughing. Brianna never knew that Frita's name stood for a Cuban hamburger.

As Sam went to put her phone back down on the counter, Siri said, "No thank you, I don't want a Frita."

Sam chirped, "See Brianna, this Frita is so intolerable, even Siri doesn't want a Frita." Brianna really needed the laughs after the horrible day. She still couldn't believe that Christian's family was left to deal with all this chaos. She bid Sam goodbye, and together they hoped that things would return to normal soon and they could all go back to their day-to-day.

Friday, June 12, 2020

Toby spent those first few weeks meeting with a wide variety of people at The F Place. His HR Business Partner role was a perfect cover for gathering intelligence for his investigation. He was also amused that Frita had asked him to come into the office on Fridays and debrief with her at the Exec Club over lunch. She did not hide her infatuation with him in the least. Toby was glad, as this would give him an opportunity to observe Ms. Fernandez's character firsthand.

"Hello, Toby; please sit down. How were your first two weeks? I want to hear all about them," gushed Frita

"Good afternoon, Frita. They have been fabulous. I got to meet with several of our executive leaders, including Brianna Grimaldi, Karen Goldman, and Isaac Davis," said Toby.

"Excellent. Please do not keep me waiting. How was your meeting with Brianna? What juicy news do you have to share with me today?" said Frita as she leaned forward in her chair.

"Honestly, Frita, it was pretty uneventful. She was friendly, professional, and welcoming. Although she did seem to get her feathers ruffled when I asked her how HR could better serve her," said Toby, ever so innocently.

"You asked how HR could serve her better?" asked Frita with genuine curiosity.

"Why, yes, we are a service organization, aren't we?" said Toby authoritatively with a smile.

"Toby, it is a little more nuanced than that. We don't serve the masses as much as we serve the few. We are here to support our CEO, Board of Directors, and shareholders. They need to know that our most valuable assets—our people—are being effectively managed and, well, controlled," said Frita.

Toby looked at Frita with a curious face.

"It is more governance than service. Does that make sense, Toby?" asked Frita.

"Frita, you are a genius. I am so honored to learn and grow from you. Are there any other words of wisdom you could share with me?" asked Toby.

"Toby, you are going places. I am really impressed that you asked me such a question. The biggest advice I will share with you today is to be supremely careful who you align yourself with. But do not worry; if you stick with me, the opportunities for you here at The F Place will be virtually limitless. Now, let's get back to Brianna. What else did she say to you?" said Frita.

"Understood. As for Brianna, she shared the highlights of her vision of growth through Transformation. And then she said that she could really use some HR support to restructure her team given that she lost so many of her leaders in the RIF. She said they were limping along right now, many still in shock with what happened," said Toby.

"And what did you say to her?" asked Frita with a smile.

"I agreed to spend a half day with her next week to strategize. Frita, given what you said about service, should I bow out of that meeting with Brianna?" asked Toby.

"No, dear. Please go ahead and join her. Then, you can fill me in on all the details next week. What about Karen Goldman; how did your meeting with her go?" asked Frita.

"Karen was fifteen minutes late for our call and seemed pretty distracted. Her only request of me was to provide an update on the dozen or so open requisitions in her team. Speaking of that, may I ask you a question, Frita?" asked Toby.

"Toby, you can ask me anything, boyfriend!" said Frita.

"Can you help me understand why we laid off more than five thousand people last month and yet we have such a huge list of new requisitions? The Talent Acquisition team seems incredibly overloaded and stressed, as far as I can tell. But I am the newbie and I defer to your infinite wisdom," said Toby.

Frita smiled. She loved how deferential Toby was to her. She was already starting to imagine how she could use him to help grow her power even more in The F Place.

"Toby, did you know that the questions people ask say more about their intelligence than the statements that they make? You continue to impress me! Let's just say that the layoff was about cleaning house. All of our new hires are laser-focused on strategic positions that we need so that we can be *FIRST* in the market," said Frita.

Toby knew he was gaining her trust and decided to see how far he could push the envelope.

"Thanks, Frita. That is a brilliant strategy. The F Place is so lucky to have you as our People Officer. In the few minutes that we have left, I would like to speak with you about Isaac," said Toby.

"I would love to keep talking with you, but I have to go back to my office to join a video call with the Young Leaders

Employee Affinity Group. I don't really want to go, but I do need to make an appearance every now and then," said Frita.

"No worries, Frita. Is there anyone else joining you in your office for that meeting?" asked Toby

"No, it is just me, myself, and I," said Frita as she stood up to leave.

"Well, would you mind if I joined you? I have considered joining that group myself, and I would love to hear what inspirational words you will share with them," said Toby.

"The pleasure is all mine, boyfriend! Let's go!" said Frita.

Frita and Toby made their way to Frita's office. Toby was impressed with how luxurious her office was with the mahogany desk and bookshelf, the leather sectional, and the 77-inch Sony smart TV hanging on the wall.

When they arrived, Frita closed her office doors and told Toby to make himself comfortable on the sofa. She then asked if he would like a drink. After all, it was Friday afternoon. She poured two glasses of Sauvignon blanc and handed a glass to Toby.

Frita then took her laptop to her desk, connected to the video call, introduced herself, and said, "Thank you for being here. You all represent the *FUTURE* of The F Place. With your talents and ideas, we will surely make The F Place *FIRST* in the marketplace!"

After staying on the call for about ten minutes, she said, "My sincere apologies, but Michael needs me to attend to an urgent matter. I have to run. Keep up the great work, and have a fabulous weekend!"

Toby stood up and said, "Frita, I can catch up with you next week if you need to leave."

"I don't need to leave you! That was just my excuse to exit that silly meeting. Now, where were we?" asked Frita as she sat down a little too close to Toby.

She held up her glass to toast, so Toby raised his also.

"To the FUTURE!" said Frita. And they clinked their glasses.

"Now, Toby, please do continue. Tell me all about your meeting with Isaac," said Frita.

"Can I speak freely with you, Frita?" asked Toby.

"Of course you can, boyfriend!" said Frita.

"Isaac seems pretty young to be an Associate Vice President on the Executive Team. What is his story?" asked Toby.

"Isaac joined The F Place about three years ago. Indeed, he is young, but one of the best Cyber Security Leaders in the world. Three years ago, he sold his cybersecurity firm for more than $100M," said Frita.

"I remember reading something about that. So, why did he decide to join The F Place?" asked Toby.

"That was all Michael's doing. Michael's and Isaac's fathers went to Harvard together. When Michael became CEO, his disdain for John Browning, the previous CIO, was just too much. Michael needed someone in that role that he could trust, and Isaac was on the top of his list," said Frita.

"I can see why Michael would want Isaac, but I still don't understand why Isaac chose to work with us. After selling his company, he could have done anything," said Toby.

"Yes ... and he chose to work here. I cannot share the details, but he does have one of the best executive packages that I have seen. Let's just leave it at that," said Frita.

She stood. "Toby, I need to go to the little girls' room. Can you please give me a minute and then we can pick up where we left off? OK?" said Frita.

"Sure thing, Frita," said Toby.

As soon as Frita exited her office, Toby knew he had to act quickly. He walked over to her desk and hacked into her computer. Using the thumb drive in his pocket, he installed spyware on her computer. Then he quickly returned to the sofa.

When Frita walked into the room, she shut the door again and smiled. Toby could smell her overpowering perfume and noticed that she had freshened up her makeup, too. It was 3:45 in the afternoon.

She turned off the lights to her office, pressed the button to close the shades to the windows and slid herself right next to Toby. It was obvious that she wanted him to kiss her and, if he wanted to keep building her trust, he would have to indulge.

"Crikey! The things that I do for this country! I better win a Medal of Honor for this one," he thought to himself as he planted a long, slow, juicy kiss on her mouth.

After Toby returned home, he went straight to the bathroom to brush his teeth. He then gargled with mouthwash for several minutes to remove all evidence of Frita from his mouth.

Toby called Nathan to give him an update. "Nathan, I am in. And you do not even want to know what I had to do in order to make it happen. Disgusting!" said Toby.

"You took one for the team. Nice work, Toby!" said Nathan with a chuckle in his voice.

"I am going to start reviewing her files this weekend. Please get the cyber team ready," said Toby.

Over the next several weeks, Toby managed to meet one on one with every Executive Team member except for Michael. Every Friday, he diligently met with Frita over lunch to give her the debrief. For the most part, he shared information that was harmless, but occasionally he would throw her a bone to keep her satisfied. She kept trying to lure him back to her office, but he always found an excuse to escape with a "rain check."

Friday, June 26, 2020

Jimmy's surveillance of Frita's laptop was enlightening and pointed to the fact that she was a power-hungry woman who thought that she should be the next CEO. The way that she spoke to and about people reminded him of that evil witch Cersei in *Game of Thrones*. But he was going to need more than just Frita's professional correspondence to crack this case wide open. He needed something more, so he decided to take a risk and reach out to Jimmy Capone directly.

After three attempts to get a virtual meeting with Jimmy Capone, Toby finally got Jimmy's meeting acceptance notice.

When Jimmy joined the call, Toby introduced himself and said that he was working on a confidential employee engagement project for Michael and Frita. He indicated that he recorded all these calls so that he could be fully present in the meeting and make sure every bit of feedback was captured. Despite his discomfort, Jimmy knew that he could not decline this request.

"So, Jimmy, how long have you worked for The F Place?" asked Toby.

"From the day the doors were opened in 2001. Michael and I go way back. I am surprised that he did not mention anything about this confidential project to me," said Jimmy.

"You got me, Jimmy. Actually, this is a project being spearheaded by Frita. Once all the results are collected, then she will share it with Michael. To maintain their spot in the Top 100 workplaces in the U.S.A., they must keep their score above 85 percent. With the global pandemic and recent RIF activity, Frita is concerned that their score could decline," said Toby.

"OK, Toby, that makes sense. So, what exactly do you need from me?" asked Jimmy.

"Since you have been with the company for nearly twenty years, I'll bet you have an intimate understanding of the strengths and weaknesses of employee engagement. Am I right?" asked Toby.

"Yes, you could say that," said Jimmy

"Well, what do you think are the top three drivers of positive engagement at The F Place?" asked Toby.

"FOCUS, FLEXIBILITY, and FUTURE orientation," said Jimmy, repeating the company line.

"That's very insightful, Jimmy. Thanks for that. Now, what about the weaknesses, or shall we say opportunities. Where do you think the leaders of The F Place should focus on improving engagement?" asked Toby.

"I am not sure I know what you mean, exactly," said Jimmy

"Well, let's take you, for example. What are three things that Michael could do to make you more engaged and committed to doing your job well? By the way, what is your job here at The F Place? I am a newbie here and still trying to understand who does what," said Toby.

"I am the manager of Security," said Jimmy.

"Oh, like information security? IT systems and all that? You report to Isaac, right?" asked Toby.

"Yeah, I report into that pipsqueak Isaac. Oh, crap, don't you dare share that little comment with anyone, you hear me?" said Jimmy

"No problem, Jimmy. This is just you and me talking. Anyway, you were saying?" asked Toby.

"No, I am more like general security around here. I work with the Information Security guys and the Building Security guys . . . well, pretty much whatever Michael needs me to do, I get it done," said Jimmy.

"What a fascinating role you must have, Jimmy. Do you travel much?" asked Toby.

"I used to travel all of the time on the jet with Michael, but not so much this year. You know? No one is going anywhere these days. He likes to bring me along and I translate for him," said Jimmy.

"What do you mean, translate?" asked Toby.

"I speak Italian, Spanish, Portuguese, and French. So, I translate for Michael when he needs me," said Jimmy.

"Impressive! So, back to my original question. What could Michael and the leadership team do to make you more engaged and committed to do your job?" asked Toby.

"They could do three things, and this doesn't apply just to me, you know. Number one—better pay. Those executives are really making bank, if you know what I mean. They should share more of it with the rest of us. Number two—more benefits. We should have free healthcare insurance, and they need to give us more time off. Everyone is tired of working all the damn time. In Italy, they do it right. They 'work to live' instead of 'live to work.' But, here in America, it is all backwards," said Jimmy.

"Great feedback. And number three?" asked Toby.

"Michael and the Executive Team need to learn to show a little more gratitude. The employees at The F Place deserve to be appreciated . . . much more than they are today," said Jimmy.

"Thanks for your time, Jimmy. This is incredibly helpful. It was nice to meet you. Have a great day," said Toby.

"You too, man," said Jimmy.

Toby had a bad feeling about Jimmy Capone and knew that there was more to the story. He was determined to figure it out.

Fortunately, Nathan and Greg delivered on their promise to mobilize the cyber team to help Toby hack into information systems of The F Place. Toby and his analyst team spent nights and weekends reviewing thousands of documents, searching for evidence of the HappyVITA and BalanceVITA fraudulent activity. He accessed and provided the clinical trial patient names to Nathan and Greg so that they could organize agents to interview these patients and verify the claims in the "Christian dossier."

And then, Toby discovered that a large subset of data had been archived to servers in The F Place Chinese data center and removed from the U.S. data center completely. When he tried to access the data in the Chinese data center, his access was denied.

CHAPTER 10

Choosing Freedom Over Fear

July 2020

"When a man is denied the right to live the life he believes in, he has no choice but to become an outlaw."

—*Nelson Mandela*

Saturday, July 4, 2020

ARI, CONAN, AND Brianna watched the July 4th celebration from Brianna's apartment. Justin was unable to join them due to an emergency that arose earlier that day. As Brianna watched the colors light up the sky, she reflected on the founding of the country and the Declaration of Independence.

"Life, liberty, and the pursuit of happiness. Those words are as true right now as they were more than 200 years ago. Why do I feel like such a prisoner when I live in the 'land of the free and the home of the brave'? Maybe I should draft my own Declaration of Independence and leave The F Place, regardless of the financial and legal trouble this would cause me. I am so tired of feeling like they own me," Brianna said to herself.

Sunday, July 5, 2020

The weekend flew by way too quickly, and now it was Sunday afternoon. That feeling in Brianna's gut was there again. Monday would be here before she knew it. She tried not to think of work and just be present with Ari, but that sinking feeling kept creeping back.

Monday, July 6, 2020

After lying in bed for several hours wide awake, Brianna got up at 4 a.m. on Monday and decided to start the day. She went for a run to clear her head and awaken her body. Normally that did the trick, but not today. Brianna's "spidey" sense told her that something just was not right.

On the way into work, she listened to a podcast about "Choosing Freedom Over Fear," and she was determined to stay positive and make it a great day. After walking the dark hallways to her office, Brianna got settled and reflected on her goals.

The Q2 financial bookings were 11 percent below plan, a little better than Q1 but still behind where they needed to be. Brianna believed that there had to be another way to grow without evangelizing HappyVITA for depression or prematurely promoting BalanceVITA for bipolar disorders.

Well before 8 a.m., Brianna received a call from Bruce Ferguson, head of supply chain at Forrester Drug Cooperative in Florida.

"Good morning, Brianna. I hope you and your family are safe and healthy?" asked Bruce.

"Hello, Bruce, so nice to hear from you. Unfortunately, I lost my father a few months ago due to COVID. This thing really became real for me in a very personal way. It has been hard, but the rest of my family is healthy, and we are moving forward. How about you and your family?" Brianna asked.

"Brianna, I am so sorry to hear about your father. My 20-year-old nephew is in the ICU right now with COVID. Young and healthy one day and in the hospital the next day. It is really unbelievable. Everyone else is good, though," said Bruce.

"Wow! That is unbelievable. I hope he recovers soon. So, what can I do for you today, Bruce?" asked Brianna.

"Right, about that. I am looking forward to seeing you at 9 a.m. for our meeting with Michael, Edward, and Veronica. The meeting caught me a little by surprise, and I wanted to find out if there is anything I should be prepared for," said Bruce.

Brianna had always invested in her relationships with people. Over the years, she had developed some incredibly trusting relationships with her customers, and Bruce was no exception. But given what he just revealed, Brianna realized that Michael had set up this meeting without her . . . intentionally. Thus, she was sure he was trying to encourage Bruce to participate in the BalanceVITA clinical trials.

"Bruce, I am glad you reached out. Unfortunately, I was unable to travel this week due to a personal commitment that I simply could not change. I know that you guys are anxious for us to get BalanceVITA to the market, and we are working diligently to do so. My advice to you is to wait a little longer until we have FDA approval—hopefully later this year—rather than join the clinical trial now," said Brianna.

"Thanks for the perspective, Brianna. I guess I will wait and see what Michael has to say about all of this. Talk to you later. And hey, I really am sorry to hear about your dad," said Bruce.

After hanging up with Bruce, Brianna called Veronica Ross, the head of Southeast Sales at The F Place.

"Good morning, Veronica," Brianna said after Veronica picked up the phone. "Where are you today?" she asked.

"Uhhh . . . in Florida; why do you ask?" inquired Veronica.

"What are you doing in Florida? I thought you told me you weren't comfortable flying yet," said Brianna.

"I am still not comfortable flying commercially. But Michael offered me a ride on the corporate jet," said Veronica.

"Oh, really? And what is the purpose of your business travel?" asked Brianna.

"Michael, Edward, and I are going to meet with Forrester Drug Cooperative this morning," said Veronica.

"Go on . . . ," said Brianna.

"Last week, Michael asked me to set up a meeting so he and Edward could discuss the BalanceVITA clinical trial with Forrester. He specifically told me *not* to tell you. I knew I should have told you, but . . . it is intimidating. He's the CEO!" said Veronica defensively.

"Well, good luck with your meeting, Veronica. Break a leg!" said Brianna before she ended the call.

Brianna called Denise, who was Michael's new Executive Assistant, to get time on his calendar with him first thing in the morning. This whole situation was wrong on so many levels, and she was going to let Michael have a piece of her mind.

Tuesday, July 7, 2020

The next morning, Brianna walked into Michael's office promptly at 8 a.m., ready for a fight.

"Michael, after everything we have been through together all these years, how could you do that to me?" Brianna asked.

"Do what to you, Brianna?" asked Michael with a smile.

"You know exactly what I am talking about. You went around me to meet with Bruce Ferguson yesterday. Why would you do something like that?" asked Brianna.

Michael smiled and handed her a single sheet of paper. "Here is a $500M order for BalanceVITA from Forrester. I got done in one morning what you were unable to do in nine months."

Brianna was furious and decided it was better to say nothing than something that she would later regret. So, she stood up and walked out of Michael's office without uttering a single word.

When she got to her office, she called her attorney Roberta and asked to meet with her after work.

Roberta and Brianna met at their usual hole in the wall. After finishing their first drink, Brianna brought her up to speed on the whole situation with BalanceVITA. She explained her quality concerns and desire to protect herself from the inevitable storm that will be coming with BalanceVITA, not to mention her growing concerns with the HappyVITA conspiracy. After brainstorming with Roberta, Brianna knew what had to be done. She was between a rock and a hard place, but she was not going out without a fight!

Wednesday, July 8, 2020

The next day, Michael stormed into Brianna's office with a document in his hand. He was fuming. Brianna stood up, looked him in the eye, and said, "I see you got my memo. I suggest you read every word of it and reconsider your plans for BalanceVITA."

The memo that Brianna had Roberta send as her counsel was distributed to Michael and the entire Executive Team. As an officer of the company, it is their duty to live up to the company values and obey the law. Expanding the BalanceVITA clinical trials without addressing the known quality issues is unethical and could result in significant liability and even death. Roberta and Brianna had decided not to say anything about HappyVITA in the memo because her life could be in danger if they knew that Brianna knew about their illegal clinical trials of the past.

Brianna reached out to Bruce at Forrester Drug Cooperative to discuss her concerns with BalanceVITA one more time and off the record. While he appreciated the call, he indicated that Michael had preemptively shared her position with him and assured him that Forrester had nothing to worry about. Michael also offered him a significant discount, and the profit margins were going to be huge. Brianna had a clear conscience with Bruce because she'd said what she needed to say. Then she tried her best to wash her hands of this inescapable disaster.

Friday, July 17, 2020

The F Place Reports Q2 2020 Results

New York City, New York—July 17, 2020—Today, The F Place announced financial results for the second quarter ending June 30, 2020.

- Second-quarter worldwide sales of $4.8 billion decreased 11 percent year over year

- Due to uncertainties regarding the impact and duration of COVID-19, The F Place will not provide new annual guidance for 2020 at this time

"We remain *FOCUSED* on our vision to become the global leader in pharmaceuticals and have taken *FAST* action in Q2 to adjust our cost structure by 20 percent in response to the market decline. We are optimistic that our BalanceVITA clinical trials will be wildly successful and that we will receive FDA approval this year," said Michael Vitali, President & CEO.

[Read More]

CHAPTER 11

F Is for Family

August 2020

"The two most important days in your life are the day you are born and the day you find out why."

—*Mark Twain*

Sunday, August 16, 2020

BRIANNA HAD JUST settled into her bed with a glass of merlot and a book when her phone rang. It was Veronica, which was unusual. Immediately, Brianna knew that there must be some kind of emergency.

"Hello, Veronica; it is really late. Is everything OK?" asked Brianna.

Brianna could hear sobbing on the line. Veronica tried to speak, but Brianna could not understand a word that she was saying.

Softly Brianna said, "Veronica, I cannot understand you. Where are you?"

Veronica took a deep breath to compose herself. "Sorry,

Brianna. I am just a mess. I have been here in Florida with Forrester all week. Several of the BalanceVITA clinical trial patients have been hospitalized and are in the intensive care unit."

"That is terrible, Veronica. I am so sorry to hear that," said Brianna.

"That's not the worst of it, Brianna. This morning one of the patients died. And then, this afternoon another one died. It is simply awful. Forrester is blaming it on us, and I do not know what to do. Please help me!" said Veronica.

"Since you brokered this deal with Michael and Edward, I suggest you try calling them," said Brianna. She felt bad, but she thought to herself, "You know, sometimes the truth hurts." Besides, there was no way that Brianna was going to get herself tangled in this mess.

"I knew you would say that, Brianna, and you absolutely have every right to do so. I have been trying to reach them all evening. Goodness, Brianna, I have left messages and multiple texts. No response. You are always good in a crisis. What do you think I should do, Brianna?" asked Veronica.

Brianna thought for a second and paused, "Veronica, for starters, don't you ever, and I mean ever, go behind my back again. We are a team, and we are in this together. You need to remember that. Now, I will get out on the field with you . . . in the rain, in the mud, to fight the good fight and win the race. Other leaders are merely spectators. This is a tough lesson, Veronica," said Brianna.

"I know, Brianna. And, for what it is worth, I really am sorry for putting you in this position. It won't happen again. You have my word," said Veronica.

"Thanks, Veronica. I will take it from here and keep you posted," said Brianna.

Brianna immediately called Michael's mobile.

"Good evening, beautiful Brianna," said Michael in a provocative voice.

Brianna could tell that he had been drinking for a few hours already. "Hello, Michael. We have a big problem on our hands. Where are you right now?" asked Brianna.

"I am at Love and War in Texas. The restaurant, not the state! Guess what, baby, I am all alone, and I was thinking that maybe you would want to join me?" asked Michael with a little hope in his voice.

Brianna really did not want to join Michael, but she needed to get this mess cleaned up and contained. "OK, Michael. I'll be there in twenty minutes."

When she walked through the doors, Brianna immediately spotted Michael at the bar. His tie was loosened, and his jacket was tossed next to him in the empty barstool. He looked like he could pass out any minute. Brianna couldn't believe that she had actually looked up to this man at one point. Now he looked like a lost drunk. She walked up to him casually and put her hand on his shoulder so that she wouldn't startle him. "Hello, Michael. How much have you had to drink tonight?" asked Brianna.

Michael looked up to see Brianna. He thought to himself that she looked so hot in her skinny jeans and silk blouse. Her hair was up in a clip and a few strands had slipped out. Come to think of it, he had never seen her with her hair up like this. He was immediately aroused by her look.

"Well, hello there, pretty darling. You can call me Mikey. You know I love it when you call me Mikey," he slurred. Then he started to straighten up and grabbed her hand. "I'm sorry, Brianna, I don't know; I lost count. What does it matter, anyways? The point is that you're here now. Would you please sit down and join me? Take that silly mask off so that I can see your beautiful face," he said as seductively as he could manage.

Brianna sat down and started assessing the situation and then quickly looked at the bartender and made a sign to cut him off. She ordered two glasses of water and a cup of coffee for him and a hot water with lemon for herself. Brianna knew she needed him to focus so she shook him.

"Michael, I need you to sober up. We have a big problem on our hands with BalanceVITA at Forrester!" said Brianna.

Ignoring what she had just said, Michael just looked at Brianna and smiled. His gaze was that of a young man who wanted so badly to impress her. He looked at her tenderly and then reached over to push a loose hair strand near her eye. "You are such a beautiful woman. Do you remember that night a couple of years ago? I sure do!" said Michael softly.

Brianna was exasperated with how the conversation was going. "Yes, Michael. That should never have happened. You are a great guy and all, but you are my boss, and we need to keep our relationship professional."

Deep down inside, Brianna was so upset at herself for indulging him the one time. It was so long ago. When would he let it go and understand that she was not interested in him in that way at all? Then she thought why bother. Michael was so drunk he would probably not even remember their conversation tomorrow. Instead, she shrugged and let him finish talking, as there was no stopping him.

"Hey, Brianna. Beautiful Brianna, do you want to come home with me tonight?" asked Michael.

Brianna replied in a stern voice, "No, Michael. We need to discuss the emergency situation with Forrester. Please drink your coffee and sober up now!"

"No matter what happens between us, beautiful Brianna, please remember that I will always love you," said Michael.

Brianna was dumbfounded and wished he would stop calling her "beautiful Brianna." She did not know where this was all coming from. He had been such a jerk to her these past few months, and now this? She truly hoped that Michael would not remember this part of their conversation tomorrow.

She tried her best to sober him up, but he was too far gone. In that moment she decided it was best to discuss the matter with him the next day. So, instead she called for an Uber and made sure he got in OK.

Monday, August 17, 2020

As soon as Brianna arrived at the office, she set up an urgent meeting with Michael, Edward, Kathleen, and Veronica to discuss the situation at Forrester.

Brianna then texted Michael. "Good morning, Michael. I hope you are sobered up. As we discussed last night, I need your help with the emergency at Forrester. Please come to my meeting this morning. I need your support."

Promptly at 10 a.m., Brianna kicked off the meeting.

"Thanks Michael, Edward, Kathleen, and Veronica for joining this call on such short notice. Veronica is on site with Forrester in Florida, and we have an emerging crisis that we need to fix. Veronica, would you please bring everyone up to speed on the latest details of the BalanceVITA situation?" asked Brianna.

"Thanks, Brianna. As of this morning, we now have twenty-six BalanceVITA clinical trial patients hospitalized. Three people died yesterday, and five more died overnight! I need your support to fix this!" said Veronica, trying terribly not to cry.

"Veronica, what evidence do you have that these patients died from BalanceVITA? I mean, could COVID-19 have played a part in this?" asked Kathleen.

"Kathleen's right. We are in the middle of a global pandemic.

These deaths are more likely to be COVID related than BalanceVITA," said Michael

"I don't . . . ," Veronica started to say.

"Michael and Kathleen, with all due respect, how can you say that? These are patients who participated in our clinical trial. Whether you will admit it or not, we know that BalanceVITA has quality issues. Now is the time for us to step up and do the right thing!" said Brianna.

"Hold on to your horses, Brianna. That is pure speculation. You have no facts to back up these wild claims of yours and, quite frankly, they are getting old. Why don't you just stay in your lane and let me do my job!" said Edward.

"Edward, I would be delighted to see you actually do your job. So, get on with it, already will you?" said Brianna firmly.

"Now, now, children. Let's all play nicely together. Kathleen, please reach out to Forrester's General Counsel to align on details of the COVID versus BalanceVITA. I am sure you can make our little problem here go away," said Michael.

"Of course; consider it done, Michael," said Kathleen with a smile.

"And Brianna, I expect you to get in line and support the company's legal position on this matter. I'd better not see another memo from your attorney or else. Is that understood?" said Michael not being able to look her in the eye.

Brianna was furious and refused to acknowledge or answer Michael's question.

"Good. Then this matter is settled. Now if you'll excuse me," said Michael and adjourned the meeting.

That evening Brianna met up with Kate at their usual Indian restaurant. She explained the complex situation unfolding at work.

"I just don't know what to do. I have invested fifteen years in The F Place, and I have bet my retirement on them. However, things have gone south over the past year, and I simply refuse to compromise who I am to stay at The F Place. There is so much happening, and I just need clarity. How can I find clarity? What is the right thing to do? How can Michael and Frita preach about the values of the company and say they expect others to live by them, yet they completely disregard them?" Brianna asked.

"Those values are just marketing words to them. They aren't principles to live by," said Kate.

As Brianna let that sink in, she felt sick again. She just could not agree to this, but then Kate's voice brought her back to the present.

"What is your life purpose, Brianna? Why do you believe you are on the Earth, right here, right now?" Kate asked.

"What could that possibly have to do with the screwed-up situation at The F Place?" Brianna asked.

"I suggest you take a couple of days to really think about your life purpose. When you have clarity of that, your next right move will become evident," said Kate.

Tuesday, August 18, 2020

The very next day, for the first time since Brianna could remember, she called in sick to work. She slept in and stayed home for several days, and she spent those days reading, praying, and reflecting on her life. Her whole life. She read Viktor Frankl's book *Man's Search for Meaning*. Frankl had survived a concentration camp by imagining the meaningful outcome of his life after the camp.

Brianna spent the day in deep reflection:

"I need to imagine my life beyond The F Place. My identity should not be wrapped up in a company."

"The F Place sucks up most of my time, and I only have leftovers to give to my family. Is the sacrifice worth it?"

"Why do I work so hard and so long at The F Place? What am I trying to prove? I am enough!"

"What is my life's purpose? What is my WHY?"

"My family is my WHY. I would give up everything to have both of my children back. Having a child is like having your heart beating outside of your body. I would give my life for them both."

"I believe I am here to shine my light and serve others through my generous giving, teaching, and leadership. I am a servant leader."

Kate was right; gaining clarity of purpose certainly puts the rest of the world into perspective.

"If I cannot live my life's purpose at The F Place, then either The F Place needs to change or it is time for me to leave, regardless of the consequences," Brianna said out loud to herself, determined to be strong and courageous.

Monday, August 24, 2020

When Brianna went to work the next week, she was determined to keep her life's purpose at the forefront of everything she did.

On her way home after a long Monday, Brianna received a call from a number she did not recognize. Hoping it was not spam, she went ahead and answered it.

"Is this Brianna Grimaldi?"

"Yes," Brianna confirmed.

"Brianna, this is Philip O'Connor with *The New York Times*. We have a story that is breaking tonight concerning the untimely deaths of forty-seven patients due to the BalanceVITA clinical trial of The F Place. Would you care to comment?"

Brianna pulled her car to the side of the road, took a deep breath, and said, "Philip, thanks for your call. I recommend you speak with our CEO, Michael Vitali, and our Chief Products Officer, Edward Ferris, for comment. Good luck."

She then called Michael and Edward to give them a heads-up, not that it was appreciated.

Tuesday, August 25, 2020

Upon awakening at 4:30 a.m. the next day, Brianna quickly checked the news. On the front page of all major networks was the headline about the killer new BalanceVITA clinical trials of The F Place. Despite best efforts to contain the fallout, The F Place stock price had dropped 45 percent by midday.

People are Dying to join The F Place Clinical Trial

NEW YORK CITY, N.Y.—August 25, 2020—Unnamed sources have confirmed that 47 people have died in the last 48 hours after participating in The F Place's clinical trial for BalanceVITA, a mood-stabilizing drug for bipolar disorders.

However, The F Place is disputing these claims, calling them "fake news" and "misinformation."

"We remain focused on our vision to become the global leader in pharmaceuticals and have taken fast action to fight back against these malicious rumors," said Michael Vitali, president and CEO.

"We are flexible and cooperating with authorities as well as the medical community at large. These deaths are tragic, but we are confident that the data will show that they were caused by COVID-19 and not our innovative new drug line BalanceVITA," said Kathleen Kane, senior vice president and chief legal officer.

[Read More]

CHAPTER 12

Focus on the People

September 2020

"Your people come first, and if you treat them right, they'll treat the customers right."

—*Herb Kelleher*

Saturday, September 12, 2020

FRITA HAD FINALLY managed to get a hair appointment with Sam, who was Brianna's hairstylist. Frita was furious that she had to pay her almost a thousand dollars for a simple visit to her brownstone, as Frita did not have time to venture out. She wondered if Brianna paid the same. It did not matter, though; she wanted to surprise Toby and get a fresh cut for the leadership team retreat in St. Thomas.

Finally, Sam arrived at Frita's place. As Sam waited for someone to answer the door, she thought about how odd it was to have received the call from some random lady named Tracy asking if she was "the Sam that cut Brianna Grimaldi's hair."

No one had ever called her and asked her about a client like that. Most people would introduce themselves and say, "Hey I was referred to you by so and so."

Sam was quickly let in by Frita's house manager, who led her up to Frita's master suite. Inside there was a dressing room already set up with a makeup chair and a professional glam countertop. The house manager inquired if Sam would like a beverage, and Sam politely declined. Then in waltzed Frita and inspected Sam as though she were interviewing her for some important job.

Frita sat down in the chair and commanded, "Well let's get to it, missy girl. I don't have all night." Next Frita pulled out an 8-by-10 picture of Brianna. She had asked Tracy to scratch out Brianna's face so that only the hair style would show, but she had forgotten. So instead, Frita put her hand on Brianna's face and tried to cover it as best as she could. She told Sam to replicate the look and make her look sexy. Of course, Sam knew that it was Brianna in the picture, but she decided to play dumb. Instead she expressed her concern to Frita about her wanting to go from being a platinum blond to a brunette like Brianna. Brianna had a very distinct hair color that was hard to attain. Brianna's color was a medium ash brown hair. Sam advised Frita against such a drastic change, but Frita insisted that it could be done.

Sam started to mix the color and apply it thoroughly. She finished the coloring process and began to cut Frita's hair. As she started to snip the back, Frita's phone rang, and she saw that it was Toby as his hunky picture flashed on her phone. Sam had the scissors lined up to trim the back pieces when, without warning, Frita reached forward to grab her phone. This caused Sam to miss her angle and cut a big chunk of hair right into the middle back of Frita's head.

Frita missed Toby's call and was furious with Sam. Sam, on

the other hand, was furious with Frita for being so careless. When Sam told Frita what happened, Frita started screaming at Sam. In order for Sam to be able to even out Frita's hair to make it look somewhat normal, she ended up giving Frita a bob.

Frita was so angry. She had wanted to have the perfect hairstyle for the trip to St. Thomas since she knew that Toby was going to be there. Instead, Brianna's hairdresser had sabotaged her look and given her a messy bob, not to mention the hair color, which turned out to have a lot of red highlights. Frita could not blame her for the color as Sam had warned her about it.

Sunday, September 13, 2020

As Frita was checking in to the hotel, she saw a group huddled in the corner of the lobby and recognized that they were from The F Place. She made her way over and greeted everyone. Edward let out a chuckle and said, "Wow, Frita, I see you updated your hairstyle. Looks like you lost a lot of hair there."

Frita nervously touched her hair and then looked at Toby and clumsily replied, "No, my hairdresser mistakenly just gave me more head." The group was speechless, and everyone except Toby quickly murmured excuses of why they needed to get ready for the next day. Toby decided to play with Frita, and just as everyone left, he whispered to her, "I like your hair."

Monday, September 14, 2020

Bright and early Monday morning, Michael welcomed the group. "Welcome, everyone. Thank you for making your travel arrangements to St. Thomas so quickly. With a crisis of this magnitude, I passionately believe that we need to be *FOCUSED* and *FLEXIBLE*. We are going to do this together and will be stronger for it. No distractions whatsoever, people!" said Michael.

Michael looked around the luxurious banquet room at the Ritz-Carlton and asked, "Who are we missing, Frita?"

Frita glanced around the room nervously and did a mental check of everyone. One by one she looked for each person who was to have attended the meeting.

Torsten, the Chief Medical Officer, was there in his wrinkled khaki shorts and stained, button-down white shirt.

Edward, the Chief Products Officer, was in the back of the room wearing his three-piece suit and tie, talking on his phone.

Shanice, the Chief Diversity Officer, could not be missed wearing a tight-fitting bright orange floral dress.

Tom, the Chief Operating Officer, was in his usual casual attire—jeans and a black T-shirt.

Isaac, the Chief Information Officer, was wearing shorts, a tank top, and sandals.

Karen, the Chief Financial Officer, was dressed in her designer suit and jewelry.

And then there was the legendary Albert Weinstein, sitting alone and looking smug as usual. Albert was dressed in his usual smart attire as if he had just finished a photo shoot with GQ magazine. He looked poised and confident in his linen suit and monogramed Cartier cuff links. Michael had insisted that Albert join the Executive Team's offsite meeting, despite Frita's protests.

Lizzy, Denise, and Toby were in the back of the room while talking with the hotel manager.

Frita had wanted Toby to accompany her on this trip, but she knew that would be too obvious. So, she had suggested to Michael that Toby, Lizzy, and Denise should join the offsite to ensure everything went smoothly. Michael agreed that this would be a great idea. Frita was irritated, as none of them were much help as there she was, stuck doing roll call. She thought to herself, "It's worth it, though, because I have Toby to look forward to." As Frita's mind drifted off to Toby, she thought about the fact that she had strategically put him in the suite right next to hers.

"Earth to Frita! Who are we missing?" asked Michael again impatiently.

"Looks like we have everyone except for Brianna and Kathleen," said Frita.

"I believe Brianna is not going to arrive until this evening. She and Veronica are still in Florida with Forrester. She sent an email out about this last week," said Lizzy.

"Well, isn't that convenient," said Frita.

"Does anyone know where Kathleen is?" asked Mark.

"My records show that she should have arrived last night. I will step out and see if I can reach her," said Lizzy.

"Frita, let's get this show on the road. Take it away!" said Michael.

"Thank you, Michael," said Frita. "Let's start by aligning on objectives and expectations for our time here together. We will go around the room and each person has no more than five minutes to describe your objectives for the week. Toby will capture them on the easel for all of us to see."

She turned to Michael. "Let's start with you," said Frita

"I have three objectives for the week. First, develop our new-and-improved messaging strategy and launch plan for BalanceVITA, which should become the premier drug for bipolar disorder. Things have gotten out of hand in the media, and we need to control the narrative and get that damn product launched already! Second, review the Q3 financials. I have gotten my ass chewed out the last two quarters, and I won't tolerate any more surprises. Finally, let's have some fun. I am taking the guys golfing on Friday. You ladies can do whatever you like!" said Michael.

"Torsten, what about you?" asked Frita.

"I am fully aligned with Michael. We need to resolve our differences with BalanceVITA and accelerate the FDA approval. I am committed to doing whatever is necessary to make that happen," he said with a nod to Michael.

"Thank you, Torsten. Karen, you're next." Said Frita.

"Michael, I don't appreciate your comment about the financials. My team and I provide you and the Executive Team with financial flash reports every week, so there should be no surprises for you in that regard. But I do agree with you that we should review our prediction for the Q3 results, as things are getting uglier every day. As I have been saying for months, we need top-line growth. And where is our Commercial leader? All I know is that she is not here!" said Karen.

"Karen, we have spoken about this before. Watch your tone with me! As for Brianna, she will be here later tonight. She is with Forrester right now," said Michael.

Just then Kathleen strolled into the room looking frazzled and distressed. "Sorry for being late. My plane had mechanical problems, and I spent the night in the Miami airport. I am never flying commercial again!"

"Thank you for gracing us with your presence, Kathleen. Shanice, you're up next. What are your objectives for the week?" asked Frita.

"Thank you, Frita. My goal is to ensure that we incorporate diversity and inclusion into everything we do," said Shanice.

"Shanice, thank you for reminding us all how important diversity and inclusion is to our *FUTURE*. We must be *FOCUSED* on making D&I part of our culture! Isaac, what are your goals for the week?" asked Frita.

"I would like to provide an update on a number of our

strategic IT projects to ensure we are aligned on the $1B budget for IT next year," said Isaac.

Karen nearly spit out her coffee as Isaac spoke. She grumbled under her breath, "Not on your life."

"Tom, over to you, boyfriend!" said Frita while winking at him.

Tom looked questioningly to Frita and wondered how she could get away with all her sexist comments. "I plan to review my footprint expansion plan and answer any questions you all may have," he said tersely.

Karen looked up from her phone and stared straight at Tom. "Tom, I told you to shift the expansion out by at least twelve months. With the turmoil we are in this year, we cannot possibly expand. Michael, did you agree to this?" asked Karen.

"Calm down, Karen. Stop being such a Karen! We can proceed with Tom's plan if we are *FAST* and *FOCUSED*! So, I expect you to hear him out this week, got it?" said Michael.

"Edward, it is your turn," said Frita.

"I am here to fully support Michael's objectives. It is all about BalanceVITA and our quarterly results. If we don't deliver on those two, we are all screwed!" said Edward.

"Kathleen, now that you are settled, can you please share with us your goals for the week?" said Frita.

"I have two main goals this week. First, we need to discuss and align on the legal action plan for BalanceVITA. Secondly, I plan to provide an update on our litigation progress. As you know, more than 10 percent of the employees who were laid off are suing The F Place. We need to discuss this as an Executive Team . . . without the extras," said Kathleen, looking around the room at Toby, Lizzy, Denise, and Albert.

"Thanks, everyone. As your Chief People Officer, my goal is to create a *FAST* and *FLEXIBLE* culture that is *FOCUSED* on people. As such, I would like to discuss employee engagement with you. We need a plan in case our survey results this month show any kind of decline. Because . . . if they drop below 85 percent, we will fall off the top 100 workplaces list, and that would not be good for me . . . or any one of us!" said Frita

"Frita, what about the others? In the spirit of inclusion, I would like to hear about their goals for the week," said Shanice.

"Thank you for continuing to remind us to be FOCUSED on diversity and inclusion, Shanice. Sure, let's start with you, Lizzy. What are your goals for the week?" asked Frita.

"Thanks, Frita and Shanice. I am here to support Michael and all of you, of course!" said Lizzy nervously.

"I am here to make sure things run smoothly for you all this week at the hotel," said Denise.

Toby then stood up and declared "Hello, everyone. It is so nice to meet you in person after mostly virtual calls for the past several months. I am here to learn more about the business from each of you so that HR can be an even better partner to you than we are today."

Frita smiled like a proud mother with Toby's comment. And then her eyes locked with Albert's.

Albert stood up and walked to the front of the room, stepping right in front of Frita. He was immaculately dressed from head to toe. "Hello, everyone. For those that don't know me, please allow me to introduce myself. My name is Albert Weinstein, and I was with The F Place from 2001 to 2017. I held a variety of roles throughout my career, including the Chief Strategy Officer from 2007 to 2017 for Alexander Wood. When Michael became CEO, he wanted to use my diverse talents in other ways, so I am now working in the basement with a red stapler. All kidding aside, I am your designated strategic consultant this week, at your service!" said Albert with a straight face.

"Very funny, Albert. You always were the jokester. In all

seriousness, I asked Albert to join us this week because of his vast knowledge of our company, products, customers, and the marketplace. Albert will be retiring at the end of this year, so we should be honored to have him with us one last time! Think of this week as your farewell party, Albert!" said Michael.

Toby was flabbergasted at how dysfunctional the Executive Team was. He had captured six pages of objectives for the week and very few of them were aligned with one another.

Minutes felt like seconds. Hours felt like minutes. Toby swore he could hear the sound of the second hand ticking back and forth, back and forth. "There goes twelve hours of my life that I will never get back," thought Toby to himself as they concluded for the day.

"Thanks, everyone. See you promptly at seven downstairs in the restaurant. We have a private room for dinner," said Frita.

Brianna arrived at the hotel just before 10 p.m. She decided to make a quick appearance at dinner and then wanted to crash.

When she arrived at the restaurant, she was escorted to their private room.

"Good evening, everyone!" said Brianna

"Hello, beautiful Brianna—you finally decided to grace us with your presence," said Michael, slurring his words.

"Well, well, well. It's missy girl. How is Forrester doing?" asked Frita, clearly intoxicated and leaning into Toby's lap.

Tom, Edward, and Torsten were huddled together at the end of the table and laughing obnoxiously. Karen and Kathleen were gathering their purses and getting ready to leave. Everyone else had already eaten and gone.

Michael stood up to greet Brianna, tripped on his chair and fell flat on his face. Frita tried to help him, but he was having none of that. He braced himself with both hands on his chair and slowly stood back up.

Brianna was thankful for the distraction and quickly said,

"Sorry, everyone. I just arrived a little while ago, and I am really exhausted. I wanted to say a quick hello. I want to be ready for our big day tomorrow, so if you all will excuse me, I am going to head to bed now. What time are we meeting tomorrow again?"

"Nine a.m. sharp, girlfriend!" said Frita a little too quickly. Brianna knew Frita would be glad that she wasn't hanging around them tonight.

Tuesday, September 13, 2020

Brianna had trouble sleeping that night. She had so many things swirling around in her head concerning the BalanceVITA patient deaths. That evening the media ran a story saying that more than four hundred people had died from the BalanceVITA clinical trials. Brianna knew that the real number was even higher! Brianna was certain that The F Place would continue to spin the story and blame these deaths on COVID-19.

At 4:30 a.m., she concluded that it was no use trying to sleep. Instead she would get up and go for a run. Doing so always energized her body and refreshed her spirit.

After her shower, she decided to have an early breakfast by herself before going to the hotel meeting room. She ordered a coffee and a cheese omelet with fresh jalapeños. Then, she settled into the quiet corner booth to read a few chapters of Tony Robbins' book *Unlimited Power*. No one else was in the restaurant at the time.

A few minutes later, she heard a man's voice speaking to the waiter. She knew that voice. There was a time when she knew that man very well. They were partners, but then he pretty much disappeared from the face of the earth.

"Albert? What are you doing here? Oh, my goodness, it is so good to see you! How long has it been? At least three years?" Brianna asked.

"Brianna, I am so happy to see you! How are you? How have you been?" asked Albert.

"Why don't you join me for breakfast? We have so much to catch up on," said Brianna.

"Nothing would make me happier," said Albert.

After the waiter brought their food, Brianna decided to move the conversation beyond the superficial. "Albert, what happened to you? One minute, you were the Chief Strategy Officer and the next . . . I don't even know what you are doing these days. You completely disappeared," said Brianna

"Brianna, you would not believe me if I told you," said Albert.

"Albert, with what has been going on at The F Place lately, trust me, I would believe anything," said Brianna.

"Brianna, I have done my time, and Michael is finally going to pay me . . . uh . . . my bonus at the end of this year. I cannot do anything to jeopardize that. I am sorry. Let's talk about you; how are the kids?" said Albert.

"Not so fast, mister. What do you mean by bonus?" asked Brianna.

"Brianna, I swear if you breathe a word of what I am about to tell you, you could ruin my life even more. Do you understand?" asked Albert.

"Albert, we have known each other for fifteen years! You were my mentor. I would not be where I am today without you. How can you doubt my trust?" asked Brianna.

"People change, Brianna. You are the Chief Commercial Officer now. I am sure you have had to betray a few people or compromise a few of your morals to make it so far up the ladder," said Albert.

"No, I have not. That is not who I am. You can trust me with your life. I promise," said Brianna.

"Very well, Brianna. Michael and Frita are not who they

seem, and they have turned The F Place upside down since Alexander moved on. Frita was clearly very intimidated by me because I saw through her charade. But then she convinced Michael that I wanted to take him out. In a million years, I could never have imagined Michael would buy her load of crap. But he did," said Albert.

"Albert, what did Michael do?" asked Brianna.

"Michael valued my product, customer, and marketplace knowledge, but he saw me as a threat. So, when I discovered something funny with the HappyVITA clinical trial data and asked a few questions, he and Frita kicked me to the curb," said Albert.

"What does that mean, Albert?" said Brianna.

"They eliminated my role and my entire team; don't you remember that?" asked Albert

"The F Place announcement said that you were leaving to start your own luxury travel business and that your team was being decentralized into the other functions. Is that not what really happened?" asked Brianna.

"Yes and no. They eliminated my role and disbanded my team. A few months later, Michael realized the error of his ways and forced me into a three-year consulting contract with a lucrative payout at the end. I should have said no, but my hands were tied. After all was said and done, I had given my best years to The F Place. All those long hours, the blood, sweat, and tears. My wife divorced me, and my kids are grown and gone. If only I had it to do over again, things would be so different," said Albert.

"Oh, Albert. I am so deeply sorry. But I am confused; what do you do for The F Place now?" asked Brianna.

"Anything that Michael needs me to do," said Albert.

Brianna sat there stunned and speechless. What kind of

company treats its best and brightest people in this manner, she wondered.

"I have one last piece of advice for you, Brianna," said Albert.

"Yes, please tell me, Albert!" said Brianna.

"Get out of The F Place while you still can," he said.

CHAPTER 13

The Funeral

October 2020

"Keep your friends close, and your enemies closer."

—*Sun Tzu*

Thursday, October 1, 2020

Brianna received a confidential meeting invitation from Alexander Wood, The F Place Chairman of the Board. He asked her to use discretion and meet him at the Plaza Hotel the next afternoon.

That evening, Brianna thought back to her first year at The F Place. She was a project manager in the Quality organization and viewed herself as nobody special. She was in survival mode in her personal life back then but had a fire in her belly to succeed professionally. Every Friday morning, she would leave the house early and go to La Madeleine for breakfast and quiet personal-development reading time. One morning in early October 2006, she saw Alexander Wood walk through the doors and sit down at the table right next to her. She knew that he was the President and CEO of The F Place, but he knew nothing about her. When his breakfast arrived, she decided to have courage and introduce herself.

"Hello, Mr. Wood. My name is Brianna Grimaldi, and I am a project manager at The F Place. I just wanted to tell you that we all think you are an amazing leader, and I am honored to work in your organization," said Brianna with as much confidence as she could muster.

"Well, the pleasure is all mine, Brianna. It is nice to finally put a face to a name. Albert Weinstein and Michael Vitali have already told me so much about you. Would you like to join me for breakfast? I would love to hear your feedback," said Alexander.

Brianna tried to keep her composure, although she was utterly shocked that Michael and Albert had spoken about her to Alexander! "Yes, sir. I would be honored," said Brianna.

"Please call me Alexander," he said as he stood up while she joined his table.

After she was seated, Alexander turned to her with a look of sincerity. He asked, "Brianna, what is the one thing that you love most about your job at The F Place?"

"Sir . . . I mean Alexander, that's a good question. I love that Quality is a priority in everything that we do. In the end, when we deliver Quality products, we can fulfill our mission of improving the mental health and lives of patients everywhere. So, I feel like my work truly matters! Does that answer your question?" asked Brianna a little shyly.

"Yes, it most certainly does. Great answer, by the way!" Alexander said. "You know, creating a one-of-a-kind company culture was part of my vision when we founded the company in 2001. It makes me incredibly happy that our culture is recognized and embraced by new employees like yourself. So, now comes the more difficult question. What is the one thing that the leadership team, myself included, can do to improve The F Place, Brianna?"

"Wow. Well, I can't speak for all employees, but I know that I would love to learn more about our long-term strategies and how the various parts of the organization work together to execute them. Right now, perhaps because of my role, I have a limited view of the bigger picture. And I believe that when our employees have clarity of our strategy, they can better enable us to make it a reality," said Brianna.

"Brianna, you have no idea how valuable your feedback is. You represent the next generation of leaders, and we need to listen to your ideas for the future," Alexander said. "This is not announced yet, but I have asked Pat Pierson to create a global Emerging Leaders Mastermind group next year that would include twenty or so associates under 30. The purpose of this mastermind group would be to incubate innovative ideas for the future of The F Place. Would you be interested in joining?"

"I would be delighted!" said Brianna with growing confidence.

"Excellent, I will let Pat know. And I will make sure that we invest more time in our employee town halls to share our strategic plans. You are right; all employees need to understand this stuff—not just the executives!" said Alexander.

And just like that, Brianna became a bright and shining star on Alexander's radar. Up until his retirement, Alexander and several members of his leadership team personally met with the Emerging Leaders Mastermind group once every quarter, which gave Brianna and the other young professionals a safe space to share their ideas and constructive feedback for the Executive Team.

By the time that Brianna was promoted to Director of Services in 2010, she had been serving as the leader of the mastermind group for a few years. One of their most promising ideas was to expand The F Place portfolio beyond pharmaceuticals into natural and preventive remedies, such as vitamins, probiotics, and supplements to improve the mental health and lives of people everywhere. Brianna and the Emerging Leaders Mastermind had a strong passion for this idea, but Michael Vitali and Edward Ferris shut it down, emphasizing that the future of The F Place was the successful launch of HappyVITA.

Over the years that followed, Brianna never let go of the portfolio expansion strategy. She had even done her research and selected a few small companies that The F Place could acquire to jump-start the vision. However, she never seemed to be able to get senior leadership support for moving the idea forward.

Brianna's mind shifted back to the present and she reflected upon why Alexander wanted to meet with her. She decided that she would not sugarcoat anything and would share her true perspective on anything and everything that Alexander wanted to discuss, including the continued bookings misses, the HappyVITA conspiracy, the BalanceVITA quality debacle, and the recent Voice of the Customer feedback. She also decided to bring a copy of Christian's HappyVITA dossier and her July 8 Legal Memo about her significant concerns with launching BalanceVITA prematurely.

Friday, October 2, 2020

Brianna left the office at 3 p.m. on Friday afternoon to meet Alexander. While she felt a little guilty leaving early, most everyone in the office had been gone for hours.

She walked into the Plaza Hotel fifteen minutes early. She was quickly ushered to a small, private room where Alexander was already seated. He stood up as she walked in, and they smiled and nodded pleasantly at one another. Brianna sat down across from him. She was still trying to get used to not shaking hands these days.

Alexander was already drinking a beer, so she decided to join him and let him order her a glass of champagne. They exchanged pleasantries for a few minutes, and then he put the moose on the table and asked her the question. Brianna wasn't expecting him to say, "What is really going on at The F Place, Brianna?"

Brianna took a deep breath and started, "Alexander, before I begin, I would like to ask your permission to speak freely. By that I mean, no sugarcoating, just the cold, hard facts. Would that be OK with you?" She paused briefly to make sure she had a positive read on his body language and then picked up where she left off. "You and I have known each other for fifteen years. That is a really long time. I want you to know that I trust you with my life. The bottom line is that there are things you need to know."

Alexander nodded in agreement and told Brianna that he would not have taken the time to meet with her and be here in this moment if he did not want the real, uncensored story. Brianna knew that to be the truth.

So she continued, "In that case, let me start by saying that we have a real-life goat rodeo on our hands. I'm not kidding. The public issues with BalanceVITA are the tip of the iceberg, and there is something much more sinister going on with HappyVITA. As you know, I started my career in the quality organization, and I can sniff out quality issues like a K-9 cop sniffs out drugs. I have been raising my concerns for the last year and I simply could not understand why Michael and Edward were not treating this as a priority. More than four hundred people have died, for God's sake!"

She saw that Alexander was listening intently, and so she continued. "It was not COVID-19-related; it was BalanceVITA. No matter how you spin the story, you just cannot put lipstick on that pig," she said. "The degradation of our brand due to the BalanceVITA disaster has been accelerating. I have personally met with our key accounts, but the ones that haven't left us are concerned. Here is the Voice of the Customer package that my team and I prepared, which provides you with supporting details and data behind their concerns. Additionally, here is a legal memo that I sent to the entire Executive Team in July warning against launching BalanceVITA prematurely into the marketplace. Michael, Edward, and the team have pushed me out of their little circle and some days pretend that I don't even exist. I have worked my way up in The F Place for the past fifteen years, and I am not going out without a fight."

"Brianna, this is a lot to digest. You said you have documentation. Please let me take a moment to read it," said Alexander.

Alexander then spent the next hour poring over the BalanceVITA materials.

"Brianna, the customer feedback is good, and we should address it. But the rest seems more like speculation. Do you have any cold, hard facts about the BalanceVITA quality issues? Any clinical trial data at all?" asked Alexander.

"I wish I did, Alexander. But, as I mentioned, I am being pushed out because I don't support the company line." said Brianna.

"Brianna, until we have evidence, this is simply a matter of 'He said, she said.' How do you actually know if those deaths were caused by COVID-19 or BalanceVITA?" asked Alexander

"Alexander, given what I know about HappyVITA, I know that something more is going on with BalanceVITA, even if I don't have all of the supporting evidence . . . yet," said Brianna.

"Right, you said something sinister is going with HappyVITA. That is a pretty significant allegation. How do you know this? Is it also your intuition, or do you have any facts to back it up?" said Alexander.

Brianna took a deep breath. She knew that if she shared what she knew about HappyVITA and Alexander was part of the conspiracy, her career and her life would be over. However, she had known Alexander for fifteen years and trusted him with her life. The leader and man that she believed he was would have no part in the HappyVITA conspiracy.

Brianna had made a copy of Christian's dossier and provided it to Alexander. As she handed it to him, Alexander commented, "Brianna, you are as white as a ghost. What is going on?"

"Alexander, before I begin, I would like to ask you a question. Will you please tell me what you know about HappyVITA?" asked Brianna.

"Brianna, considering the fact that I was the Chief Executive Officer when we launched HappyVITA, that is a strange question to ask of me. But, given our relationship I will indulge you," he said. "After 9/11, anxiety and depression in the United States grew significantly. We saw an opportunity to help people with their anxiety and depression while growing our new business by developing a new anti-depressant drug. We conducted our preclinical research from 2001 to 2005, our clinical research from 2005 to 2009 and obtained FDA approval in September 2010. HappyVITA is one of the selective serotonin reuptake inhibitor (SSRI) drugs and is the biggest cash-cow drug at The F Place," said Alexander.

"All of that sounds about right to me. HappyVITA obtained FDA approval in nine years, whereas the process typically takes twelve. How did the team accomplish such an incredible feat?" asked Brianna.

"The short answer is that I put the right leaders in place.

Michael Vitali was head of Product Development at the time. He and his team did a fabulous job! What are you getting at, Brianna?" asked Alexander.

"Would it surprise you to learn that some corners were cut during clinical trials?" asked Brianna.

"Why, yes it would, Brianna. What kind of corners are you talking about?" asked Alexander.

"I have cold, hard evidence that The F Place paid undocumented immigrants large sums of money, well beyond patient care costs, for participation in the clinical trial," said Brianna.

"Brianna, you must be mistaken. This cannot be true. Michael would never do anything like that," said Alexander.

"Alexander, not only is it true, that's not the worst of it. There are hundreds of suicides from HappyVITA patients that The F Place has made simply disappear. It's been the world's best vanishing act," said Brianna.

Alexander sat there stunned for a moment, gained his composure, and said, "Brianna, I find this incredibly hard to believe. But, show me this evidence of yours."

Brianna then handed over Christian's dossier to Alexander and said, "Within this packet, you will find hundreds of stories that substantiate my claims. This material was pulled together by Christian Boyd as part of our Voice of the Patient Transformation initiative. I met with Christian two days before he was going to take this evidence to the FBI. Do you know what happened to him after that?"

"No, I don't. Christian is your VP of Commercial Transformation, right?" asked Alexander.

"He was my VP of Commercial Transformation. Christian and the entire Transformation team were let go as part of our RIF in April . . . along with many of my top leaders," said Brianna.

"What are you talking about, Brianna? Why would you let those leaders go? They were the catalyst for driving true and sustainable change within the company, including the incredible innovations incubated by the Emerging Leaders Mastermind. If you ask me, that Transformation team of yours represent the future of The F Place," said Alexander.

"Exactly, Alexander. They were the future of this company, but let me be absolutely clear; it was most certainly not my choice. You have to understand that it was Michael and Frita who made the decision and executed the RIF without me. I wanted no part in that circus," said Brianna.

"This is simply shocking, and I don't agree with these actions. Perhaps I should speak with Michael about bringing back Christian and your Transformation team," said Alexander.

"Alexander, it is too late," said Brianna.

"It is never too late, Brianna. I can be very persuasive," said Alexander.

"It is too late because Christian is dead. He was in a terrible car accident the day before he was going to meet with the FBI and share this information. He died a few weeks later, and his family has been treated like second-class citizens by The F Place throughout this entire ordeal. It is heartbreaking," said Brianna, trying her best not to tear up in front of Alexander.

"Brianna, there are too many coincidences in this story. I am going to take this dossier and read it from cover to cover. Then let's meet together again tomorrow," said Alexander.

"Thank you, Alexander. One more thing you should know. After Christian's accident, I shared this dossier with the FBI, and there is an undercover investigation happening as we speak. So, you and I need to be very careful about keeping this information between us. Our lives could depend on it," said Brianna.

Saturday, October 3, 2020

Early the next morning, Brianna saw Alexander walk into the diner. His head hung low, his eyes were red, and the anguish on his face was obvious. He looked like he had not slept last night.

"Good morning, Brianna," said Alexander

"Good morning, Alexander. Now that you have read the dossier, do you understand what I was telling you about The F Place?" asked Brianna.

"As much as it pains me, I see exactly what you were saying. And I blame myself. I was the one who chose Michael over David to succeed me. Clearly, I bet on the wrong horse. And now there is a cancer growing in the company I spent so much of my blood, sweat, and tears building. We are going to fix this," said Alexander.

"What do you think we should do?" asked Brianna.

"Brianna, we need to keep you out of this as much as possible. You need to carry on at The F Place as usual . . . to the extent that you can amid a conspiracy, a global pandemic, and a highly charged election year. Please give me the contact info for your guy at the FBI. I will contact him directly and will do everything in my power to fix this mess before it is too late," said Alexander.

"Thanks for your support. You know, The F Place has not been the same since you stepped down as CEO," said Brianna.

"I've got your back, Brianna. I promise," said Alexander. Then he stood up, told her to stay strong, and walked out.

Thursday, October 8, 2020

Brianna had trouble sleeping almost every night that week. The tension and stress in the office was at an all-time high. Brianna arrived in the boardroom fifteen minutes early for the October executive leadership meeting and took her seat.

Frita walked in and sat as far away from Brianna as she could. She would not make eye contact, either. She preaches about creating an employee-focused culture, but words without actions are simply useless.

Edward walked in and looked like he had just seen a ghost. What other skeletons in his closet is he hiding?

Karen strolled in and sat down next to Brianna. Brianna remarked to herself that Karen was so passive-aggressive. Her thoughts about Karen were that she's usually nice to your face and then backstabs you when you least expect it. The power that she holds as CFO is tremendous, second only to Michael and Frita. One would have expected Karen to be more concerned with the long-term financial implications of product quality issues, but she has proven time and again that her vision is only as good as the current quarter's numbers. Her reputation is at stake, and she does not like to be challenged by the Board or the analysts during the quarterly earnings calls.

Brianna glanced over at Tom, who had just spilled his coffee down his shirt. He had bumped into Kathleen walking into the boardroom. "Where is his head right now?" thought Brianna.

Isaac came into the room with a stack of documents. He looked frazzled and stressed, which was unusual for him. He was usually calm, cool, and collected.

Michael walked in seven minutes late, sat at the head of the table, and looked around the room. He started, "Who are we missing?" He looked around again and paused. "Where is Tom?"

Kathleen responded and said that he was in the bathroom cleaning his shirt. Michael tilted his head quizzically and moved on. Lizzy sat down next to Michael, ready to do whatever he needed her to do.

Michael stood up and walked to the front of the room.

Karen shared a slide that showed how far they had missed the first three quarters of this year. He walked over and stood right in front of Brianna.

"Brianna, nothing else we do matters if you and your team are unable to bring bookings in the door. Why do you keep missing the mark this year? It hurts all of us, and it will hurt our pocketbooks this year," said Michael.

"Michael, I respectfully disagree. I believe this is the time when we need to rise up and live out our values. They need to be more than words on a page. When our products fail, people can die . . . and they have. I cannot sell products and solutions to our customers if I do not have the confidence in their quality. Edward, will you please provide us with an update on your quality improvement plan for BalanceVITA?" said Brianna.

Edward and Michael looked at each other and nodded. Michael then stated, "Brianna, stay in your lane. You do your job, and Edward will do his!" said Michael.

"Michael, you are the CEO of this company. For the sake of our future, I suggest you start acting like our CEO instead of. . . ." Brianna decided to stop herself from finishing that sentence. She simply stood up, gathered her things, and walked out of the boardroom. She went to her office, picked up her briefcase and purse, and left to finish the day at home. There was no value in being in the office anyway, despite Michael's classification of the Executive Team as "essential." Everyone else at headquarters had been working from home since March.

On the drive home, Brianna kept replaying the recent events over in her mind. She had a nagging feeling again and quickly realized that the common thread between HappyVITA and BalanceVITA was Michael. "What was his motivation for cutting corners? What could it be?" pondered Brianna.

Then she shifted her attention to Edward and mentally went

through the different scenarios. She thought, "As the Chief Products Officer, why does Edward not even seem to care? "

It was Kathleen next. Brianna prompted herself to think about what her motive may be. She thought, "Rather than seeking to mitigate the legal risks with the clinical trials, why is Kathleen singularly focused on being the spin-master queen?"

Then there was Frita. Brianna always had a bad feeling about her but continued to question herself. "Why does Frita seem to have so much political power without delivering an ounce of value to this company?" She concluded that all of this just didn't add up.

When Brianna arrived home, she set up her things in her home office and turned on her laptop. After logging in, she received a notice that IT was installing a software update. Although this seemed strange for 11 a.m., she clicked OK and expected it to take a few minutes.

While waiting for the update to complete, Brianna went to the kitchen and made a fresh cappuccino. Justin had given her a cappuccino machine for Christmas last year, and she savored the smell of fresh-ground coffee beans and the sound of the milk frothing. She took a deep breath and took in the moment. Coffee in hand, she returned to her home office.

When she logged into her laptop, a red screen appeared with a seventy-two-hour countdown timer. The screen said that the files had been encrypted and that she had seventy-two hours to pay $1 million dollars or all the files would be lost forever. Brianna had heard about these ransomware attacks, but honestly thought Isaac, with his healthy IT budget and cybersecurity expertise, had them covered.

Brianna immediately called Isaac and got his voicemail. He is probably still in that dreaded executive leadership meeting in the boardroom. So, she texted him and shared the details. Still no answer. "Are you kidding me?" she thought to herself.

Brianna called her assistant Anna to get her to contact IT. When her assistant answered, she sounded flustered and stated that her computer had just been hacked. When she described what she was seeing, Brianna realized that they were experiencing the same thing. Brianna then asked her to immediately contact Isaac's second-in-command, Jeffrey Young. In the meantime, Brianna would try to connect with Isaac again.

While trying to reach Isaac, Brianna got a call from Veronica. She was terribly upset and said that she thought she had been hacked. Brianna calmly explained her hypothesis that The F Place had been the target of a cyberattack. Brianna told her she would contact her when she had more information. OK, now they had three independent data points. This is not good! She decided to call Michael directly. No answer. Sent a text. No response. Brianna reached out to every single member of the Executive Team, and no one would take her call or answer her texts. What the hell was going on?

Anna called back and said she left two voicemails and three text messages for Jeffrey. No response. Brianna thanked her and told her she would be in touch as soon as she figured out more definitively what was going on.

Brianna quickly finished her coffee, grabbed her things, and made the forty-five minute drive back to the office.

On the elevator ride up, Brianna wondered what she would find upon entering the office this afternoon. Everything about the day was simply awful. She badged in and walked quietly towards the boardroom. She could hear everyone in there, and their voices were extremely loud. She thought it strange that the voices did not sound concerned. Rather, they sounded as if they were celebrating something.

Yes, thought Brianna after second-guessing herself—she had just heard Michael make a toast to Kathleen . . . followed by the sound of clinking glasses. She questioned herself again; was she dreaming, or did she just walk into an episode of *The Twilight Zone*?

She kept her footsteps very quiet so that she could move closer to hear what they were saying. "Next, I'd like to propose a toast to Isaac. When we needed you most, Isaac, you came through for us!" said Michael.

"Here, here," said Frita.

In that moment, Brianna froze. Although she did not know exactly what was going on, she knew that it was downright evil . . . unethical at best or, more likely, criminal. So, she turned around as quietly as she could and left the office . . . for the second time that day. She did not need anyone to know that she was there that afternoon. Her life might just depend on that.

On her drive home, Brianna wanted so badly to call Justin, but he was in surgery. Her heart was racing, and she knew she needed to do something; she just was not sure what she could or should do. So, she called Kate. Good old Kate. She was always so wise. "Kate, I need to talk to you . . . in person. It is incredibly urgent. Can you please meet me at my house?"

Brianna sat in her favorite wingback chair by the fireplace. Her heart was racing, adrenaline still flowing through her veins. She tried to slow her breathing down, but it was not working. "I wonder if this is what a heart attack feels like. Am I having a heart attack? No, this is probably a panic attack. If I am alive in one hour, I guess we will know for sure. What am I going to do?" Brianna said to herself.

In the middle of her panic, the doorbell rang. Kate was finally here. Brianna showed her the laptop (the countdown timer now said 66 hours and 27 minutes). She explained what she had discovered in the boardroom and asked Kate what she thought she should do.

Kate gave her a big hug and told her to calm down and breathe deeply. She then advised that Brianna get her attorney Roberta on the phone. As usual, Roberta picked up her call on the first ring. Brianna started to speak and then just lost it. She was crying and sobbing such that she could no longer speak. So, Kate proceeded to relay the story to Roberta. Roberta promptly said that she could be at Brianna's house in thirty minutes and told Brianna not to speak to another soul until she arrived.

When Roberta arrived, Kate met her at the front door and let her in. By this time, Ari had become curious about what was going on and had joined them. Kate took her to the side and gave her the abridged version of the story. While Brianna really wanted her daughter to see her as a strong woman who could overcome anything, Brianna thought she could learn a little something from being a spectator in the unfolding events . . . even if that meant seeing her mother in a weak and vulnerable state. Thus, the four of them sat at the dining room table and discussed how Brianna was going to manage this situation.

To get a break from the drama of the day, Brianna turned on the news. Big mistake. Just before going on a commercial break, the news anchor said, "Next up, we will hear from Michael Vitali, CEO of The F Place, on how he and his team are fighting back against a devastating cyberattack."

"Just like our country does not negotiate with terrorists, I refuse to negotiate with cybercriminals. We will not pay their ransom! I have the best and brightest information security professionals, including our very own Isaac Davis, working to defeat this cyberattack. The FBI have also mobilized special cyber agents to assist us."

"I cannot believe that he is already spinning this story in the media," said Brianna. But why? It just does not make sense.

Regardless, it was crystal clear that Michael and the rest of the Executive Team did not want Brianna in on whatever they had cooked up.

The F Place Stands Strong Against Cyber Attack

NEW YORK CITY, N.Y.—October 8, 2020—Today, The F Place announced that they were the victim of a malicious cyber-attack.

"We remain *focused* on our vision to become the global leader in pharmaceuticals and have taken *fast* action to fight back. Just like our country does not negotiate with terrorists, I refuse to negotiate with cyber criminals. We will not pay their ransom! I have the best and brightest Information Security Professionals, including our very own Isaac Davis, working to defeat this cyber-attack. The FBI have also mobilized special cyber agents to assist us," said Michael Vitali, President & CEO.

[Read More]

Thanks to Roberta, Brianna was able to meet with Nathan Price of the FBI again that night about 9 p.m. By then, she had composed herself and had simply become numb. She explained the story of today's events for the third time and showed Agent Price her laptop. He sounded skeptical when she told him about overhearing the boardroom celebration. However, he said he would work with the other members of the FBI team to get to the bottom of this and determine if there was any connection between this and the HappyVITA investigation already underway. Brianna thanked him for his help . . . what else could she do?

After Nathan left Brianna's house that night, he immediately contacted Greg Butterfinger and Donald Clooney (a.k.a. Toby) and asked to meet first thing in the morning.

After consuming a bottle of wine with Kate and Roberta, Brianna finally collapsed in bed about 11 p.m. She never heard back from anyone at The F Place. She thought to herself "Who the F knows what is going on in that place?" That night, she had the most unsettling dream.

I woke up in a cold sweat, my heart pounding in my chest. In all my thirty-eight years on this Earth, I have never had a dream so vivid. Was it stress induced due to everything crazy going on in the world today, or was it a sign of something to come? Either way, I cannot get the image of my own funeral out of my mind.

It was a chilly, rainy November in New York City. The church was filled with everyone I knew. My beautiful 18-year-old daughter Ariana (Ari) had such sadness in her eyes that my heart seemed to shatter into a million pieces. My 16-year-old son Eshan was sitting at the end of the aisle with his head in his hands, slowly shaking his head from left to right repeatedly. My ex-husband, Antonio, stood in the back of the room with a remorseful expression on his face, as if he wished he could rewrite the last ten years of our bitter estrangement. My mom Sonia was standing next to my dad . . . wait, my dad, Milan, passed away months ago due to COVID-19. My little brother Grayson was there, staring into space, his face as stone cold as a statue. All of my family, friends, colleagues, and neighbors filled the pews. So much black—everyone was wearing black from head to toe, including their face masks.

I walked down the same aisle that I had walked eighteen years ago to marry the man I thought was the love of my life. I was so young back then, with a life full of promise. And now, I was coming face to face with my own mortality. I saw my casket, beautiful oak with ornate designs . . . but, nevertheless, a casket. An oversized picture of me sat on top of the casket. Why did they pick that picture? I never liked that one. Red roses and white lilies, my favorites, filled the space.

I sat down on the front row, prepared to watch my own funeral. What would they say about me? Did my short life make a difference in this world? If I had known my life would only last for thirty-eight years, I would have done so many things differently. I would have loved more, followed my dreams, given more, grown more in my faith, and left a true legacy. I should not have sold my soul to The F Place, trading most of my waking hours for a healthy paycheck, a retirement fund, and company stock.

Friday, October 9, 2020

The following morning, Nathan filled Greg and Donald in on the cyberattack celebration as shared by Brianna last night. As he was undercover within The F Place, Toby was already aware of the attack and had his suspicions but no concrete facts yet.

Donald reminded them about the data that had been archived to the Chinese data center. With the strained U.S.-China relations, the odds of getting access to that data center were very low.

After discussing many different options, they wondered if the best one would be to offer one of the other executive leaders a deal in exchange for their testimony. While Donald had been working on the inside for a few months, his recommendation was that Brianna would be the most suited to determining which executive Leader would roll over and talk.

So, the three of them decided that Nathan and Donald (Toby) would bring Brianna into the plan and get her perspective before proceeding further.

Nathan called Brianna at noon to see if she could meet him later that evening. They agreed to meet up at 7 p.m. at a pizza joint on 4th Street.

At 7 p.m. sharp, Brianna walked into the pizza joint with her mask on and headed to the back where she saw Nathan in a booth. He nodded to her to join him. She also noticed another man sitting across from Nathan.

When Brianna got closer, she realized the man sitting with Nathan was Toby. "That is strange," she thought.

When Brianna sat down to join them, Toby smiled at her and said, "Hello, Brianna. I'm sure that you're wondering why I'm here. I know that we have a few things to bring you up to speed on, and we will."

Nathan quickly reminded Brianna, "Brianna, before we begin, we need you to understand that you must keep everything we discuss here completely confidential. Your life and ours may depend on it. Do you understand?"

"Yes, I understand. At this point, nothing would surprise me," said Brianna.

"Brianna, Toby is an undercover agent with the FBI. He is one of our finest, and he is on our side. He has been gathering evidence for our case for the past few months. Toby is not his real name, but that should not concern you," said Nathan.

"Interesting. So, when can we lock these guys up? Every day gets stranger, and I am so sick and tired of working with criminals. It is just so surreal!" said Brianna.

Nathan and Toby looked at each other.

"What are you waiting for?" asked Brianna.

"Well, it is complicated. Do you know about the Chinese data center, Brianna?" asked Toby.

"Maybe. I think Isaac may have shared something about that last year. But I honestly don't care about where we manage our IT systems. I just need them to function," said Brianna.

"The F Place has moved a large volume of data over to the Chinese data center. Even the FBI cannot access that with the current state of U.S.-Chinese relations," said Toby.

"And how does this relate to the cyberattack? The celebration in the boardroom?" asked Brianna.

"We know that this is all related and that the cyberattack is a smoke screen for the movement or disappearance of data. But what data exactly and what crime they are hiding still needs to be uncovered with actual evidence that will stand up in a court of law," said Nathan.

"I get it. So, how can I help?" asked Brianna.

"We were hoping you would ask that," said Toby.

"After looking at all options, we believe the best path is to offer a deal to one of the other executive leaders in exchange for their testimony against Michael and the leaders of The F Place. Who do you think would roll over and talk on the record with us?" asked Nathan.

"What would happen to the person who talked?" asked Brianna.

"They would get a lesser sentence or perhaps even immunity," said Nathan.

"That is unacceptable! These guys are all criminals, and I am living in a war zone. People have died. No one deserves a reduced sentence, let alone immunity," said Brianna. "Isn't there another way to bring down this house of cards?"

"Brianna, we need proof that the cyberattack was intentional in order to destroy evidence. We need to know why they did it, how they did it, and who did it. With the complexity of China involved, we can only get this evidence if someone on the inside talks," said Nathan.

"What if I could get someone to talk?" asked Brianna.

"It would just be 'He said, she said,' unless we had that talk recorded as evidence," said Nathan.

"So, I would have to wear a wire and record the conversation?" asked Brianna.

"Yes, that is what would be required. But, I don't advise that. It is too risky for you," said Toby.

"But if I could do it, we would have the evidence that we need, right?" asked Brianna.

"Yes, we would," said Nathan.

"OK. Please give me a few days to think. Let's meet up again next week," said Brianna.

Monday, October 12, 2020

Two days later, Brianna, Nathan, and Toby met at the Starbucks on Main Street. "I have given this a lot of thought, and I am going to do it," said Brianna. "I've decided that I am going to wear a wire, and I am going to bring justice to The F Place. I have worked there my entire career, and I believe in that place and the people. Somehow the leadership has gotten corrupt, but I still have hope in the company, and I know how I am going to do it."

"Brianna, are you certain? You are playing with fire. This is dangerous territory that we're on here. Just exactly how do you think you can accomplish this?" asked Nathan.

Brianna had thought about all of this and even talked it over with Kate to make sure that she had thought through all the different angles. She looked at Nathan and then proceeded. "How do you kill a snake?" Nathan looked back at her puzzled. "You cut off its head," said Brianna coldly, for emotional effect.

Thursday, October 15, 2020

Days later, Brianna put on her favorite Lululemon running gear. She thought about the first time she had purchased a pair of Lululemon leggings with Ari. Ari was obsessed with the brand, like many other teenage girls. Ari had insisted that Brianna be a cool mom and start wearing some hip workout clothes, and thus Brianna's collection of Lululemon gear. She intentionally chose the lavender print high-waisted leggings, a racerback bra, and a fitted crop top that showed the straps from the back. She put her hair up in a high ponytail to accentuate her oval face and doused herself with Coco Chanel parfum, even though she was going for a run. She had to make sure that everything on this excursion was going to run smoothly. She then headed to Central Park precisely at 6 a.m. She knew that Michael ran there every day, come rain or shine. Occasionally, Brianna would manage to run into him on the days she started her jogs later at the park.

She knew exactly where to go and put in her AirPods as she waited near a bench. Brianna knew that Michael always started his runs there because it was the entry point to the street that he lived on. Brianna decided to get rid of some of the nervous energy that she had in her and she began stretching her legs. She was fully gearing up for the run, especially as she saw him in the distance coming in her direction. As soon as she saw him, she looked the other way and started to slip off her ponytail holder and shake out her hair. She wanted him to notice her and come up to her first.

As she started to put up her hair again, Brianna acted surprised when she heard Michael greet her, "Good morning, Brianna, what brings you here?"

"Oh, hey, Michael, you caught me off guard. Good morning to you. I have been coming here for months now just to get a change in scenery. I love running in Central Park. With all the stress, it's been a great reliever for me to get some fresh air. I am actually really surprised that we haven't run into each other in a long while," said Brianna with a big smile.

Brianna continued her stretching. She made sure to bend over and touch her feet a few times so that Michael would notice her. She wanted to be sure she got an invite to join him, so she unzipped her hoodie and tied it around her waist.

Michael looked at her admiringly and asked, "Brianna, would you like to run with me this morning?"

Brianna paused and flashed him a flirtatious smile again and replied, "I thought you'd never ask, Mikey."

Michael looked pretty pleased with himself as they began their six-mile run around the park. "How are things on the home front, Michael? How is Tanya? How are the kids, Rachel and Rebekah? After all this time, hopefully things have improved between you and their mother," asked Brianna.

Michael picked up speed and glanced at Brianna briefly. "Brianna, I assumed you already knew this. Tanya and I split up last year," said Michael.

Brianna was surprised and quickly replied, "Michael, I honestly had no idea. I am sorry to hear that. You two were together for, what, two years?" Brianna wondered if that's why Michael had flirted with her so much this year and made several attempts to ask her out.

He interrupted her thoughts with, "Yes, nearly two years. We still see each other once in a while, but we are no longer committed, if you know what I mean. She really has let herself go, which is wrong on so many levels. Sorry, Brianna . . . TMI. Anyway, you know my twins just started university at Columbia—definitely not the best freshman college experience with everything online right now. As for their mom, as long as she gets her alimony check every month, she is happy," said Michael.

Brianna could tell he was remorseful for the way that it had ended with his third wife, Tanya. Although Michael valued having a beautiful woman by his side, he had never meant to hurt her. Brianna offered, "That must be difficult for you. How are *you* doing, Michael? I mean how are you really doing, Mikey? We have known each other for nearly fifteen years. As someone that has known you for so long , I really do care about you," said Brianna.

"Thanks, Brianna. That is really nice of you to say, and I would like to believe it," said Michael. He added, "Well, what about you? How are you and that guy that you're with? What's his name, and how's he doing? Jason, is it?"

"It's Justin," Brianna replied and then gave him a look of despair. She continued, "Justin and I have seen better times. I thought things would be better once I moved to New York City, but we still don't see each other all that much. Especially with him working around the clock at the hospital, well, let's just say that things could be better," said Brianna. She felt pretty proud of herself as she knew she sounded pretty convincing.

Brianna noticed that Michael had perked up when she shared that last bit of news with him.

"I am sorry to hear that, Brianna. Any man would be lucky to have a woman like you. I've always thought that you could do so much better than him. Oh, forget that I said that. It is none of my business," said Michael.

"Do you really mean that, Michael?" asked Brianna with a flirty tone in her voice.

"Of course I do. You are the total package, Brianna," said Michael.

Brianna stopped running for a moment. She gave Michael an adoring look and sweetly piped, "Thanks so much, Michael. You know, we should do this more often. I forgot how good it feels to be with you . . . with no one else around. Just you and me. Just imagine what we could accomplish together if we could talk like this at work!" said Brianna.

"You are absolutely right, Brianna! Why don't we have lunch together tomorrow and we can talk through this whole BalanceVITA situation again . . . just the two of us," said Michael.

"Great idea! Just tell me when and where. I will be there!" said Brianna.

Friday, October 16, 2020

The next morning, the Q3 earnings were published. Brianna expected Michael to be more stressed out and anxious about the results than he seemed. "What Machiavellian scheme does he have up his sleeve? Well, I am going to find out!" she thought to herself.

The F Place Reports Q3 2020 Results

NEW YORK CITY, N.Y.—October 16, 2020—Today, The F Place announced financial results for the third quarter ending September 30, 2020.

- Third-quarter worldwide sales of $3.9 billion decreased 21 percent year over year
- Due to uncertainties regarding the impact and duration of COVID-19, The F Place will not provide annual guidance for 2020

"We remain *FOCUSED* on our vision to become the global leader in pharmaceuticals and have taken additional *FAST* action in Q3 to adjust our cost structure by 10 percent in response to the continued market decline. We expect our BalanceVITA clinical trials to successfully conclude soon, and we should receive FDA approval next month," said Michael Vitali, President & CEO.

[Read More]

That afternoon, Brianna walked through the doors at Anton's restaurant at 2 p.m. sharp. Nathan and Toby had helped her with her wire, which was carefully secured in her purse. The hostess led her to a private booth in the back where Michael was already seated. He was dressed up more than usual and his cologne was a little too strong.

"Hello again, Michael. Fancy seeing you here today," said Brianna with a flirtatious tone in her voice.

"Hello, beautiful. Please join me!" said Michael.

Brianna sat down across from Michael. It was obvious he had already been drinking. He looked up at Brianna and asked, "Brianna, do you have any big plans for the weekend?".

"You mean . . . other than work? No big plans. I will be home in my beautiful penthouse . . . all alone. What about you, Michael?" she casually asked.

"I leave for Vegas in a couple of hours. I am playing in a private invitation-only poker tournament again this weekend," said Michael.

Brianna arched her eyebrows ever so slightly and coyly inquired, "Really? I didn't know you played poker. I don't know much about it. How much do you need to play?"

Michael quickly responded, "These private tournaments are very limited and expensive. It costs me $100K to play, but I almost always win back that money and more. Maybe you should come watch me play sometime?"

Flirtatiously, she responded, "Oooh! How fun! Yes, give me a little notice next time and maybe I can join you. I would be scared to death to spend that kind of money in poker." She paused and continued, "You must have the lucky touch, Michael!"

Amused, he responded, "Brianna, it takes a lot more than luck to win at poker. It takes skill. If you are interested, I could teach you."

"I would love that!" beamed Brianna. "Now, shall we order some food for lunch and then talk about how we can resolve our differences with BalanceVITA?" she asked.

"It is Friday afternoon after a long week, including the earnings call this morning. Could we please punt the BalanceVITA conversation until next week? I am just not in the mood. Besides, an argument between us would really ruin my appetite," said Michael.

"Listen, it doesn't have to turn into an argument. Let's just talk this out like mature adults . . . like friends," said Brianna.

"I am afraid it will take more than just talk to get you and I to see eye to eye. And I just don't have it in me today after all," said Michael.

Calmly Brianna inquired, "What do you mean? I'm a reasonable person. Let's just talk. We can start with the things that we agree upon and work through the rest."

Michael started to get a little frustrated. With a deep sigh he continued, "Brianna, you of all people should understand that The F Place needs BalanceVITA to be successful in the marketplace. This pandemic has wreaked havoc on our business this year and we need this win . . . in a big way. If we don't get it, this could be the beginning of the end for The F Place."

Brianna stood her ground and replied, "I understand that we have a lot at stake with BalanceVITA, but launching prematurely is a gamble that we cannot afford to take."

Michael looked into Brianna's eyes and said, "Brianna, I am going to stop you right there. I said I don't want to talk about this today, and I mean it. If you really want to have THIS conversation, then join me in San Francisco next week. I am leaving Vegas on Sunday night and flying there directly. I can have the jet pick you up." Deep down inside Michael hoped that she would accept his invitation.

Meanwhile, Brianna realized that she could not push him any further today. So she quickly replied,

"OK, Michael. Let's do it. Tell me what time on Sunday and I'll be ready."

"The jet will be ready for you at Teterboro Airport. Departure at 1 p.m. sharp on Sunday," said Michael.

Brianna had no intention of flying on the corporate jet with

Michael. However, she went along with Michael at the time because he seemed so excited about her joining him.

Sunday, October 18, 2020

On Sunday morning, Brianna texted Michael at 8 a.m. "Michael, I am so sorry, but I won't be able to make it to the jet at 1 p.m. as planned. My dog Conan is recovering from surgery and he pulled out his stitches again last night. I have to take him to the vet today and I am not sure how long it will take. As soon as we are finished, I will grab a commercial flight and meet you in San Francisco. We can meet up for breakfast tomorrow".

"Fine, I see how it is," texted Michael at 8:02 a.m.

Later that afternoon, Brianna, Nathan, and Toby boarded their flight to San Francisco. Nathan had booked the hotel room right next to Brianna's so they could conduct surveillance.

Monday, October 19, 2020

On Monday bright and early, Brianna texted Michael several times, but he never responded. So, she went down to the restaurant and decided to work, hoping that he would eventually come down.

About 10 a.m., Michael finally strolled in. He looked like he had slept in his clothes and his eyes were bloodshot. Brianna took a breath to compose herself.

"Good morning, Michael. Late night, huh?" said Brianna cheerfully.

"You don't know the half of it, Brianna," grunted Michael.

"Well, sit down and tell me all about it. And let's get you a coffee, too," said Brianna. "How did the poker tournament go for you this weekend?"

Michael shook his head and then put his head on the table.

"That good, huh?" asked Brianna.

"It was a bloodbath. Can't you see the blood stains on my clothes?" said Michael.

"Oh, no! How much did you lose?" asked Brianna.

"Everything." said Michael.

"Everything? You mean your $100K?" asked Brianna.

"No, I mean everything. How could I be so stupid?" said Michael to himself.

"I don't understand. What's going on Michael?" asked Brianna.

"I was on this winning streak . . . like never before. I was all the way up to four-hundred grand. Then I got a straight flush. So, I went all in," said Michael.

"And then?" asked Brianna nervously.

"An ass from Canada had a royal flush and stole the game from me," said Michael.

"So you lost your one hundred grand and what you had won? That's awful but not everything," said Brianna.

"Nope. I don't give up that easily. I signed a marker with the house for one hundred thousand to keep playing. And each time I lost, I signed another marker. I was sure that I would at least eventually break even," said Michael

"But you did not break even, did you?" asked Brianna.

"No, I am in the hole five hundred thousand, and it is due in thirty days," said Michael.

"Wow! Michael, that is a lot of money. But you are a remarkably successful and wealthy man. I am sure you can figure something out," said Brianna.

"Brianna, I don't have any assets. Each of my ex-wives committed highway robbery and took large sums of my wealth. Everything else I have lost. I don't even own my Manhattan apartment . . . I am renting it. My life hasn't sucked this badly since Juliette broke my heart two weeks before I graduated from the U.S. Naval Academy," said Michael.

He could never understand why whenever he felt insecure about something his mind would instantly drift to Juliette. They had met during their junior year in high school. She was the first woman he had ever loved. She was beautiful and smart, the total package, and the object of every high school boy's fantasy. And she had chosen him. Just like his mother, Juliette adored him, stroked his ego, and made him feel like God. Michael and Juliette were inseparable their last two years of high school and were crowned prom king and queen. When she left for Stanford and he went to the Naval Academy, they promised to stay committed to one another, get married after graduation, and live happily ever after.

But Juliette turned out to be unfaithful, just like every other woman Michael had ever known. She found someone else, broke up with Michael, and married that other guy six months later. To add insult to injury, his buddies at the Academy had constantly harassed him when he would talk about her or show her picture to them. They would say, "Man, there is no way that this woman is your girlfriend. She is way too hot! But, if it makes you feel better, keep on pretending, buddy!" He had been so excited to finally introduce Juliette to his friends at graduation, and then she had dumped him two weeks earlier. For years afterwards, whenever he saw his friends, they would always ask him how his pretend girlfriend was doing. Well, Michael would show them; he would show everyone. He would be so successful that he could get any woman he wanted!

"Michael, I am so very sorry to hear all of this. I am here. How can I help you?" asked Brianna. Brianna knew that she had to tread lightly because Michael seemed so vulnerable.

Michael's thoughts shifted back to the present. "Thanks,

Brianna. We are supposed to be meeting with GenTech this afternoon about BalanceVITA. But I just cannot do it. Would you please have Denise cancel the meeting? Then, what I would really like to do is play hooky today. Would you play hooky with me?" asked Michael.

"There is nothing that would delight me more. Why don't you have some breakfast, and we can plan our day?" said Brianna.

After Michael freshened up, they met downstairs in the hotel lobby. As they looked out over the bay, the sky was still orange and smoke-filled from the wildfires.

"Does the bad luck ever end?" said Michael, seemingly to himself.

"It is still pretty bad out there. What would you like to do on our hooky day, Michael?" asked Brianna.

"Come to think of it. I would much rather go back up to my suite, watch something on TV, and just chill. Will you join me, Brianna?" asked Michael.

Brianna had no choice at this point. "Of course, Michael, I would be delighted," said Brianna.

They made their way up to Michael's suite at the Ritz-Carlton, which was luxurious. Brianna noticed that Michael was getting text messages, and she needed to keep him focused on her.

"Michael, this is your hooky day. Turn off your phone! The F Place can survive one day without you and me!" said Brianna.

"OK, only if you turn yours off, too, Brianna," said Michael.

"Deal," said Brianna.

They ordered a pot of coffee and two big bowls of popcorn. Then, after a brief debate about what to watch, they settled in on the sofas to binge-watch the first season of *The Office*. Michael needed something to laugh about, given the high anxiety in his life.

Brianna made herself comfortable with a blanket on one couch and Michael settled in on the other.

A few episodes in, Michael came and sat next to Brianna. They were both laughing hysterically, and if someone did not know better, it would have seemed they were old friends.

After finishing the six episodes in Season 1, Michael declared, "It's time for happy hour. What do you fancy to drink, Brianna?"

"I would love a nice merlot. What about you, Michael?" asked Brianna.

"Merlot it is," said Michael and he rang his butler to bring up two bottles of their best merlot and a refill of popcorn.

The butler arrived within minutes and poured them their wine. Taking a sip of her wine, Brianna gave Michael a sultry look and smiled. "Cheers to making time for fun, Michael!" said Brianna.

They watched another four episodes, and, for a short while, Brianna got lost in the storyline while she nursed her glass of wine. She almost forgot why she was there in the first place and realized she needed to move things along with Michael before he drank too much and passed out.

"Michael, if you were a character on *The Office*, who would you be?" asked Brianna, acting a little tipsy.

"Good question, beautiful! Let me see . . . Michael Scott, the well-intentioned, self-centered manager is a likable guy and has a great name, but unlike me, he is not smart. Then, there is Dwight Schrute, the nerdy salesman by day and beet farmer by night, but he is so ridiculous it's sad. Nope, I am definitely not a Dwight. Well, that leaves Jim Halpert, the intelligent, lovable guy who gets a kick out of practical jokes. I guess I would be Jim. What about you?" said Michael.

"Am I Angela Martin, the stuck up, cat-loving accountant who is head of the party planning committee? I think not! No, my character starts off shy but then grows in assertiveness. She is smart, creative, and artistic. And . . . she falls in love with Jim. I would be Pam Beesly," said Brianna.

"Oooh . . . that means our screen characters hook up, Brianna. What do you think about that?" asked Michael, clearly intoxicated.

"You mean like we almost did several years ago, Mikey?" said Brianna amused.

Michael inched his way closer to Brianna and put his arm around her. She was uncomfortable but kept her cool. "Yes, something like that," said Michael excitedly.

"You were a mentor to me for years, and now you are my boss! I respect you far too much to damage our professional relationship, Mikey," said Brianna with a sly smile.

"This would not damage our relationship, Brianna; it would enhance it. Take us to another level," said Michael.

"How so, Mikey?" asked Brianna, leaning in closer.

"It would make us closer, more intimate. Just imagine what we could do together, Brianna. We would be a force to be reckoned with in the industry!" said Michael, slurring his words.

"That does sound appealing. But, in all honesty I thought that it was you and Frita who were the force to be reckoned with. You seem to trust and value her so much more than you do me these days. I mean, I know that she is older than me, certainly more wrinkly than me, but wiser? I would think not!" said Brianna nervously. Brianna knew that Michael loved to play the part of being the chivalrous man and she had hit a soft spot with him.

"Brianna, you know as well as I do that it is really lonely at the top. Frita has been there for me these last couple of years. I owe her for that, and I do trust her," said Michael.

Brianna knew this was the turning point moment and that

she had better make sure it turned out in her favor. Brianna coyly responded, "Well, you and I have known each other for a long time. I feel a certain way about you, but I'm not sure it's being reciprocated in the same way. You know I don't like to play second fiddle," Brianna teased. "So, you have to make a choice, Michael. It's pretty simple. Close your eyes and imagine the three of us are characters in *The Office*. Frita is Angela, I am Pam, and you are Jim. Who do you trust more? Angela or Pam?" said Brianna flirtatiously.

Michael looked into Brianna's eyes and said, "If given the choice, I choose you . . . Pammy . . . hands down, every time." said Michael.

Brianna smiled and leaned in towards Michael. "Michael, you are the CEO of The F Place. Of course you have the choice. So, please tell me what is really going on with HappyVITA, BalanceVITA, and the cyber-attack? You have kept me in the dark for far too long, Mikey!" Brianna said, and she gently touched his face.

Michael looked at Brianna, speechless. "Don't you trust me, Mikey?" said Brianna, leaning in so close that she could smell the wine on his breath.

"Yes, but . . . it's a long, complicated story that I don't want to think about it on our hooky day. Can't we discuss this tomorrow and enjoy the evening together, Brianna?" pleaded Michael.

"Michael, this is so tempting, but it is clear that you don't really trust me. You are just saying what you think I want to hear. So . . . I think it is time to call it a night. I'll see you in the morning downstairs for breakfast at seven," said Brianna.

"Please don't go, Brianna. I meant what I said. You and I could be a force in the industry. Together, we can do anything. You have to believe that," said Michael

"Only if you trust me with your life," said Brianna.

"I do. How can I possibly make you understand that, Brianna? I know I've been hard on you, but that's because you are special and, well, you are so black-and-white. Sometimes there are shades of gray," said Michael.

"What do you mean? Give me a specific example, Michael," said Brianna.

"You keep resisting the launch of BalanceVITA. Don't you understand that our future depends on this product being successful . . . no matter what?" said Michael. "You are more focused on checking all of the boxes than you are ringing the cash register. With the inevitable recall of HappyVITA, we have to get BalanceVITA out there now!"

"What do you mean, recall? This is the first time I have heard that!" said Brianna.

"I cannot talk about this; I am sorry that I said anything," said Michael.

"No, you cannot do that. Tell me what the hell is going on! And tell me now, Michael! You said you trust me!" said Brianna.

"I am trusting you with my life. We are in the cone of silence. If you ever say that I told you about this, I will deny it until my last breath. Agreed?" said Michael.

"Agreed. Please continue. What is going on with HappyVITA?" asked Brianna.

"Oh Brianna, where do I begin? Three years ago . . . ," said Michael. Just then the hotel phone rang.

"Don't answer it, Michael. Please continue. What happened three years ago?" asked Brianna.

They tried to ignore the phone, but it kept ringing. Finally, Michael stood up and answered it.

"Hello," said Michael.

"Frita, what is going on?" said Michael, surprised to hear from her. Even though Brianna was sitting on the couch opposite of Michael, she could hear Frita's voice coming through as she was so loud.

"Michael, I've been calling you all day. Why aren't you answering my calls or text messages?" inquired Frita impatiently.

"I don't know why my calls are going to voicemail. My phone must have died," said Michael.

Frita went on to tell Michael she needed to talk to him.

Michael thought there was no way he was going to get into a lengthy discussion with Frita when he had Brianna waiting for him on his hotel room couch. Instead he said, "Listen, it's been a long day, Frita. I just finished a late dinner and am going to bed. Let's talk tomorrow."

Frita was persistent and asked him if he was drinking. To which Michael responded tersely, "Yes, Mother, but only a couple of glasses of wine."

Brianna pretended to be reading emails on her phone while the two of them continued their phone conversation. She couldn't believe the way Frita was interrogating Michael. Just then Frita must have asked him another question, which Brianna couldn't make out to which he snapped, "No, I am not drunk again, Frita!" said Michael. He paused and barked back at her, "Why would you ask me that?"

Brianna could tell that Michael was getting really angry at Frita when this time he yelled into the phone, "Yes, I asked her to join me. She is our Chief Commercial Officer, and GenTech is one of our biggest customers!"

He listed again for a moment.

"You need to stop second-guessing me," said Michael.

After another exchange, he firmly said, "No, I am not going to have that conversation right now. I am hanging up, Frita, as I'm done with this conversation. I'll see you back at the office on Thursday. Good night." Michael slammed down the phone.

Michael refilled his glass of wine and sat down right next to

Brianna. "I'm sorry about that. Where were we, sweetheart?" He continued to put his arm around her, leaned in and kissed her ever so softly.

Brianna carefully pulled back from Michael and said, "Mikey! What was that for?"

"Did I not say to you, if given the choice, I would choose you? Well, I just proved that to you. So, you need to show me how much you appreciate what I just did by giving me a little kiss," said Michael playfully.

"Not so fast, mister. We need to finish our conversation about The F Place. Once we get the work stuff out of the way, then we can . . . play!" said Brianna in a flirty tone.

Michael groaned and said, "You are going to be the death of me, woman . . . ," under his breath.

Brianna picked up her glass of wine, leaned into Michael and said, "You were saying . . . three years ago?"

"Three years ago, in July, I became CEO of The F Place. I worked my entire career to make it to the top. I came from humble beginnings and earned every red cent of my wealth. Do you know about the situation with David Church?" asked Michael.

"I remember David. But what situation are you referring to?" asked Brianna.

"Alexander Wood had been grooming both of us. I was the heir, apparently, and David was the spare. But, when push came to shove, it was a much closer call than I would have liked," said Michael.

"What do you mean?" asked Brianna.

"Once it was clear that Alexander was going to retire, David laid it on thick. He brought in more new business that year, than the previous three years combined," said Michael.

"Why did that matter if you were anointed as the heir?" asked Brianna.

"Sometimes you are so naïve, Brianna. It matters because Alexander started to question whether David should get the throne instead of me. And under no circumstances could I let that happen," said Michael.

"Oh, my goodness, Michael. What did you do?" asked Brianna.

"What does a good captain do? Of course, I called in the big guns," said Michael proudly.

"What does that mean?" asked Brianna.

"It means that I called in a favor with my man, Jimmy Capone. He dug up dirt on David for me and made sure that Alexander just happened to learn about those skeletons in David's closet. And voilà . . . the rest is history," said Michael.

"Holy cow, Mikey!! That sounds like something from a movie. What is with Jimmy? All I know about him is that he is an Italian-American guy from the Bronx, a little rough around the edges, and that he works in IT," she said in dismay. Brianna knew that by stereotyping Jimmy, she could get Michael to take the bait and open up more about his relationship with Jimmy.

"Yeah, that's Jimmy boy, all right. He and I go way back. We went to middle school together and have been fast friends since then. We're brothers, Brianna. We take care of each other. You know? He scratches my back and I scratch his. That's how it's always worked with us, even when we were kids. We're tight, Jimmy and I," said Michael fondly.

"OK, but how is all of this related to HappyVITA and BalanceVITA?" asked Brianna.

"Don't you see, Brianna? That was a huge favor I called in with Jimmy. Once I became the CEO, he made sure that I knew that I was in his debt . . . forever. And with Jimmy's connection to the mafia . . . ," said Michael.

"Are you serious, Michael?" said Brianna.

"Serious as a heart attack," said Michael.

"So, what . . . Jimmy was blackmailing you?" asked Brianna.

"You could put it that way. Like I said, Jimmy and I go way back. Did you ever wonder how we were able to get HappyVITA launched to the marketplace so quickly?" asked Michael as he took several drinks of his wine.

"Well, Mikey, I just assumed that it was your incredible leadership vision, drive, and focus on excellence," said Brianna, trying to lighten the mood.

Michael looked into Brianna's eyes and smiled. "Yes, it was certainly all of those things and then some. To accomplish something like that, you have to cut corners here and there. You cannot always go by the book, if you know what I mean," said Michael.

"What does that have to do with Jimmy?" asked Brianna.

"Jimmy was my secret weapon. If I said to jump, he asked how high. If I said to get the clinical trials done in months, not years . . . he made things happen," said Michael.

"What did he do with the clinical trials, Michael?" asked Brianna nervously.

"He found willing participants who had financial hardships and gave them an incentive to participate in the HappyVITA clinical trials," said Michael.

That was a light bulb moment for Brianna. She realized that Jimmy was Dr. George, and the willing participants were the undocumented immigrants like Jose and his family. Her heart started to pound in her chest so loudly that she feared Michael would hear it beating. But she kept her composure on the outside.

"So, you cut a few corners, Michael. But think about all the people who have been helped by HappyVITA. The good outweighs the bad, right?" said Brianna as she leaned into Michael.

"Exactly! Sometimes you have to sacrifice the lives of a few to benefit the many," said Michael.

"What does that mean, Mikey!?" asked Brianna. She could tell that Michael was really drunk by this point and hoped that he would continue spilling the beans.

"It is not my fault that all of those people committed suicide. They would probably have done so with or without HappyVITA. Instead, I focus on all of the people that we have helped," said Michael.

"Is that why you believe a HappyVITA recall is inevitable?" asked Brianna.

"It is only inevitable if the incriminating documents are made public," said Michael.

"What incriminating documents?" asked Brianna.

"The ones that Jimmy thought he could hold over my head. I think I have those buried far away in China. But there is always a risk. You never really know who you can trust!" said Michael.

"Michael, you are so clever. . . . I am having trouble keeping up with you. What do you mean buried in China?" asked Brianna.

"I was inspired by former Secretary of State Hillary. She was able to delete thousands of emails without consequence. I did the next best thing for The F Place, I made thousands of incriminating records disappear. So, Jimmy and his 'family' as well as our government cannot touch us with a 10-foot pole," said Michael.

"How did you make those records disappear, Mikey!?" asked Brianna.

"Brianna, you really are so naïve, and that's one of the many things I love about you. I made those records disappear through my leadership, teamwork, and a timely cyberattack," said Michael.

"Oh, Mikey, your leadership is clear. What do you mean by teamwork? Who helped you?" asked Brianna.

"Brianna, enough with the questions. It is time to move from work to play," said Michael.

"Mikey, just answer this one last question. Who helped you?" asked Brianna as she leaned in and kissed his cheek.

"The entire Executive Team except for you, Brianna. That's what I love about you. You are my good girl to the core. I know you and I never once thought that you would be willing to join us in the 'gray zone,'" said Michael with complete sincerity.

Brianna acted as though she was hurt that he left her out. She tilted her face towards him and asked, "Everyone else was in on this?"

"Yes, everyone except for you, my darling. In a way, I thought I was protecting you. But now I realize I should have confided in you all along. Can you ever forgive me?" asked Michael as he reached over and squeezed Brianna's thigh.

"Of course I can, Mikey! I'll tell you what, I'm going to go to my room to freshen up. I brought a special outfit for this trip that I want to put on for you. You stay exactly where you are. I don't want you to go anywhere. I'll be back soon, love," said Brianna as she poured him another glass of wine. Brianna grabbed her purse from the coffee table and walked out of Michael's room without looking back.

As Brianna walked through the doors of her hotel room, she collapsed in the first chair she saw. She gently pulled the wire out of her purse and whispered right into the microphone. "Please tell me that you guys got all of that. I am about to have a heart attack and need to get out of here now."

There was a knock on Brianna's door. Her heart started pounding so loudly, she was sure the entire hotel floor could hear it. She started praying that it was not Michael. She had not told him her room number, but still she was a little worried.

Who could blame her? Then she peered through the peephole and saw that it was Nathan. Brianna let out a huge sigh of relief and opened the door and quietly let him in.

Nathan smiled at her and said "Nice work, Brianna. We got everything we need and then some. You are absolutely right. We need to leave now, as in ASAP. Grab your things, and we will meet you downstairs by the pool entrance in exactly five minutes," said Nathan. "I'll stay up here while you gather your belongings to make sure that you get to the elevator safely."

Tuesday, October 20, 2020

Just before 6 a.m. Tuesday morning, Brianna walked through her front door and went straight to her bedroom. She, Nathan, and Toby had planned what she would say to Michael about her untimely exit from San Francisco.

Brianna texted Michael. "Mikey! I am so sorry about last night. I lay down on my bed to close my eyes for a few minutes and fell asleep. I was jolted out of my sleep when my hotel phone rang, and it was my daughter on the line. She is in the hospital and they believe it is COVID. I am on my way to the airport now. Can we please take a rain check?"

Given that it was 3 a.m. on the West Coast, Michael was drunk as a skunk last night, and his phone had been turned off, she figured he would not read her text for several hours.

She drifted off to sleep and did not wake up for another twelve hours. She checked her phone and had many unread messages, including one from Michael.

"I hope Ari is OK. I miss you already. How about dinner on Friday night at my place?" Michael texted.

Before responding, Brianna called Nathan.

"Nathan, please tell me that everything is going to proceed as planned . . . just like we discussed." Brianna pleaded.

"Brianna, stay calm. Everything is in motion. You just have a few more days and this will all be over," said Nathan.

"OK, thanks, Nathan. I don't know how I can ever repay you," said Brianna.

"You don't need to repay me, Brianna. This is my job. It is what I do!" said Nathan.

With that reassurance, Brianna responded to Michael's text. "Thanks, Mikey! Friday night sounds amazing."

Brianna planned to work remotely on Wednesday to focus on catching up on work that she had missed during the last few days.

Thursday, October 22, 2020

Brianna woke up at 4:30 a.m., determined to get in a long run before heading into the office. She thought to herself, "This is going to be a day that will be remembered forever." She started feeling a little anxious and, as she always did, took a few deep breaths to calm herself.

As she stepped out on to the street and made her way to Central Park, the crisp, cold morning air hit her and further activated her mind. She wondered how the day would unfold and wanted to fast-forward a bit, and then she was reminded of a quote she had read from Vera Nazarian: "Would you like to know your future? If your answer is yes, think again. Not knowing is the greatest life motivator. So, enjoy, endure, survive each moment as it comes to you in its proper sequence—a surprise." Wise words, she thought, as she knew better than anyone else that life is fleeting and impermanent. As she ran, her mind drifted to the events that had taken place this year— 2020 was such a chaotic year and looked nothing like she had envisioned at the start.

While there were a few bright spots in her life, as she

thought about The F Place, it was all disquieted and repulsive. The global pandemic, the unnecessary layoff of thousands of employees, the corporate political warfare, the betrayals, the fraud, and the never-ending toxicity. "Is this really my life?" she asked herself. What Brianna wanted most was the freedom to write her one-of-a-kind life story without having to choose between a meaningful career that makes a positive difference in the world and being a loving and generous mother to her treasured children.

Brianna thought about Michael. He was so intelligent and driven, handsome and charismatic, yet lacking in integrity and emotional intelligence. He had so much promise early in life, but somewhere along the way, he had lost himself and had become a broken man who left a trail of broken people in his wake.

Her thoughts quickly shifted to Frita. Brianna's skin crawled at the thought of her. Frita was conniving, self-centered, boastful, vain, patronizing, and just pure evil. It was unbelievable for Brianna to think of how that woman stirred up conflict everywhere she went. She seemed to grow in power every time she belittled someone else. She had sarcastic comments about everyone except for Michael and the Board. While at times they seemed small, they were designed to hurt people.

As Brianna's pace evened out, her attention turned to Edward next. She thought of how Edward was a pawn in all this and did not even know it yet. Then there was Isaac. He was so young, and when he had joined The F Place, there was such a promising future ahead for him. That kid has so much potential . . . all of which he had wasted on The F Place. Brianna inhaled the fresh air deeply and cringed at the fact that each and every single one of them had crossed the line, one inch at a time. Well, today, they would all regret the day that they walked through the doors of The F Place.

Brianna made her way back to her place to get ready. She was thankful that the run had helped her to clear her head and given her an extra boost of much-needed mental energy. Given the significance of the day, Brianna decided to dress up and look her absolute best. She knew exactly what she would wear to make her entrance. Brianna thought about how in her Indian heritage, white was the standard color for the grieving members of the deceased. She decided to dress herself in an off-white wool suit with a cream-colored silk blouse underneath it. She recalled that she had the suit custom-made in Singapore during her last visit there with Michael. They had gone to see several potential customers there as Singapore's pharmaceutical market had been anticipated to grow to almost double digits over the next fifteen years. Michael had insisted that Brianna meet with his tailor on that trip. Brianna still remembered that trip fondly. She could not believe how the tailor had turned around four custom-made suits for Brianna within twenty-four hours and the price was so reasonable. During that visit Brianna recalled how Michael would always look at her so appreciatively. Brianna had made it clear to him a long time ago that their relationship was going to be purely professional.

Brianna worked hard for her body. At 5 feet, 5 inches, 127 pounds, Brianna looked like she was barely 30. She loved to dress up for work and often shopped abroad so that her wardrobe would not be replicated by anyone else in her circle. Looking at herself in the mirror, she knew that she looked professionally stunning. Her long brown hair glistened from the bright light from her closet chandelier. She quickly glanced at the time and slipped on her jewelry before she swiftly made her way to The F Place.

As usual, Brianna arrived in the boardroom early to do her final preparations before the executive leadership meeting. Michael walked in a few minutes before 8 a.m. and went to his usual spot at the head of the table. He looked at Brianna admiringly and smiled. "Good morning, Brianna. Wow, don't you look stunning today." Brianna smiled back at him, fully knowing that the suit she had on would remind him of their trip to Singapore. When they had gone to pick up the suits, Michael had told her that this was his favorite out of the lot. She joked to Michael, "I wish I would've known then to ask your tailor to make me a matching mask for each of my suits."

Michael laughed but could not take his eyes off Brianna. He thought to himself, "She truly is a stunningly beautiful woman." He admired the way that she was always so sure of herself. She was everything he wanted in a life partner: smart, gorgeous, funny, and one of a kind. Then like an awkward schoolboy he nervously whispered across the room, "Brianna, I have to confess. I cannot wait for tomorrow night!"

Brianna winked and flashed back a playful smile at him, "Thank you, Mikey. I am flattered. Indeed, tomorrow night will be very memorable and unlike anything you have ever experienced before!"

Shortly after, the rest of the Executive Team walked in and took their places six feet apart in the boardroom. They were supposed to be wearing masks, but as usual no one bothered to do so. At 8 a.m. sharp, Michael kicked off the meeting and then handed it over to Frita.

"Thank you, Michael. As you all know, employee engagement has declined by 17 percent this year. This is not just an HR problem; this is a leadership problem," said Frita.

Brianna decided that she would jump right in and get to it. "Frita, I wholeheartedly agree with you. This really is a leadership problem that needs to be fixed. How do you propose we fix it?" asked Brianna.

Frita looked at Michael, expecting him to jump to her rescue, but he was nodding his head in agreement with Brianna.

Irritated now, Frita looked away and turned to snap at Brianna "Well, sweet pea, we will get to that shortly. My team has worked tirelessly now for weeks to prepare this employee engagement packet. I need each of you to review it and put together your improvement plan," commanded Frita.

"So, Frita, if I understand correctly, and I certainly do, as you've made it abundantly clear for everyone here—are you really telling us that you do not have a plan? You came into this meeting today simply to tell us that we need to create a plan?" The others looked on in disbelief. Someone was finally going head-to-head with Frita, and for the first time ever Frita looked a bit nervous. Brianna knew all eyes were on her now, and she had commanded everyone's attention around the table. For added effect Brianna leaned back in her chair and crossed her arms. "Frita, please help us to understand exactly what value you and your HR team are adding to this process?" questioned Brianna confidently.

Frita started to twitch in discomfort. She regretted wearing her Spanx today. Between the wide Gucci belt that she had on her trousers, the Spanx, and the three-inch stilettos, she was feeling a bit suffocated. She had overslept this morning and was mad at herself for not taking the time to look as good as Brianna. She was having trouble concentrating on the conversation at hand and was taken aback by Brianna. She started to think to herself, "How dare she interrogate me like this? Who does she think she is?" After all this was said and done, she would make sure Brianna never returned to The F Place again. She wanted to lunge at Brianna and drag her out of the boardroom.

"I am sure that it was her looks that got her this far," thought Frita. Well, little did she know that Michael was on Frita's side. "Oh yes, Michael," she thought to herself. Frita knew that Michael would back her up. All she had to do was give him the cue that she normally did. She cleared her throat and flashed him a pleading look as if she was a poor little puppy dog that needed a pat on the head. It worked every time, and she expected that he was going to jump in and shut Brianna up once and for all.

Much to Frita's dismay, he did not. Frita paused again and wondered what had gotten into Michael today. He seemed so distant yet content. She did a mental run-through of all the events that had led up to this moment. She had told Michael exactly what she planned on doing, and he had given her the green light. Yet here he was just letting her fall down this slippery slope without even offering her a hand.

Frita decided she would play the video that she had asked the communications team to develop for her. Soon after this meeting she would ask her assistant to send it out company wide. It was Frita sharing the takeaways from the employee engagement survey. Frita was pretty proud of herself as she was going to teach this group a thing or two about engagement. Before she asked Denise to play the video, she told the group that her HR team had the highest employee engagement out of all the organizations at The F Place. The video was only a few minutes long, and that would give Frita the time she needed to collect her thoughts and recompose herself.

Why was Michael not looking at her, she wondered? Then Frita glanced in Brianna's direction and felt intimidated for the first time. "Look at her, just sitting there so comfortably. She's busy looking at her phone instead of paying attention to my video," thought Frita.

Just then it was the army of footsteps coming down the hall that caught everyone's attention at the same time. Michael turned to Lizzy and asked her to see what the commotion was about. As Lizzy started to get up, the doors to the boardroom were flung open, and suddenly inside the boardroom there were a dozen or so FBI agents who quickly barged in. There was no mistaking that these were FBI agents. They were all dressed alike in dark blue nylon jackets with the prominent yellow letters "FBI" on them.

Frita screamed out loud first. Tom blurted out next, "What the hell is going on here? Is that the FBI? Why are you here? What is happening?"

Kathleen jumped in, saying, "Quiet, everyone." Brianna was so relieved to see the blue jackets coming in. She looked in Michael's direction first. He was looking around the room in total dismay and shock. She could see how scared and upset he looked. Next was Frita; there was an instant breakout of sweat on her face, and she looked like she was about to have a heart attack.

All eyes moved to the front of the room towards agents Nathan Price, Donald Clooney, and Greg Butterfinger. They stood there for what seemed like countless minutes as the rest of the agents took over the entire boardroom and spread out in equal distance. They all had dark blue masks on. They seemed to be respirators. Agent Price stepped forward a few inches, flashed his badge and put his hand securely over his holster.

"All right, everyone stays exactly where you are. Do not move. This meeting is over. You are all under arrest," said Nathan firmly. He continued to read them their rights: "You have the right to remain silent. Anything you say can and will be used against you in a court of law. You have the right to an attorney. If you cannot afford an attorney, one will be provided for you. Is that clear?"

Isaac and Frita looked at Kathleen and asked her to do something. Kathleen began, "Officer, I am the Chief Legal Officer for The F Place. What is going on here?"

Nathan replied, "Ms. Kane, we know exactly who you are. Let me remind you that you are under arrest, and you do have the right to remain silent."

Frita locked eyes with Donald Clooney. "Toby, what the F?" she asked. And then everything that had transpired between them flashed between her eyes.

Everyone looked helpless and confused. There was nothing to do but comply with the agents. FBI agents proceeded to handcuff each of The F Place executive leaders, except for Brianna. Agent Donald (a.k.a. Toby) had quietly and securely moved Brianna to a corner in the front of the room and told her that he would call her later to check in on her. Brianna watched in disbelief at the arrests taking place in front of her. She finally felt such a huge sense of relief. It had been such an incredibly long stretch of ongoing stress these past months, and finally it was all coming to an end for her. She wished Donald would have taken her to her office instead of her having to witness all this.

The few employees who were in the office that day had gathered outside of the boardroom, their faces in shock as they watched their executive leadership team being walked out in handcuffs. Most of them had their phones out and took photos as one by one each leader was being escorted out. The FBI had to slow it down as there were only two elevators. Little did Brianna know that within the hour, The F Place leadership team arrest would be all over social media.

"Get your hands off me. Wait, what about Brianna? Why isn't she in handcuffs, too?" screeched Frita.

Frita looked confused again as she saw Brianna standing in the front corner of the boardroom. She scowled at her. Brianna decided that this would be a good time to give clarity to Frita on what was happening. As she started to make her way across the room, Brianna thought to herself, "God, I better say what I have to say now, because who knows if I'll ever see Frita again?"

Nathan saw Brianna walking towards Frita and quickly

gave her a thumbs-up to let her know that it was OK. Brianna walked up and stood a few feet from Frita. Frita looked so hideous and angry. Her belt had somehow loosened and the double "GGs" on her belt were hanging sideways. She looked so disoriented and disheveled. Brianna wished so badly she could have Frita see her full expression so she could see her reaction, but because the FBI had made her wear her mask, she looked at Frita in the eyes.

With as much calmness as she could find within herself, Brianna started. "Frita, I am not in handcuffs because unlike you, I am not guilty of any wrongdoing here. My hypothesis is that you're going to have plenty of time to think about all the ways you did not live out the five Fs in our F Place core values. Instead of being FIRST, you're now last. Instead of being FAST, you're now slow. Instead of being FOCUSED, you're distracted. Instead of being FLEXIBLE, you're rigid. Finally, your FUTURE, well I'd say it looks a little bleak! Also, I guess employee engagement is no longer your problem because by the looks of it out there in the hall, people seem pretty engaged with their phones and are dying to get a picture of you walking out of here in those metal bracelets with your hands behind your back."

Without another thought Brianna started to head towards her office and ended up locking eyes with Michael as he was being escorted out. Brianna started to feel sorry for him. She was quickly reminded of how careless and reckless he had been with his decisions. As soon as that realization hit her, she started to look away from him.

Michael on the other hand was still in shock. He was speechless and he knew that there was no point in saying anything, not a single word. The words that the FBI agent blurted out still echoed in his mind "You have the right to remain silent. . . ." As he saw Brianna leave the boardroom, he knew that he had underestimated her, and she had outsmarted him. This was her way of giving him, Frita, and the rest of the leadership team the one-finger salute. It was the checkmate of the century! The one thing Michael never doubted of Brianna was how clever she was.

Less than an hour later after the arrests of the century, Brianna's phone rang, and it was Alexander Wood. "Brianna, I understand that today has been quite an eventful day at The F Place," Alexander said.

Brianna snorted. "That's the understatement of the year, Mr. Wood."

Alexander sounded serious when he said, "Brianna, you and I need to talk about the future of The F Place. Would you please meet me at the Four Seasons for lunch at noon tomorrow? I'll have my secretary send a car for you."

Alexander had spent the last couple of weeks working with Nathan Price and the FBI to ensure that justice was delivered, no matter what. After discussing the situation with Brianna and reading through the "Christian dossier," Alexander had been overcome with guilt and anger. He was the one who had groomed Michael all those years and selected him over David Church. The only question in Alexander's mind was how deep within the organization the corruption went. Regardless, Alexander realized that hundreds and possibly thousands of people had died because of The F Place . . . indirectly because of his own decisions. Once Alexander and Nathan had their game plan in motion, Alexander called an emergency Board of Directors meeting one day before the FBI takedown.

"Mark, Brian, Isabella, Lexi, Parker, Olivia, Jacob, and John, thank you for joining me on such short notice and for using discretion. What I am about to share with you must be kept with the strictest of confidence due to the ongoing FBI investigation. I will forewarn you, what I share with you today will sound more like something out of a blockbuster Hollywood thriller than a global pharmaceutical company . . . but it is absolutely true, and it happened on my watch," Alexander declared as he kicked off the meeting.

Alexander proceeded to bring the Board up to speed on the latest developments of the case, including the fact that they had just secured critical evidence that would likely result in the arrest and prosecution of the entire Executive Team with the exception of Brianna Grimaldi. The eight Board members sat in complete shock as they digested the unexpected news from Alexander.

Finally, Brian Hughes broke the ice and spoke first. "Alexander, I am finding all of this a little difficult to believe. How in the hell could something like this happen at The F Place? I am utterly flabbergasted!"

"Believe me, Brian, I have been asking myself that same thing. Here is my assessment of the situation, based upon where things stand at this time. Our first mistake, or shall I say, *my* first mistake was endorsing Michael for CEO. Hindsight is twenty-twenty, and I can see now that there were red flags and signs of his dysfunctional power-hungry behavior, which I had mistaken for honest ambition. As soon as I stepped down to retire in July 2017 and passed the baton to Michael, he pushed out all but two of the Executive Team leaders. As the new CEO, it was his right to put his own fingerprints on the company and set up his own leadership team, but I had hoped that he would have built upon the foundations of the past rather than essentially starting from scratch with a new Executive Team. But that alone would not have created the situation we are in today," said Alexander.

"OK, Alexander, we promoted the wrong CEO for the job. We all know that the tone is set at the top; the company culture will be a reflection of the CEO. But how did we end up with murders, corruption, fraud, and an FBI investigation?" asked Isabella Busseau.

"Firstly, the company mission and values that we created back in 2001 have become nothing more than marketing words, and, quite frankly, I am disgusted by that. Those were fundamental elements of the one-of-a-kind culture that I personally spearheaded with Pat Pierson and The COMO Group when The F Place was founded. Secondly, I believe the force multiplier in this corrupt circus was Frita Fernandez. I was irritated by how Michael treated Pat and probably should have injected myself into that situation. But Michael was adamant that he needed Frita as his Chief People Officer to implement his vision of Transformation for the company. He and Frita had known each other for years and he trusted her. So, against my better judgment, I trusted him," sighed Alexander.

"Alexander, you handed him a well-oiled machine when he took over. There wasn't anything he needed to fix, per se; he just needed to keep improving. And yet, how many Board meetings did Michael share with us that he was going to grow through Transformation? He had a grand plan to accelerate new product development, expand the China hub, and optimize processes and systems while reducing costs, but it seems to me that what he really did was Transform the company into the ground. What am I missing here?" asked a clearly frustrated Parker Reid.

"Michael gave far too much power to Frita and her HR organization. When HR is led by leaders with a servant's heart who truly love people . . . like Pat Pierson . . . they can create an employee-focused culture with low turnover, high employee engagement, and outstanding organizational wellness. But, when HR is led by leaders motivated by money, power, or dare I say sex, rather than serving, it can end in disaster.

Think about it—HR has access to all employee compensation, performance reviews, succession plans, training plans, personality assessments, and even leadership coaching and performance improvement plans. In the wrong hands, that kind of information can destroy a company from within," said Alexander.

"We have all met with Frita on numerous occasions. She sure seems to me like she loves her job and is a people person. What makes you think that her negative influence within The F Place has been such a key factor in this situation?" asked Lexi Bellissimo.

"Because the FBI has revealed new information to me about her past, which I am not at liberty to share with you, unfortunately," said Alexander.

"OK, then what else can you share, Alexander?" asked Olivia Cheval, clearly frustrated.

"I believe that the slippery slope started with HappyVITA. When I was CEO, I pushed Michael and his team to accelerate the timelines. Every good leader should challenge their team to accomplish more than they believe is possible. What I didn't expect was that Michael would authorize illegal activities in order to rise to my challenge. We should have had better checks and balances. As a leader, I should have gone deeper and looked under the covers to understand how the team was shaving time from the FDA approval and launch. That's on me. I have since learned that Michael pushed Edward Ferris, Torsten Schmidt, and Jimmy Capone to cross several illegal lines to deliver that product. And people died because of it. I also have a sneaking suspicion that Michael was doing something questionable with the books, which is why he had a revolving door of CFOs. That's being investigated right now, but I am pretty certain that we will have financial restatements in our future," said Alexander.

"That's just great! The F Place is going down, and we all know it!" exclaimed Mark Trivedi.

"Not so fast, Mark. I believe we can move forward from this. Please stay with me. I have a few more revelations to share and then we can talk strategy," requested Alexander.

"OK, let's move on," said Brian.

"As I was saying, I learned from the FBI that Kathleen Kane, the Chief Legal Officer, is also Michael's personal attorney. I honestly had no idea about that either. Clearly, he was circling the wagons to protect himself legally on all fronts. The FBI also shared that Michael and Frita have confirmed ties to the late Jeffrey Epstein. Something tells me that this scandal has some very evil roots! But we will let the FBI do their job and sort all of that out!" said Alexander.

"I don't know about you all, but my head is about to explode. Is there anything positive that we can hang our hats on, Alexander? Anything at all?" asked Jacob Messi.

"Jacob, I am glad you asked, because that is where I wanted to go next. Although Michael and Frita managed to bring the rest of the Executive Team into their corrupt little scandal, there was one leader who stood alone and did not join in. And that leader is Brianna Grimaldi. She joined The F Place right after college, held a variety of progressive leadership roles, and worked her way up to Chief Commercial Officer. You all have spent a little time with her since she we promoted her in 2018. Unlike Michael and Frita, Brianna is the real deal. She knows her stuff, she has phenomenal relationships with our customers and she genuinely cares about the people of The F Place. She invests in the people around her and inspires them to greatness. For the past ten years or so, she has been the highest exporter of talent across virtually all functions within the company," said Alexander.

"I'd like to believe that—I really would. But with everything that you've revealed here today, how can we know for certain that Brianna is innocent and squeaky-clean from the corruption of The F Place?" asked John.

"Because she risked everything two days ago to help the FBI collect evidence to prosecute Michael, Frita, and the rest of the Executive Team. She has more integrity, intelligence, courage, and empathy than any other leader that I know. And ladies and gentlemen, if we want The F Place to survive, she must be our next CEO! She is the only one who can turn this ship around. Otherwise, we need to right these wrongs as best we can and close our doors forever," said Alexander.

Friday, October 23, 2020

The following day, Brianna walked into the Four Seasons. She had arrived a few minutes early, and as she was being escorted to the table, she found that Alexander was already seated. What surprised Brianna was that four other Board of Directors members were with him.

Alexander got up to greet Brianna and smiled. He offered, "Please sit down, Brianna. I hope that you don't mind that I've invited a few of my colleagues to join us. I believe you met all of them at our last couple of Board meetings." Brianna smiled and greeted Olivia, Lexi, Parker, and John by name. Handshakes were a thing of the past, so instead they tapped elbows and they all had a laugh.

As Brianna settled in, Alexander started. "We have much to discuss today. I know I've surprised you by bringing in members of the Board, but we have an important matter that requires us all to be here," said Alexander. He went on to indulge Brianna in a little detail that he had been hiding. Alexander had been working closely with the FBI and was well aware of the evolution in the case, including her wiretap in San Francisco earlier in the week. He had been asked by Greg Butterfinger not to disclose anything to Brianna. "Given everything that has transpired, what are your plans for the future, Brianna?" asked Alexander.

"With a few notable exceptions who shall remain nameless, I love the people of this company. I believe in The F Place, and I want to help rebuild it so that we can truly shine a light and help the people of this world," said Brianna.

"In full transparency, Brianna, none of us would blame you if you wanted to pack your bags and leave The F Place forever. However, we were hoping that you would want to stick around and play a key role in turning this company around. It truly is a shame that we are in this position today, and the Board, myself included, certainly takes the blame for promoting Michael, but none of us could have predicted that things would come to this," said Alexander.

"Alexander, John, Lexi, Olivia and Parker, I appreciate that you made the time to meet with me today. This week has been the most insane week of my life, and 2020 as a whole has been so chaotic, stressful, and frightening, to be honest. Call me crazy, but even though Michael, Frita, and the Executive Team are sitting in jail cells right now, I still believe in The F Place. So, you can count on my full support in making our company great again!" said Brianna with a slight smile.

Alexander smiled back at Brianna and then made eye contact with John, Lexi, Olivia, and Parker. "Brianna, you have no idea how pleased we are with your decision to stay at The F Place. What is the first thing you believe this company needs in order to get moving in the right direction?" asked Alexander.

"Well, clearly we need a new President and CEO, someone with rich industry experience and who has the utmost integrity— someone who will right all of these wrongs and create a new vision of the FUTURE for the company. Alexander, we need you to come back and join us!" said Brianna with passion.

"Brianna, I agree with almost everything you just said. Yes, we need a new leader, but no, that leader is not me. My time has already come and gone. It is time for a new leader to rise up and lead. And the Board and I believe that new leader should be you!" said Alexander with pride.

Brianna took a deep breath and composed herself. She did not see that coming, although she probably should have. As if on cue, she smiled at them warmly. "I'm truly honored that you would consider me for this vital role. This company means so much to me, and I know firsthand the potential that it has. All of that being said, with the departure of Michael and the Executive Team, this is a huge shake-up! Not just for our thousands of employees but also for our customers and investors. It is going to take a herculean effort to turn things around. Our stock has already plummeted by 70 percent. I wish I could give you a definitive answer today, but I'm going to need some time to think things over. Nevertheless, it goes without saying that I will lead this company in the days and weeks ahead until we are fully aligned on my future role and strategy going forward," said Brianna.

She could tell that the others were surprised by her response. Who wouldn't jump at the opportunity to take on such an incredible role? But Brianna knew that if she was going to be successful, she needed to get full alignment and backing on her plan.

Alexander nodded at Brianna, and she continued. "While I sincerely appreciate the vote of confidence, I will need the full support and backing of the Board for my plan if you want me to lead the turnaround of The F Place. So, please give me a little time to formulate my proposed strategy. I mean it—I will need your unconditional support! We will need to transform the company from a culture of fear and lies to a culture of freedom and truth. I know that this will be an incredibly difficult and expensive journey, but with your support and the help of a trusted partner, I believe we can do it. Let's reconvene in three weeks," said Brianna with passion and assertation.

Alexander, pleased with himself, turned to his colleagues and said, "Ladies and gentlemen, I rest my case." The others nodded in agreement. Alexander grabbed Brianna's shoulder and said, "This is exactly why you are the right leader for this role. We wouldn't expect anything less from you, Ms. Grimaldi. Would it be fair if you gave us your formal response by the middle of the month? Also, given that the elections are coming up and that we still have a lot of cleanup to do in the media from the blowup with Michael and the team, it probably makes sense for us to take our time before we make any public announcements to our investors."

Alexander beamed at Brianna and added, "We fully expect you to say yes when we meet next, and we will be ready to celebrate. It goes without saying, we wouldn't be having this conversation with you if we didn't believe that you were the right woman for the job."

Brianna thanked them again for the consideration. They finished their meals and agreed that they would all reconvene in three weeks' time. She told the group she'd be in touch soon. She couldn't wait to run out the door and call Justin, her mother, her kids, and Kate to share this incredible news.

As she walked out from her meeting, she got a text from Eshan "Mom, I miss you. Ari said you are having a big Thanksgiving dinner; can I come?" Brianna's heart pounded hard, and she immediately responded to him. "Eshan you have no idea how happy I am to hear from you. I love you, and of course I'd love nothing more than to spend Thanksgiving with you and Ari."

Book Discussion

CONTINUE WITH US on the journey of The F Place. Would you like to learn more about what happens to Michael, Frita, and the rest of the leadership team after the epic FBI bust? Are you curious about how The F Place will Transform under Brianna's leadership?

If you want to keep with what's happening at The F Place, visit us at www.thefplace.com.

1. Did the characters seem believable to you? Why or why not?

2. Did the characters remind you of anyone, personally or professionally?

3. Which character did you relate to the most and why? What impact did that individual have on you?

4. How were the values applied by the various characters, and how did it impact the people and culture?

5. Have you ever encountered someone like Frita, and what did you learn from the book that would better help you to work with this kind of personality?

6. Similar to Alexander, have you ever had to courageously admit that you made a wrong decision? How did you own that decision, and what would you do differently today?

7. How did Michael's leadership style affect the culture and the performance of the company? How will you apply this lesson in your circle of influence?

8. What lessons did you learn about personal Transformation? How will you apply these lessons?

9. What lessons did you learn about professional Transformation? How will you apply these lessons?

10. Could the story have taken place in your workplace and/or your personal life?

11. How did you feel about the parental styles and the long-term influence that they had on the characters?

12. To what extent do you believe that people can change their mindset from what they learned in childhood?

13. Kate was a trusted promise partner to Brianna. What impact did that have on Brianna as she was undergoing her Transformation? How do you leverage your trusted circle of influence in your Transformation?

14. Given that several relationships in the book ended in divorce, what are the pros and cons of each scenario? What can we do individually and collectively to improve harmony within our communities, post-divorce?

15. What do you believe were three pieces of evidence that demonstrated successful Transformation in the book? How can you apply these lessons to your own Transformation?

16. The F Place under Brianna's leadership will inevitably need to undergo a Transformation. What do you believe be three critical success factors of true Transformation in the future for The F Place?

BONUS CHAPTER
The Future Looks Bright

November 2020

"There are far better things ahead than any we leave behind."

—*C.S. Lewis*

Sunday, November 1, 2020

BRIANNA WAS STILL heady with excitement at the thought of taking on the role of CEO. She knew that in less than two weeks, she would present her proposed strategy to Alexander and the Board. And if they supported it, she would accept their offer to serve as the next President and CEO of The F Place.

She was optimistic that they would back her Transformation strategy, but she needed to be sure. The world seemed in such disarray with the election just a couple days away. There was so much tension all around with the Presidential election. People were raging across the country in the hopes of pushing their political party. Outside of The F Place, most of the conversations focused on the upcoming election.

That led Brianna to think about the implications that the politically charged environment would have on The F Place. She certainly had her work cut out for her, but her confidence was growing every day. She smiled as she thought about how much progress they had made since she kicked off the strategic brainstorming and planning session with her trusted inner circle just one week prior.

"Thank you all for being here tonight on such short notice. Before we begin, I would like to propose a toast. Here's to true friends and partners who stick with us through thick and thin," said Brianna as she leaned into Justin, who was sitting next to her.

Justin, Kate, Roberta, and The COMO Group partners, Myles and Noelle, raised their glasses. "Here, here!"

"By now, you have seen the viral social media posts and videos about The F Place. Tonight, I am going to share with you the other part of the story," said Brianna.

Almost spitting out her wine, Kate said "You mean, there's more? The F Place is going down!!" They all laughed.

"Yes and no. While many leaders at The F Place were corrupt, there is still hope. I believe that we can turn that company from a place of fear, fraud, and lies to a place of freedom, growth, and truth. But it is going to require a huge Transformation, starting with the company culture," said Brianna.

"And this is why I asked each of you to join me tonight. The Board of Directors has asked me to be the President and CEO, and I need your help. Are you with me?" asked Brianna.

They all raised their glasses and declared a resounding "YES!"

"Good. Because we need to carefully manage the narrative with the media, set up an interim leadership team, and build our Transformation strategy quickly. I need to present my plan to them in three weeks and, if they support it, then I will accept the role of president and CEO of The F Place," said Brianna.

"Brianna, this is aggressive, but we can do it. The F Place needs The COMO Factor. It is our proven methodology for professional and personal Transformation. I know you know what our values are, but they're worth repeating for the team." said Myles.

"C is for Clarity. Brianna, it starts with gaining clarity on what you envision for The F Place. We need to develop a high-definition vision for the company and communicate it broadly inside and outside the company," said Noelle.

"O is for Ownership. You need to visibly take ownership for the future of The F Place . . . within the media and with the customers and employees of the company. They need to see you truly leading by example, and they will follow," said Myles.

"M is for Meaningful Mindset. The F Place takedown has many similarities to Enron. You will have to acknowledge the failures of the past and somehow right those wrongs; then focus the media, your customers and your employees on the future. Give them hope and show them that true Transformation is possible," said Noelle.

"The last O is for One-of-a-Kind. You already know what makes The F Place one of a kind. It is the people. So, you need to inspire them, get rid of any pirates, remind the marketplace of your strengths, and become your customer's trusted advisor," said Myles.

Monday November 2, 2020

Brianna was pleased with the progress that she, Kate, and The COMO Group had made developing the Transformation strategy for The F Place. Having worked with them in the past, she knew that they would be the right partners to help her define and execute her vision. And The COMO Group had already exceeded her expectations, despite the compressed timeline! During the weeks ahead, they needed to prepare the next level of detail and put together the roadmap and budget.

"Good morning, Brianna. Are you ready for our working session today? I know you are stretched thin between running the day-to-day business and developing the Transformation strategy, but together we can do this!" said Myles with a smile.

"You are absolutely right! Despite the exceptionally long hours right now, I wake up energized every single day because I know in my heart and soul that I am on a mission to turn this company around!" said Brianna.

"That's right, Brianna. When you are living your one-of-a-kind purpose, you can feel it in your soul. OK, let's get started. Let's run through our five-point strategy this morning and pressure-test it again to make sure that it is rock solid. As we agreed last week, we have a full lineup of employee and customer focus groups every day this week to get their feedback before we finalize," said Noelle.

"Firstly, we will voluntarily recall HappyVITA and

BalanceVITA from the market immediately and take full responsibility. Rather than spending hundreds of millions of dollars in lawsuits, we will provide generous settlements to all families that were affected by these products," said Myles.

"Yes, this was my first priority, and the wheels are already in motion. We are in touch with the FDA, and I have the legal team working through the details of the settlements as we speak. This is going to have serious financial consequences to the company, but I don't care. It is the right thing to do, and I know that Alexander and the Board support this action," said Brianna.

"Secondly, we are going to put our money where our mouth is and show the world that we are truly employee focused. All employees who were laid off this year will receive an additional six months of severance. We are also going to make things right for Christian Boyd's family and any other employee who was adversely affected by the corrupt and fraudulent actions of our former leaders this year," said Noelle.

"Thanks, Noelle. I would also like to add that I will declare that The F Place will not have another layoff. Instead, effective immediately, we will cut executive salaries, my own included, by 50 percent and offset their compensation loss with additional performance-based company stock. Given that our stock is at a ten-year low right now, the executives who stay with us will have the potential to reap more significant long-term rewards. This one is near and dear to my heart. If the Board does not support this, that will be a non-starter for me. How are you guys coming along estimating the total costs?" asked Brianna.

"We need a few more days to provide you with a firm number, but right now our cost estimate is upwards of $200 million," said Noelle.

"That sounds about right. Let's please continue and finalize the figures quickly," said Brianna.

"Third, in order to begin offsetting the revenue loss from the product recalls, we will proceed with your innovative idea to acquire Vitamin House and develop a personalized subscription service for physical and mental health, including natural vitamins and supplements as an alternative to pharmaceutical medicine," said Myles.

"Kate, you know that this has been a passion of mine for years, but I could never get Alexander or Michael to buy in to it. It has always been my belief that a CEO needs to lead with increased purpose and impact, both societal and economic. What do you think about this strategy?" asked Brianna.

"Brianna, you have already done your due diligence on this and have great relationships with Vitamin House. With the continued growth of subscription services in the marketplace, I believe this has the potential to be a game-changer by elevating the benefits of natural remedies like probiotics, vitamins, and supplements. You will need an innovative and comprehensive marketing strategy, and, when your customers start to see the improvements in their health, you should leverage their testimonials to the greatest extent possible," said Kate.

"Yes, you are right, Kate! Noelle, where do we stand with the financial projections of this new product line?" asked Brianna.

"Acquisition costs will be approximately $85 million. We are still crunching numbers for integration and expansion costs as well as revenue, gross profit, and net income projections. We should be ready with those by Wednesday at the latest," said Noelle.

"Excellent. As soon as you have the numbers, please let me know. This new product line is key to our survival," said Brianna.

"Brianna, just think about this for a moment. The F Place would seriously be challenged to stay afloat without your advanced planning and due diligence of this subscription service strategy. Good for you! Let's move on to the fourth pillar in our strategy, your new executive leadership team," said Myles.

"Thanks so much, Myles. That means more than you know. As for my new leadership team, I need The COMO Group's help with assessing our talent and making recommendations. We still don't know how deep the fraud goes into the organization, and we cannot let even one conspirator into the executive ranks," said Brianna.

"Don't worry, Brianna. We have your back! We have developed a custom assessment playbook that incorporates your mission and values into the screening process. As you know, we are working with an independent firm to conduct executive background checks, which includes a full scan of The F Place's email and company phone correspondence as well as public social media accounts. Where possible, we are using the HR succession planning information, but our confidence in that is understandably low. Nevertheless, we are confident that we will be able to qualify your top three internal candidates for each leadership role by the middle of next week. From there, you and the Board can proceed with your interviews before making appointments or opening select positions up for external hires. Lastly, if we encounter any individual who seems suspiciously connected to Michael and Frita's fraud, we will loop in Donald Clooney ('Toby'), as agreed with the FBI last week," said Myles.

"Knowing that I can trust you so implicitly with this process is why I can finally sleep well at night!" said Brianna with a sigh of relief.

"Brianna, you know that we are here for you! OK, let's move on to the last, but not least, element of our strategy, the Transformation office. As we have discussed, this office should report directly to you, Brianna, and should be empowered to drive, govern, and deliver on your vision for The F Place Transformation. Your Transformation will include people, process, technology, and cultural change. The COMO Group will help you to set up this office and will provide training and staffing support according to your needs. Additionally, based upon the outcome of our internal executive interview process, we expect to identify and make recommendations for high-potential leaders to join the Transformation Office. In a nutshell, Brianna, you should view the Transformation Office as the fuel for your engine of change!" said Noelle enthusiastically.

"Noelle and Myles, I trust you both implicitly and cannot thank you enough for your support. Please also make sure you reach out to the members of my Commercial Transformation team who were laid off earlier this year. I would like to offer each one of them a role in our new Transformation team. Would it be fair to say that without the Transformation Office, there is no Transformation at The F Place?" asked Brianna.

"Brianna, you are spot on! The F Place is facing the toughest and most brutal season in its history. Without a dedicated team of high-potential leaders who can drive the implementation of massive change across the organization, change will simply not happen. Your leaders need to own and lead the Transformation initiatives within their respective organizations," said Myles.

"Thanks, Myles. I believe that we have the right five-point strategy for Transformation. Let's continue refining this week and incorporating the valuable feedback from our focus groups. And I would like a deep-dive review of the financials on Wednesday. The Board has never approved a plan of this magnitude before, but I am cautiously optimistic that they will support our plan. It's far better than the alternative!" said Brianna with authority.

Saturday, November 7, 2020

On the seventh of November, the media announced the country's presumptive President and Vice President elect. Alexander had called earlier that day to check in on Brianna to see how things were progressing. Brianna decided to share the highlights of her five-point Transformation strategy with him so that she could test it out. She knew if Alexander committed, it would be much easier to get the rest of the Board behind her plan.

Meanwhile, her mother Sonia was cooking up a storm at home, getting Brianna's house ready for Diwali. They had decided to have Kate and her family over. Kate was family to Brianna, Justin, and her kids. They had to limit their social gatherings to a small group of ten due to COVID. Normally, Brianna would have had all their closest friends and family over for the Diwali celebration, but due to COVID, she wanted to be cautious and intentionally kept it small.

Friday, November 13, 2020

Brianna woke up at 4:30 a.m., feeling surprisingly rested and at peace despite the significance of the day . . . and the fact that it was Friday the Thirteenth in the year 2020. Like every other year, this one would go down in history, but for The F Place it would have a different kind of meaning if all worked according to plan. She completed a five-mile run before getting ready and heading into the office to present her plan to the Board of Directors.

Given this was Brianna's first formal meeting in her new role as the CEO of The F Place, and because The COMO Group was also attending this very important meeting, she decided to warmly greet each Board member by name. Instead of addressing everyone as "Mr." and "Ms.," she decided to warmly address them by their first names. Besides, she knew that Alexander preferred to use first names. So she began, "Good morning, Alexander, Mark, Brian, John, Isabella, Lexi, Olivia, Jacob, and Parker. Before we get started, I would like to thank you again for your vote of confidence in me. Regardless of the outcome of your decision here today, I am truly honored to have been considered as the next President and CEO of The F Place. In the room with me today are the managing partners of The COMO Group, Myles and Noelle. They are my trusted partners in this journey.".

"Good morning, Brianna. And welcome . . . again . . . Noelle and Myles. It's nice to see you again. The pleasure is ours. We are anxious to hear your proposal, so please proceed," said Alexander.

Brianna walked confidently to the front of the boardroom, where just over three weeks ago the Executive Team had walked out in handcuffs. Brianna was at peace regardless of which way things turned out. Whether she served as President and CEO of The F Place or moved on to something different, her value was not dependent upon a company. Her value was intrinsic to her identity as a unique, one-of-a-kind person in this world.

Brianna spent the next four hours outlining her five-point strategy for transforming The F Place. All in, the price tag was over $1 billion dollars, a majority which would hit their books in 2020.

"Man, those numbers are ridiculous! Don't get me wrong, we believe you, Brianna. Anyone who thinks that crime pays should take a walk through the halls of The F Place," said John.

"John, you are right, but I assure you that we are going to right those wrongs and get rid of the cancer in this company and make it great again!" said Brianna.

The Board deliberated for less than one hour and then called Brianna, Myles, and Noelle back into the boardroom. "Brianna, once again you have proven to us that you are the right woman for the job! You have the unanimous support of the Board for your plan," said Alexander.

"Thank you, Alexander, and to each of you for your support. In return, you have my acceptance of your offer to serve as the President and CEO of The F Place! This journey will be challenging, but it will be meaningful and memorable for sure!" said Brianna.

Saturday, November 14, 2020

Brianna woke up excitedly as it was Diwali and she had officially committed to the Board that she would become the first female CEO of The F Place. It was an auspicious day for her and her family, as Diwali represented extinguishing evil and replacing it with light. Diwali is the Indian festival of lights and symbolizes the spiritual victory of light over darkness, good over evil, and knowledge over ignorance. Brianna paused to reflect on the irony of how the meaning of this auspicious holiday would, today, hold the same significance at The F Place. The F Place had been under a dark cloud these past years under Michael, Frita, and the rest of the leadership. The darkness was finally going to be lifted with Brianna now stepping into the CEO role. Brianna counted her blessings.

She, Ariana, and her mom got the house ready with oil lamps and candles throughout the penthouse. It looked magical. Because Sonia had done all the cooking, Brianna managed to get some work done before Kate and her family arrived. They all had a wonderful time enjoying Sonia's hard work. Brianna couldn't help but feel her heart ache over not having

Eshan there. She had texted him earlier to wish him a happy Diwali.

Before Kate left, Brianna had reminded Kate that their Indian New Year was going to start. She had taken Kate to her vision board. It amazed them both at how powerful of a tool the vision board was. "You know, Kate, it's so true. Just look at us. What you think of and visualize in life plays an essential role in what you do in your life and how you live it," remarked Brianna. "I mean look at this here . . . how could I possibly known at the start of the year that I would get to do this?" inquired Brianna.

Brianna had listed on her vision board under her professional goals that she wanted to drive a cultural change at The F Place, and that's exactly what she was going to do in her new role as CEO. She still had some work to do to reconnect and rebuild her relationship with her son, but she was confident that it would happen very soon. Kate reminded her, with a chuckle, that she had a little extra time and that while the Indian New Year was on a lunar calendar cycle, they still had over a month before 2021 kicked in.

Thursday, November 19, 2020

Brianna, Kate, and The COMO Group spent the morning in Brianna's office putting the finishing touches on Brianna's speech before the communications team recorded her later that afternoon. Brianna was insistent about making the video so that all employees of The F Place would hear directly from her about the future of the company, rather than the fearmongering people on social media. She wanted to inspire them and give them hope by helping them understand her plan to right the wrongs of the past and help the company move forward and transform from a place of fear, fraud, and lies to one of freedom, growth, and truth. Brianna wanted to ensure that she was able to secure the trust of all associates at The F Place. The only way to do that was to be open and transparent about where they were they were today as a company and how they would work together for a successful future.

Around noon, they broke for lunch and turned on the television in Brianna's office. There were several news stations that were broadcasting stories about the possibility of election fraud. With everything going on in her own life, Brianna was tempted to change the channel. However, Kate suggested that they watch for a few minutes just to see what was going on. Those few minutes turned into more than one hour! Everyone in the room was simply speechless. They all wondered out loud, could something like that really happen in the United States of America? Brianna's thoughts drifted to the corruption and fraud that had been discovered at The F Place. She thought to herself, no one could have predicted what had occurred at The F Place.

Later that evening, Brianna settled into bed with a glass of merlot and her journal in hand. "Tomorrow, I will become the President and CEO of The F Place. I am so grateful yet incredibly scared. Franklin Roosevelt said that 'Courage is not the absence of fear but the assessment that something else is more important than fear.' Freedom is far more important than fear! I choose freedom over fear!! I truly hope I can live up to this role and make things right for people like Christian, Sara, Jose, and the countless others affected by the sins of the past. This is all so much more than I expected when 2020 began. If only I had both of my children with me, my life would be complete."

Friday, November 20, 2020

The F Place Board Names Brianna Grimaldi as President & CEO

NEW YORK CITY, N.Y.—November 20, 2020— Today, The F Place announced that its Board of Directors has appointed Brianna Grimaldi as President and Chief Executive Officer, effective immediately. Ms. Grimaldi joined The F Place in 2005 and quickly moved through the ranks within the company. She most recently served as Chief Commercial Officer, leading the company's global sales and marketing organization during its most tumultuous season.

"This is the perfect time for Brianna Grimaldi to become the next Chief Executive Officer. She has dedicated her entire career to The F Place and has proven to be an outstanding innovative, resilient, and ethical servant leader during the most challenging time in our history. Today's pace of change is exponential, and I am confident that Brianna will lead the charge with Clarity, Ownership, a Meaningful Mindset and in her One-Of-A-Kind way that is second to none," said Alexander Wood, Chairman of the Board.

Ms. Grimaldi and The F Place Board of Directors want the public to know that they are committed to the company's Transformation, which includes the elimination of a select number of senior leaders whose vision is not aligned with the new direction of the company.

> "I joined The F Place 15 years ago because I wanted to change the world. Under my leadership, The F Place will right the wrongs of our past and once again become the global leader in pharmaceuticals by providing wholistic solutions that improve the mental health and lives of people everywhere. True Transformation is hard, but with the best People on our team we can deliver Sustainable Results!" said Ms. Grimaldi.

That evening as Brianna left the office, she received a text message from Eshan.

"Mom, I just saw the news that you are the President and CEO of The F Place. How did that even happen??" said Eshan.

"Darling, I'm so happy to hear from you. As for The F Place, that is a really LONG story. Let's just say that I stayed true to myself and I chose freedom over fear. How are you, sweetheart? I miss you and love you so much," texted Brianna.

"I'm good, Mumsy," texted Eshan. Just as Brianna started to respond, she received another text from him.

"I miss you. I can't wait to visit you next week for Thanksgiving," wrote Eshan.

Acknowledgments

TRUE TRANSFORMATION CAN make a positive impact on individuals, teams, and businesses. When individuals and organizations are able to successfully achieve Transformation, the results can be extraordinary. Our vision for this book is to use the art of story to communicate a framework that both individuals and organizations can use to learn about the power of true Transformation. Our hope is that as you read this book, it will inspire you to embrace your one-of-a-kind self to drive true Transformation with sustainable results.

Over several decades of experiencing our own personal and professional Transformations as well as leading and championing massive enterprise change, we have realized that we are passionate about helping individuals and organizations alike to reach their true potential. Over the years we have been privileged to learn about how mindsets and behaviors can make or break a vision. We are thankful to be able to share these lessons with you in a creative way.

We owe an enormous debt of gratitude to those who generously gave of their time to provide us with detailed and constructive feedback on our book. Those who are in our inner circle we would like to mention by name:

Sharyn Albertson, Mark Algar, Mark Behnam, Alexia Belvis,

Parker Belvis, Suzie Bergman, Samantha Chiaverini, Kimberly Church, Jason Church, Maria Clara, Jason Clark, Tom Diez, Tom Doyle, David Dye, Judy Guidry, Petra Hajdu, Claudia Herrington, Ronnie Mandal, Catherine Mehra, Suwan Mehra, Carrie Nauyalis, Vibhu Passi, Sonia Patel, Ingrid Schaffenburg, Ashok Shah, Brian Strobush, Olivia Strobush, Rupal Trivedi, Sonia Valy, Kate Visconti, Karen Wever, Jacob Wood, Tangalene Wood, and Brad Young.

The members of this inner circle generously invested their time to read early drafts of the book and to discuss character development, key concepts, and plotlines concerning the transformative lessons learned. This priceless feedback truly enabled us to provide you, our reader, with what we hope will be an entertaining yet effective way to learn about personal and professional Transformation. Last but not least, our inner circle has been immensely supportive of us throughout the writing our first book.

A special thanks to Jacob Guidry, The COMO Group Creative Director, and Kimberly Chamiok, The COMO Group Director of Business Development and Marketing, for their creativity, commitment, and support for the vision of *The F Place* book.

We would like to express our deep gratitude to Ashok Shah, who has been a leader of Transformation long before Transformation was "a thing." Ashok is recognized in the industry as a thought leader in Transformation and has also authored several books on this topic. He has been an incredible mentor for the past fifteen-plus years. We are honored to have him write the foreword to *The F Place*. Ashok has decades of experience and wisdom with personal and professional Transformation and fully understands the purpose and vision of our book.

We are also incredibly thankful for Mark Algar, who is one of the best people-centric leaders we have ever had the pleasure of working with. Mark has invested more than twenty years in mentoring and coaching us and countless others in his personal and professional circle. Mark is another industry Transformation powerhouse who has positively led and championed Transformation globally and specifically across Canada, the United States, New Zealand, France, and India. After retiring a few years ago, Mark practiced what he preached and transformed himself into a professional artist. You can find his one-of-a-kind artwork at MarkAlgarFineArts.com.

There are two other special leaders we would like to recognize, although we have not met them personally . . . yet! First, Dave Ramsey has positively influenced millions of people to achieve financial peace, and we count ourselves blessed to be among them. If we had not followed his program, The COMO Group business and *The F Place* book might never have been created! Secondly, we would like to thank Donald Miller for his StoryBrand and Business Made Simple programs. We applied his StoryBrand framework to develop this book, and this helped us accelerate our time to launch! We are also honored to be part of his Business Made Simple Inaugural Certified Coaching program.

We would also like to thank our parents for providing us with their unconditional love, encouragement, and support to believe that we can shine our light and change the world.

A special thank-you to our children for continuing to be our "why" and our torch that inspires us to live our best lives and to share that gift with others: Isabella, Brianna, Grayson, Lexi, Myles, Olivia, and Sarah.

Finally, without the support of our life partners Mark Behnam and Brian Strobush, we would not be able to deliver this so quickly. Their willingness to put up with us throughout the arduous process of writing our book while balancing our family and start-up business was priceless. They spent countless hours reading and reviewing our story, while providing us with continuous encouragement and support.

CPSIA information can be obtained
at www.ICGtesting.com
Printed in the USA
LVHW011029060221
678541LV00003B/15/J